US Election
HISTORY

KEIVAN SHAKOURI

J. Kenkade
PUBLISHING
Bryant, Arkansas

U.S. Election History
Copyright © 2022 by Keivan Shakouri

J. Kenkade Publishing
5920 Highway 5 N Ste. 7
Bryant, AR 72022
www.jkenkadepublishing.com
Facebook.com/jkenkadepublishing

J. Kenkade Publishing is a registered trademark.

Printed in the United States of America
ISBN 978-1-955186-28-5

I dedicate this book to my father's soul and memory for all the great endeavors he undertook for me.

Contents

Sources
About J. Kenkade Publishing

Introduction

The historic Boston Tea Party incident in 1773 is considered one of the most important events in the beginning of the United States Revolution. Heavy taxes on various products such as tea by the British government caused many protests. Some young people in Massachusetts secretly boarded ships overnight and dumped tea into the sea. Many businessmen also objected and said that we should not pay taxes to the British government until we have a representative in the British Parliament.

In 1774, in response to the Boston Tea Party, Britain imposed punishments known as the Intolerable Acts against the Thirteen Colonies. However, the American Revolutionary War lasted from 1775 to 1783 until the thirteenth British colony finally declared independence on July 4, 1775.

This independence came after the establishment of the First Continental Congress (September 5, 1774) and the Second Continental Congress (May 10, 1775) in Philadelphia and were governed as autonomous states until 1787. That same year, after the signing of the new U.S. Constitution at the Philadelphia Convention, Delaware was the first state to adopt the US Constitution and became the founder of the newly formed United States of America. Subsequently, the rest of the states joined the constitution. New Hampshire, Massachusetts, Rhode Island, Providence, Connecticut, New York, New Jersey, Pennsylvania, Delaware, Maryland, Virginia, North Carolina, South Carolina, and Georgia were the thirteen early colonies that declared independence.

The first presidential, Senate, and House elections were held in 1789. The history of the governorships of the states, however, dates back to before that and after the declaration of independence in 1776 when they held this position for one or two consecutive terms.

The American election has its own conditions and style. Every citizen who is born in the United States and is at least 35 years old and has lived in the country for 14 consecutive years is eligible to run for president; however, if a person wants to be nominated by a party, he / she must first participate in the intra-party process (primary elections) of that party, which is according to the internal laws of that party, and if he succeeds in that process, he will be nominated as that party's candidate.

Primary elections are held in most states by primaries. In this way, registered party members go to the polls and vote for their preferred candidate in the primary presidential election. Most state parties have adopted the primaries since the 1970s.

Another method of holding primaries is the caucuses method, which is currently only used in Iowa, Nevada, North Dakota, Wyoming and Kentucky. Alaska held the Cox-style primary until 2016, after which it changed to primaries. In the Cox method, a combination of party members and leaders selects the party's final candidate in the state for the final presidential election by forming a working group. Party members and leaders gather at a venue such as a stadium, and by naming each candidate, those who wish to select him in the primaries will gather at a point in the hall, and at the end, each person will be counted as one vote.

Prior to the passage of the 22nd Amendment to the United States Constitution in 1951, there were no periodic restrictions on running for president. Franklin Roosevelt, the 32nd President of the United States, served four terms. At present, no one should be elected president for more than two terms, and no one has the right to run for more than two terms.

Each state has two senators in the senate who are elected for at least a six-year term. Senators do not have a periodic limit on their candidacy. From 1789 to 1913, the senators of each state were elected by the legislature of that state, but from 1913 with the passage of the Seventeenth Amendment, the task of electing senators was left directly to the citizens, and the conditions for running in this election are:

1. At least 30 years old
2. Have at least 9 years of US citizenship
3. Residence in the state in question at the time of the election

Representatives of the states for the US House of Representatives are also elected every two years and their participation in this election is unlimited. Depending on the population of the states, the number of state representatives varies and changes every 10 years with a statistical census. Conditions for running in this election are:

1. At least 25 years old
2. Have at least 7 years of US citizenship
3. Residence in the state in question at the time of the election

Elections for the governorship of each state are held in accordance with the laws of that state.

Elections in the United States of America can be considered as one of the most important elections of the present era, which has many direct and indirect effects on the political, economic and even social spheres of the world. However, the complexities and specific style of this electoral system in fifty states have made people and those interested in the humanities read or hear about it. That's why I prepared this book to provide a comprehensive research with new statistical data to those interested in this subject.

This book examines the history of US elections since independence in its 50 states and the District of Columbia, located in Washington, DC. In this book, in addition to general information about all fifty states, you will read in detail about the history of elections at the federal level, such as the number of representatives, senators, governors, parties, presidential electoral winners, and the course of the election from the beginning to the present.

It has been more than two centuries since the independence of the first 13 states since 1776 and the accession of other states to the law, and it is natural that the volume of statistical, historical data and documents is wide. Classifying and using them was tedious. It took me almost two years to publish the material in the shortest possible form as a ready-made book. However, the present book has some shortcomings, which I hope your corrective and critical comments will help to improve my new edition and other writings.

Special thanks to my professor Samantha Staggs and my friends Alireza Soleimani and Reza Mohajer who helped me in my scientific development and writing this book.

Delaware

The historic state of Delaware and its capital, Dover, are located in Northeastern America. Delaware was one of the original 13 states that revolted against British colonial rule, a rebellion which resulted in independence. These states declared independence and were self-governing separately on July 4, 1776. Just like the other 13 colonial states, Delaware was autonomous until ratifying the Constitution in 7 December 1787 as the first state of the U.S. and founder of the new country. "Blue Hen Chicken" was a title for the state regiment led by John Haslet in the Continental Army and well known for bravery of its soldiers. Delaware was the field of Battle of Cooch's Bridge between the revolutionaries and British colonial forces.

In reality, Delaware was a country which allowed slavery, but it was not a common phenomenon in the state. When the Civil War began, many people from the northern part of the state sided with the Union while many southerners sided with the Confederacy and joined its army. Since the governor and state legislators were Union loyalists, they voted anonymously to stay in the Union. Pea patch island in Delaware was a main center to house prisoners of war during the Civil War. At the time, Delaware was an industrial state, and its industry played an important role to satisfy the needs of the Union army. Wilmington is the most important city in the state, and through producing nearly half of the gunpowder used by the Union army, played a major role in the Civil War. During the Civil War period, workers of the gunpowder factories owned by the Du Pont family had to work day and night to satisfy the military needs. The Du Pont family, who were among the richest in the U.S through their investments, made the gunpowder industry in Delaware an important part of its' economy. Henry Algernon Du Pont, a member of the family, took part in the Civil war and because of showing competence in the battle of Cedar Creek, gained a medal of honor. Harlan and Hollingsworth ship building company equipped the Union Navy with warships and other vessels.

According to the last census, Delaware has a population of 973,764 inhabitants, of which 61.7% are whites, 23.2% blacks, 9.6% are Latinos, 4.1% are East Asian people, 0.7% Native Americans and Alaskans, 0.1% Hawaiians and other Islanders, and 2.7% are from other races.

University of Delaware is one of the 10 oldest universities in the U.S, first founded as a school in 1743 and then gradually turned into a university. Among the alumni of the university, people like George Reed (one of the legislators who ratifies the U.S Constitution) could be named.

Delaware State University, Wesley college and Wilmington University are among educational institutions of the state.

Delaware is a rich state in producing pharmaceutical products, plastics, and industrial chemicals and is known as the universal capital of chemical industries. The DuPont company, based in Delaware, is among the top chemical producers in the world. Despite its limited geographical area, Delaware is a top agricultural state and among rival states, holds a high rank in producing corns, soybean and chicken. Because of its extensive tax exemptions, Delaware has been a safe haven for many companies, and more than half of the registered companies in New York stock exchange are registered in Delaware, too.

In addition to Du Pont company, Sallie Mae (provider of financial services and education loans), W. L. GORE AND ASSOCIATES (chemicals producer) and many other corporations have their headquarters in Delaware state.

The tourist attractions of this state consist of: 1. Winterthur Museum and Gardens founded by Henry Francis du Pont. 2. beautiful Rehoboth and Delaware Beaches with white sand and restaurants and a peaceful atmosphere. 3. Hagley Museum and Library in Wilmington (which has been the main residence of the DuPont family for making gunpowder). 4. Nemours Mansion and Gardens (Alfred DuPont's present for his wife's birthday). 5. Air Mobility Command Museum which was a collection of antique airplanes. 6. John Dickinson (Writer of "12 Letters from a Farmer in Pennsylvania", known as "Penman of the Revolution") Plantation. 7. Brandywine Creek State Park with a zoo that specializes in endangered species in North and South America. 8. the Nanticoke Indian Museum in which a variety of indigenous industries are on display. 9. Delaware's Old State House in which construction was completed in 1792. 10. Grand Opera House in Wilmington which was constructed in 1871. 11. First State National Historical Park which consists of different historical parts. 12. Inn at Montchanin Village Montchanin alongside with beaches, museums, and other places of entertainment altogether make historical Delaware state a calm and pleasant tourist destination and connects every tourist with depths of American History.

1.George Ross Jr and Caesar Rodney (participants in the second Continental Congress which saw ratifying the U.S Constitution). 2. Aubrey Plaza, Teri Polo, and Ryan Philips are famous Hollywood actors and actresses from Delaware. 3. Paul Goldschmidt, Baseball player. 4. Stephen Marley, musician. These are all among famous people from the state. Joe Biden, current 46th president of the U.S was born in Pennsylvania, but a resident of Delaware has been a U.S senator for 36 years.

From 1789 to 2020, Delaware has taken part in every single 59 presidential elections held in the U.S. In these 59 contests, Democratic Party candidates have gained 25 victories, Republicans won 18 times, Federalist Party emerged victorious in 8 elections, Whigs won 4 contests, Democratic-Republican Party had 2 victories and National Republican Party scored 2 wins.

To put the history of presidential elections in Delaware under scrutiny, it would be better to divide it to 3 different parts. In the first part, from 1789 to 1848, 16 rounds of elections were held. In these contests, Federalists won 8 rounds, Whigs won 4 rounds, Democratic Republicans and National Republican each won 2 state electoral votes. In second part, 1852 until 1932, 21 rounds of elections were held, and in the first 11 rounds, Democrats won 10 contests, while the Republican Party only gained a single victory, but in the second section of this part and in 10 contests, Republicans had 9 victories versus a single victory for Democratic Party. During the Third period, from 1936 to 2020, 22 rounds of elections were held, and the Democratic Party won 14 of them, while Republicans scored 8 victories. Until 1988, a tense competition has been going on among the rival parties, and winner position switched between them, but since 1992 Democrats have won each and every 8 presidential elections in Delaware. As it could be observed, in this issue, historically, Democrats have performed better as they have won 25 rounds compared to Republicans who have won 18 rounds. Democrats continue victories in recent decades as they have won 8 recent rounds. It has turned Delaware to a Democratic leaning state.

The 2020 Democratic presidential primary in Delaware ended in favor of Joseph Biden who won 89.4% of votes while Bernie Sanders only gained 7.5%.

Republican candidate in Delaware for 2020 presidential elections was Donald Trump, who won the contest by gaining 88% of votes, while Rocky De La Fuente was able to gain 12%.

Looking to different share of Bernie sanders compared to Joe Biden votes in 2 recent Democratic primaries would be interesting. Joe Biden was a long-serving senator of the state, and his landslide victory in 2020 wasn't surprising.

Biden won the 2020 presidential election in Delaware by gaining 58.7% of votes versus 39.8% for Donald Trump, and all 3 electoral votes from Delaware were put into the Democratic basket.

From 1789 to 2021, Delaware has sent 51 elected senators to the U.S Senate. Of these, 18 senators were Democrats, 12 were Republicans, 5 were members of the Federalist Party, 2 were Whigs, one was an Opposition Party candidate, one was Anti-Jacksonian, another one was an Adam's men Party member, 2 Jacksonians, 1 was Democratic-Republican, a Pro-Administration Party member, and 7 senators switched their political affiliations during their careers. 2 of them were members of Jacksonian and Whig parties, one served as a member of the Pro-administration and Anti-Administration parties. A candidate experienced membership in Anti-Jacksonian Party, Opposition Party and Whig Party. One of senators acted as a Federalist and Pro-Administration Party member. Another senator experienced membership in the Federalist and Adams-Clay Federalist and Adam's-Men parties, and finally, one of Delaware senators in the U.S Senate served as an Adams-Clay Federalist, Adam's-men Party member,

Anti-Jacksonian and a Whig.

Surveying the U.S Senate election in Delaware shows that the first Democrat Senator was elected in 1851, and the first Republican senator gained his seat in 1889. Democrats have an upper hand in the issue and have gained 18 seats through the history of U.S Senate elections in Delaware and have kept one of the state Seats in Senate since 1973, while the other seat has been in their hands since 2001, indicating that Delaware has been a Democratic leaning state for a while. Thomas. Carper and Christopher. A. Coons are current senators from Delaware in the U.S Senate. Joe Biden (1973-2009), 46th President of the U. S, with 36 years of serving history in the Senate and William.V. Roth Jr (1971-2001) with his 30-year career, have been the longest-serving senators from Delaware.

Other than the DuPont family, Bayards are among famous families from Delaware who has held the state seat in the US Senate for many years. Senator Richard Bassett, father-in-law of senator James A. Bayard Sr., was among the first politicians who ratified the U.S constitution. 2 of senator Bayard's sons, Richard Henry Bayard and James A. Bayard Jr and 2 of his grandsons, Thomas F. Bayard Sr and Thomas F. Bayard, all have served as senators from Delaware.

From 1789 to 2021, 63 elected representatives from Delaware have entered the U.S House of representatives, of which 13 later served as U.S Senators. 23 of them were Democrats, 20 were Republicans, 8 were Federalists, 2 were Democratic-Republicans, 2 were members of the Whig Party, one was from Native American Party (also known as American Party or Know Nothing Party), one was a member of the Union Party, another candidate was a member of the Unconditional Union Party (the same Union Party which changed its name in 1861). A representative was from Pro-Administration Party, and 4 representatives changed their political affiliations during their careers. One of the representatives switched sides. Among Anti-Jacksonians and Whigs, one served as an Anti-Jacksonian and Adam's-Men Party member, one acted as a Federalist and Jacksonian, and another representative experienced membership in the Democratic Republican and Anti-Administration parties.

Delaware is a small state, and only has a single seat in the House of Representatives. The seat has been switching permanently among

Republicans and Democrats. Democrats have been on the superior side in the history of the House elections in Delaware by having 23 representatives compared to the Republicans with 20 representatives, and Democrats have kept the House seat since 2011. Lisa Blunt Rochester is the current representative of Delaware in the U.S House of representatives.

Before entering into the subject of governorship, it is necessary to mention that John Carney is the 74th governor of Delaware state, but the number of people who reached this position were 71 people. The reason for this numerical difference is that Joseph Haslet, Charles Polk Jr, and Elbert N. Carvel were the three governors who served in 2 nonconsecutive terms. For instance, Joseph Haslet served as 27th and 30th governor, and that's the reason why Delaware's recent governor, John Carney, is considered as the 74th governor, but actually, there were 71 people in 74 rounds.

Since 1777 until now, Delaware has witnessed 71 governors. 21 of these were Democrats, 16 were members of the Republican Party, 12 were Federalists, 5 were Whigs, 4 were Democratics and Republicans, 1 was from Union Party, 1 was a National Republican Party member, one was from the Native American party (also known as American Party or Know Nothing Party), 1 changed parties and joined both the Federalist party and the Whigs, and nine governors had no political affiliation. At the time of their tenure, American political parties had not yet been formed and Delaware was governed independently after the declaration of independence from Britain and joining the United States in 1787. 9 presidents of Delaware were equal to governors. Thomas Collins was the 9th governor of Delaware after ratifying of the U.S Constitution and replacing the governor title with president, but, as mentioned before, all these 9 people were recorded as Delaware's governor in history.

Some governors served for a single term, while some of them succeeded to do it twice. The First Democrat governor began his career in 1836, but the Republican Party in Delaware wasn't able to gain the governor seat until 1895. As the statistics show, through the history of Delaware, the Democratic Party has had 21 governors while Republicans have had 16 governors since 1993 to 2021. All four governors of Delaware are from the Democratic party.

John Carney, a Democrat, is currently the governor of Delaware. It would be interesting to know that one of elected governors of Delaware, Henry Molleston, was a Federalist who died before beginning his career.

Conclusion: As it was mentioned before, Democrats have won 25 rounds of presidential elections in Delaware, including all 8 recent contests compared to Republicans who won 18 rounds. Democrats, throughout the history of Senate elections, have sent 18 senators, 23 candidates and 21 governors compared to Republicans who have sent 12 senators, 20 candidates and 16 governors and right now, both senators and the single representative and the governor from the state are members of the Democratic Party. They also have an upper hand in the history of the U.S. senate elections in the state, Historically, Delaware has been a Democratic leaning state, and right now the situation is not different.

Pennsylvania

Pennsylvania is located in the northeastern United States, and its capital is Harrisburg. Pennsylvania was one of the first 13 states which revolted against the British colonial rule, a rebellion which ended with their declaration of independence and autonomy. After ratification of the U.S Constitution, Pennsylvania joined the U.S as its second state on 12 December 1787. In addition to its major role in economic and social development of the U.S, Pennsylvania was a bastion of the revolution. Philadelphia, first capital of the state, emerged as the capital of the newborn country. The text of the U.S Constitution and United States Declaration of Independence were written in the Independence Hall of this city. Pennsylvania is known as the "Keystone state". Through its industrial and agricultural capacity, Pennsylvania played an important role in the Civil War. The state sent nearly 360 thousand soldiers to the battlefields and was a main source of providing light and heavy weapons for the Union Army. Phoenix Iron Works company was a main provider of artillery for the Union. From day 1 to 3 of July 1863, Pennsylvania witnessed one of the major battles of the War, Battle of Gettysburg, which resulted in 51 thousand deaths for both sides and emerged as the bloodiest battle through the War. Gettysburg was a huge defeat for the Confederation Army and a tipping point in the course of the War in favor of the Union Army. Two years after Gettysburg, Confederation was defeated, and the War came to its end. According to the last census, Pennsylvania had a population of 12,801,989 inhabitants, of which 75.7% were white, 12% were black,

7.8% were Latinos, 3.8% were Asians, 0.4% were Native Indians and Alaskans, 0.1% were Hawaiians and 2.1% of the population were from other races.

The University of Pennsylvania was among 9 universities which were founded during the British colonial rule, and Benjamin Franklin was one of the main founders of this education institute. Today, the University of Pennsylvania is one of 8 Ivy League universities and top 10 universities in the U.S. The University had its early foundations in 1740 and was the first Medical college in the U.S. Moravian college, the 6th oldest university of the country, founded in 1742, Carnegie Mellon University, Pennsylvania State University, and Lehigh University, are all among the top universities in the World, and along with other colleges and education institutes, shape an ideal space for scientific development of students.

Nearly 60% of the state area is covered by forests, and the logging industry in Pennsylvania ranks 1st in the U.S. Wheat, barley, apple, cherry, peach, grape, cheese, ice cream, butter, meat, chicken and fish are among products of the state, and Pennsylvania is among the top states in producing mushroom, milk and egg. Apart from these, the state is known as the world snack capital, and potato chips, candy, chocolates and salty noodles are among its important products, Metal and electrical industries, machinery and coal (Pennsylvania is a top coal producer state in the U.S) along with limestone, oil and natural gas are other main products of the state.

Many big corporations like Hershey (one of the largest Chocolate, cookies, cakes and drinks manufacturer in the world), Aramark (provider of food services), Comcast (giant internet, cable TV, phones and wireless communications provider), Genesis Healthcare (Providing nursing and rehabilitation services), ALCOA)8th largest producer of Aluminum in the world), and RITE AID (drugstore chain) have their headquarters in Pennsylvania.

Pennsylvania and specially Philadelphia, because of participation in the American Revolution ratification of the Constitution and the role in the Civil War, have a strong tourism attitude which takes the tourists to the historical atmosphere of those old times. 1. Liberty Bell and Independence National Park which has many different historical parts like Philadelphia Independence Hall (saw ratification of the

Constitution for the first time) that acted as the Congress building for nearly 10 years. 2. Gettysburg National Military Park, which was a battlefield of the Civil War in 1863 (Battle of Gettysburg resulted in 51 thousand deaths during 3 days). 3. Valley Forge and Valley Forge National Historical Park (after the occupation of Philadelphia by British forces, George Washington moved his forces to this valley, but despite the sacrifices done by patriots, shortage of food, supplies and disease caused about 2 thousand deaths). 4. Eastern State Penitentiary (Prison which held people like Al Capon). 5. Intercourse village with a traditional and dreamy environment. 6. Presque Isle State Park along with its beach and lighthouse. 7. Railroad Museum of Pennsylvania in Strasburg and taking trip with old coal train are among tourist attractions of Pennsylvania, and 8. Hershey park are all sightseeing attractions taking you to the heart of the American history.

1.James Buchanan and Joe Biden, 15th and 46th Presidents of the U.S, 2. Sharon Stone, Will Smith, James Stewart (Hollywood actors and actresses) are among people born in Pennsylvania. Followers of Amish church, who are a branch of protestants, are mainly settled in Pennsylvania. They don't use modern technology, industrial products and new innovations like electricity, insurance and universal healthcare. They don't join the Army, and using cars among them is rare. Most of them use horses and carriages for transportation.

From 1789 to 2020, Pennsylvania has been present in all 59 presidential elections held in the U.S. Republican Party won 26 contests while Democrats gained 20 victories. The Democratic-Republicans had 6 wins, Federalist Party had 2 victories, Whigs won 2 contests, and the Progressive Party scored a victory. In 2 rounds of elections, 1796 and 1800, electoral votes of the state were divided between Democratic-Republicans and the Federalist Party: in 1796, Democratic-Republicans won 14 votes while Federalists gained 1, and in 1800 the share was 8-7 in favor of Democratic-Republicans.

To have a better inspection, it would be better to divide the history of presidential elections in Pennsylvania to 2 periods. First part, from 1789 to 1912, saw 32 rounds of elections in which Republicans gained 13 victories, Democrats won 6 times, Democratic-Republicans scored 6 wins, Federalist Party was able to win 2 times, Whigs had 2 victories, the Progressive Party gained a single victory, and as said before, in

1796 and 1800 electoral votes were divided among Federalists and Democratic-Republicans.

In the second part, from 1916 to 2020, there were 27 elections, and the Republican Party emerged victorious in 13 rounds, while Democrats had a better performance and gained 14 wins. Until 1988, there was a balanced cycle of wining among the 2 main parties in the state, but after that, the Democratic Party won 6 out of 7 presidential elections in Pennsylvania, and the Republican Party won only once in 2016. Through the entire history of the state, Republicans have 26 victories and seem to be in a superior position while Democrats have won 20 contests, but in recent years, Democrats won 6 out of 7 elections in Pennsylvania, and now, Pennsylvania is seen as a Democratic leaning state.

In the 2020 Democratic Party primaries for presidential election, Joe Biden was able to defeat Bernie sanders by gaining 78% of votes while Sanders got 18.5%.

In the 2020 Republican presidential primaries in Pennsylvania, Donald Trump won the candidacy by gaining 93.8% of votes while Bill Weld won 4.7%.

Finally, the 2020 presidential election in Pennsylvania witnessed a win for the Democratic candidate, Joe Biden, who got 50% of the votes while Donald Trump gained 48.8%. All 20 electoral votes from the state were gained by the Democratic candidate.

From 1879 to 2020, Pennsylvania has sent 53 senators to the U.S Senate. 21 were Republicans, 10 were Democratic Party members, 7 were Democratic-Republicans, 3 were Jacksonians, 1 was a Whig Party member, the Federalist Party had a seat in the Senate, 1 was a Pro-Administration Party member, one was an Anti-Administration Party member, a senator was from Adams's men gathering (also known as Anti-Jacksonians), and 7 were senators who switched sides during their political career in the Senate. Among these, 2 were Democrats and Republicans, 2 were members of the Democratic and Jacksonian parties, one served as Pro-administration and Federalist Party member, one experienced membership in the Democratic-Republican and Jacksonian parties, and a senator switched sides among Democratic-Republicans and Crawford Republicans.

According to the statistics shown above, a number of those senators served only as Republican Party members from Pennsylvania, in addition to those who experienced membership in other parties during their careers and their names have been recorded as Republican U.S senators, was 23, while the same number for Democrats was 14, showing superiority of Republicans in the issue.

Right now (2021), Robert Patrick Casey Jr from the Democratic Party, and Patrick Joseph Toomey Jr from the Republican Party represent Pennsylvania in the U.S Senate. This shows a tie among Pennsylvanians in their political affiliation in the Senate elections.

Arlen Specter with a 30-year record of service in the U.S Senate (1981-2011) and membership in both Democratic and Republican Parties, along with Boris Penrose with a 24-year record (1897-1921) from Republican Party are the longest-serving Senators in the history of Pennsylvania.

It's also worth noting that William Scott Vare, from the Republican Party who had a history of representing Pennsylvania in the U.S House of representatives, won the Senate seat in the 1926 elections but was removed due to allegations of corruption and voter fraud. James Buchanan, 15th President of the U.S, was once a senator from Pennsylvania.

From 1789 to 2020, 1039 representatives from Pennsylvania have made their way to the U.S House of representatives. Among them, 391 were Republicans, 330 were Democrats, 84 were Democratic-Republicans, 39 were Jacksonians, 47 were Whig Party members, 24 were Federalists, 11 were Anti-Masonic Party members, 6 were Pro-Administrations, 5 were Independent Republicans, 5 were Anti-Jacksonians, 3 were Adams's Men gathering members, and one was an Adams's men member and then an Anti-Jacksonian. Anti-Jacksonian and Adams's Men were both names for the same party, so the representative mentioned saw this name changing during his career. 4 were members of the Opposition Party, 3 were Native American Party members (also known as Know Nothing Party) members, 2 were Anti-Administration Party members, one was an Independent Democrat, 1 was a Greenback Party member, one was an Anti-Lecompton Democratic Party member, another representative was an Adams-Clay Federalist, and 72 representatives changed their political affiliations during their careers. 10 were sometimes Democrats and sometimes Jacksonian; 7 were sometimes Republicans and Opposition Party members; 6 were Jacksonians and

Republicans; 5 were sometimes Anti-Masonic Party members and sometimes members of the Whig Party; 5 were sometimes Democrats and sometimes Republicans; 5 served as Democratic-Republicans, Jacksonians, and Jacksonian Republicans, 3 were sometimes Democratic-Republicans and sometimes Anti-Administration Party members; 3 were Republicans and Progressive; 3 were Democratic-Republicans and Jacksonian Republicans ; 2 were sometimes Whig and sometimes Republican; 2 were sometimes Pro-Administration Party members and sometimes Federalists; 2 served as Whigs and Anti-Jacksonians; 2 were Democratic-Republican and Democratic Party members; 2 were Federalists, Jacksonian Federalist and Jacksonians for a while; 2 had history of being Whigs, Republican and Opposition Party members, , and one was a Whig and once a Opposition Party member; one served as a Whig and member of Adams's Men gathering; one was an Adams's Men Party member for a while and sometimes served as a Jacksonian Republican; one was sometimes a Democratic-Republican and once a Jacksonian Federalist; one had record of being a Whig and an Independent Democrat; one served as a Whig and a Jacksonian; one experienced membership in the Whig and Free Soil parties; one was once a Republican and once an Independent Republican; one served as a Democratic-Republican and Anti-Lecompton Democratic Party member, one had a record of membership in the Federalist, Adams's men and Whig parties; one served as a Democratic-Republican, Pro-Administration Party member and an Anti-Administration Party member, and at the end, a representative experienced membership in 5 different parties: Democratic-Republican, Jacksonian Republican, Adams's men, Anti-Jacksonian and Whig. 9 were representatives without clear political affiliation, or their political affiliation remains unknown to our sources.

A number of those House representatives who served only as Republicans from Pennsylvania during their careers, in addition to those who experienced membership in other parties, were 411, and the same number for Democrats was 347, showing an edge for Republicans in the history of the U.S House of representatives in Pennsylvania. But, recent years have seen a tighter competition, and currently (2021), each party holds half of the House seats belonging to the state (each 9 out of 18).

Lewis Charles Levin, one of founders of the Native American Party (also known as Know Nothing Party), who was a representative from Pennsylvania, is known as the first Jewish Person to enter the U.S House of representatives. James Buchanan Jr, 15th President of the U.S., once was a representative from Pennsylvania in the House.

From 1777 (Declaration of independence) to 1787 (Ratification of U.S Constitution), Pennsylvania had 7 Presidents of the Supreme Executive Council, which were equal to governors. In 1787, Benjamin Franklin, known as "The First American" and one of the Founding Fathers who was against slavery, served as the first United States Postmaster General and President of Pennsylvania during his political life. Philadelphia Convention (also known as The United States Constitutional Convention and Federal Convention) was held in 1787 and ended with ratification of the Constitution, and Franklin was one of 34 signers. The same year, Pennsylvania joined the U.S., but Thomas Mifflin, who joined the Federalist Party after its foundation, was speaker of the Pennsylvania House of Representatives at the time (and also a signer of the Constitution), and a year later, he replaced Franklin as 7th President of Pennsylvania in 1788. In 1790, Mifflin became the first governor of Pennsylvania after ratification of State constitution. Mifflin also served as Quartermaster General of the Continental Army during the Revolutionary war against the British colonial army.

From 1790 to 2020, Pennsylvania witnessed 47 governors. 25 were Republicans, 13 were Democrats, 5 were Democratic-Republicans, 1 was a Federalist Party member, one was an Anti-Masonic Party member, and 2 were Whigs. As it could be observed, Republicans with 25 governors, had a better performance here, and from 1861 to 1955 (94 years) only 2 Democratic Party members were able to gain the governor seat in Pennsylvania for 12 years, and the rest of governors were Republicans. But, in recent decades, the race has tightened, and the current governor of Pennsylvania, Tom Wolf, is a Democrat.

Conclusion: During the history of presidential elections in Pennsylvania, Republicans have had an upper hand and gained 26 victories against 20 wins for Democrats. But, the Democratic Party has won 7 out of 8 recent elections (including the last one in 2020). The Republican Party has sent 23 candidates to the Senate, while Democrats had 14 senators through the history of the state. Of the two current senators, one is a Republican and one is a Democrat. The race for the House is not different (411 Republicans vs 347 Democratic representatives). Currently, out of 18 (2021), each party has 9 seats in the House. At the end, Republicans were superior in gubernatorial elections, and 25 of their party members were able to become governors, while Democrats had 13 governors. But recent years has seen a stronger performance by Democrats, and the current governor of Pennsylvania is from their party. History shows an edge for the Republican party through the political history of Pennsylvania, but recent years has seen a tight race among 2 main parties, and right now (2021) Pennsylvania could be regarded as a Democratic-leaning state.

New Jersey

The historical state of New Jersey is located on the East Coast of the U.S. by the Atlantic. Trenton is the capital of New Jersey. New Jersey was among the initial 13 colonies that revolted against the British colonial rule and declared their independence, beginning the American Revolutionary War. Finally, New Jersey joined the U.S as its 3rd state after ratification of the Constitution on 18 December 1787. New Jersey was residence of the great innovator, Thomas Edison, and because of being a pioneer state of industry in the 19th century, it was known as the birthplace of the American Industrial Revolution. New Jersey was a battlefield for many battles during the Revolutionary War, and due to its essential role in that era, was called "Crossroads of the Revolution". Morristown, which hosted a continental army led by George Washington for two winters, was given the nickname "Military Capital of American Revolution". During the Civil War, New Jersey was among Northern states which shaped the Union and supported president Abraham Lincoln. About 80 thousand soldiers from New Jersey fought for the Union during the War. According to the last census, New Jersey had a population of 8,882,90 inhabitants. 54.6% were whites, 20.9% were Latinos, 15.1% were blacks, 10% were Asians, 0.6% were Native Indians, 0.1 were Hawaiians and other Pacific islanders, and 2.3% were from other races and ethnicities.

New Jersey is home to Princeton University, which is among top universities in the world and is the 8th oldest education institute in the U.S. Princeton was one of 9 universities founded during the British colonial rule (established 1746) and is a member of 8 universities of the Ivy league. Rutgers University in New Jersey is one of the other old universities in the country. Stevens Institute of Technology and Bell Labs (founded by Alexander Graham Bell) are among other famous education institutes in the state.

Regarding its arable land area, New Jersey has a successful agriculture, mostly consisted of greenhouse crops. Pharmaceutical industry, Biotechnology, IT industry, financial services and transportation are among other active economy sectors in New Jersey. Along these, film industry is one of the most active economy sectors of the state and after Hollywood, is the largest in the U.S. Actually, the first film studio in the world, Black Maria, was founded by Thomas Edison in New Jersey and was the universal capital of the film industry. Also, the first drive-in movie in the world emerged in Camden, New Jersey.

New Jersey is home to the Headquarters of many large corporations like JOHNSON & JOHNSON (one of largest pharmaceutical companies in world), TOYS R US (international toy, clothing, and baby product retailer), BED BATH & BEYOND (chain of domestic merchandise retail stores), Burlington (department store cloth and shoes retailer), PRUDENTIAL FINANCIAL (Insurance services, capital management and other financial services).

The most well-known tourist attractions of this state are as below: 1-Atlantic City and its casinos, entertainment centers and beautiful beach. 2-Victorian architecture of Old Victorian Cape May district with its beautiful beaches and lighthouse (six U.S presidents had summer residences here). 3- Delaware Water Gap National Recreation Area, located between New Jersey and Pennsylvania. 4- Princeton and the Battlefield State Park, in 1777 battle of Princeton took place here. 5- Battleship New Jersey, a museum ship. 6- 2-million-gallon Adventure Aquarium, including 8500 marine species. 7- Thomas Edison National Historical Park, including Thomas Edison's house and laboratory. 8- Morey's Piers, a beautiful and amazing water and amusement park at Cape May, all of which are included in the tourism industry of this state. These industries together help New Jersey have a reliable economy in a way that it is resided as the highest ratio of millionaire families in the U.S. in 2020.

Grover Cleveland was elected 2 times as 22nd and 24th president of the U.S. David Copperfield, famous American magician, Jordan

Burroughs, well-known American wrestler, Jerry Sebastian Lewis, American comedian, actor, producer, writer and director, Buzz Aldrin, astronaut and 2nd human to walk on the Moon, Alfred Charles Kinsey, biologist known as the "father of sexology", John Francis Bongiovi Jr, singer, actor and lyricist, and George Raymond Richard Martin, author of "A Song of Ice and Fire", novels which the series "Game of Thrones" were based on, are among well-known people from New Jersey.

From 1789 to 2020, New Jersey has taken part in every presidential election held in the U.S. In these 59 contests, Democrats had 25 victories in New Jersey, while the Republican Party scored 18 wins, Federalists won 5 times, Democratic-Republicans had 5 victories, Whig Party won 4 times, and the National Republican Party was able to gain a single victory. In the 1860 election, electoral votes were spilt among Republicans and democrats (4 for Republicans and 3 for Democrats.)

To inspect the history of presidential elections in New Jersey, we can divide it into 2 periods: The first part, from 1789 to 1892, saw 27 elections. Democrats had 10 victories, Federalists won 5 times, Democratic-Republicans scored 5 wins, Whigs had 4 victories and the National Republican Party had a single win. As mentioned above, 1860 elections witnessed a split of the electoral votes among Republicans and Democrats.

Second part, from 1896 to 2020, witnessed 32 rounds of elections. The result was 17 Republican wins while the Democratic Party had 15 victories, including 8 recent elections. As it could be observed, Democrats have an upper hand in the history of presidential elections in 25 rounds in the state, and 8 recent years have seen this trend, too.

The 2020 Democratic presidential primaries in New Jersey ended in victory for Joe Biden who won 86.1% of the votes, while his rival Bernie Sanders got 13.5%.

In the 2020 Republican primaries, Donald Trump won the candidacy by gaining 95% of the votes. Write-ins was in the second place. That means voters wrote the names of people outside the existing candidates.

Finally, in the 2020 presidential election in New Jersey, Democratic candidate Joe Biden gained 57.1% of the votes and emerged victorious, while his rival, Donald Trump from the Republican Party received 41.3%. All New Jersey's 14 electoral votes were counted for Democrats.

From 1789 (the year the first U.S Senate election was held in the state) to 2020, 67 people represented New Jersey as the U.S senators. Of these, 24 were Democrats, 21 were Republicans, 5 were Federalists, 4 were Democratic-Republicans, 3 were Pro-Administration Party members, 2 were Whigs, one was from Adams's Men gathering, one was an Anti-Jacksonian, and a Senator switched sides among Adams-Clay Republicans, Adams's Men, and Anti-Jacksonians. As mentioned before, all of these 3 names point to a single political party in different periods, and the senator actually didn't change his affiliation. The names and dates are written here to indicate the work process of the parties. 5 senators changed political affiliation during their careers. 2 were sometimes Pro-Administration Party members and sometimes Federalists, one served as a Democrat and Jacksonian, one had record of membership in the Democratic-Republican, Whig and Anti-Jacksonian parties, and one switched sides among Democratic-Republicans, Crawford Republicans and Jacksonians.

As the statistics showed, those Senators who only served as Democratic Party members, in addition to others with a record of membership in the other parties, were 25 persons, while the same number for the Republican Party is 21. This shows an edge for the Democratic Party in the history of the U.S Senate elections in New Jersey. Democrats have also been successful in recent years and decades: from 2 seats of the state in the U.S Senate, apart from 5 months in 2013 (Because of the Democratic senator's death that allowed Republicans to hold his seat temporarily), one has remained Democratic since 1979, and the other seat has been held by Democratic senators since 1959, except 9 months in 1982. Currently, Robert Menendez and Cory Booker, both Democrats, represent New Jersey in the U.S Senate.

Clifford Philip Case Jr from the Republican Party with a 24-year history of presence in the Senate (1955-1979) and Harrison Arlington Williams Jr from the Democratic Party with a 23-year record (1959-1982) have been the longest-serving U.S senators from New Jersey.

From 1789 to now (2021), 319 elected candidates have represented New Jersey in the U.S House of representatives. Among them, there were 125 Democratic Party members, 109 were Republicans, 25 were Democratic-Republicans, 16 were Whigs, 10 were from Federalist Party, 5 were Jacksonians, 4 were Pro-Administration Party members, 4 were Anti-Jacksonians, one was an Adams's men gathering member, 2 were Adams's Men and Anti-Jacksonian Party members (as said before, 2 names for the same party), 1 was an Opposition Party member, a representative was from Anti-Lecompton Democratic Party, and 14 representatives switched sides during their political careers, among these 2 were sometimes Republicans and sometimes Opposition Party members, 2 were Democratic-Republicans, Jacksonian Republicans and then Jacksonians, 2 were sometimes Democratic-Republicans and sometimes Adams-Clay Republicans and Adams's Men or Anti-Jacksonian for a while, one served as Whig and Republican, one served as Democrat and Republican, one was a Pro-Administration Party member for a while and sometimes served as a Federalist, one had record of being Whig and Opposition Party member , one served as Jacksonian Republican and Jacksonian, one was sometimes a Democrat and sometimes an Anti-Lecompton Democratic Party member, one served as Democratic-Republican and Adams-Clay Republicans, and according to our sources, 2 representatives had no clear political affiliation.

As the statistics show, those representatives who only served as Democrats, or had history of membership in other parties along this, have been 128 persons. The same number for Republicans is 113, which indicates an upper hand for Democrats in this issue in the history of the House elections. But number of service years for these 113 Republican representatives has been more than the same number for their Democratic counterparts. On the other hand, currently 10 out of 12 representatives from the state in the U.S House of representatives are Democrats (2 are Republicans), which shows wide support for Democratic Party in the House elections in the state.

Before 1776, New Jersey was a British colony, just like the other states which later became U.S states, and its ruler was a colonial official appointed by the British. But, in the same year and after the declaration of independence by the initial 13 colonies, New Jersey's state temporary constitution was ratified, which remained in place for the next 68 years and saw some changes. William Livingstone, one of the signers of the U.S Constitution at the Federal Convention at Philadelphia (1787), acted as the first governor of New Jersey for 14 years (1776-1790). His cousin, Robert R. Livingston, was U.S ambassador in France during the presidency of Thomas Jefferson and served as part of the diplomatic mission which succeeded in the Purchase of those lands which later shaped the nowadays U.S state of Louisiana.

Since 1776 to now (2021), 56 elected governors and 15 acting governors have served in the state. Some of them, like John Farmer Jr, had temporary posts (Farmer only acted for 90 minutes on 8 January 2020), and in another case, Richard James Codey served as acting governor of New Jersey for 5 days in January 2002 (10-15 January) but became 53rd elected governor of the state in 2004 and held his seat until 2006. We won't discuss the history of acting governors here.

Among 56 elected governors, 28 were Democrats, 17 were Republicans, 4 were Federalists, 4 were members of Whig Party, and 3 were Democratic-Republicans. As the statistics show, Democrats have been superior in this issue, and the current governor of New Jersey, Phil Murphy, is also a Democrat.

Garret Dorset Wall was elected as governor of New Jersey in 1829, but declined to serve Thomas Woodrow Wilson, 28th President of the U.S, also had served as governor of New Jersey during his political life.

Conclusion: As it could be observed, the Democratic Party has shown a better performance during the political history of New Jersey: It won 25 presidential elections (including 8 recent ones) while Republicans had 18 victories, Democrats had 25 U.S senators from New Jersey while Republicans had 21, and both current New Jersey seats in the U.S Senate are held by Democrats. Republicans had 113 representatives in the House with more years of service than Democrats who sent 128 fellows from the state to the House, but today (2021), 10 out of 12 House seats belonging to New Jersey in the House are in Democratic hands. Democrats also have a stronger performance in history of gubernatorial elections in New Jersey: 28 of elected governors in the state were Democrats, while 17 Republican Party members were able to gain the seat, and current governor of New Jersey is a Democrat. All these facts indicate that New Jersey has been a Democratic bastion during most of its history, and today (2021) has the same political attitude.

Georgia

Georgia state and its capital, Atlanta, are located in the southeast of the U.S. The state was originally named in honor of George II, King of Britain. The state was among the initial 13 colonies which declared their independence during the American Revolution in 1776. Georgia joined the U.S. after ratifying the Constitution on 2 January 1788 and became the 4th state of the country. On 29 December 1778, the state witnessed the beginning of the capture of the historical city of Savannah, one of the major incidents of the Revolutionary War. During the Civil War, Georgia joined the Confederation and sought secession from the Union.

Today (2021), Georgia has a population of 10.617.423 inhabitants. Demographic composition of the state can be seen in these numbers: 52% of the population is white, 32.6% are blacks, 9.9% are Latinos, 4.4% are Asians, 0.5% Native Indians and Alaskans, 0.1% are Hawaiians and people from other Pacific islands, and the rest 2.2% are from other races and ethnicities.

The University of Georgia is among the oldest universities in the U.S, and Emory University is one of the most credible universities in the world in medical sciences and biotechnology, and the Georgia, Institute of Technology is one of the best technical and engineering education institutes in the U.S. These are among important universities and colleges in Georgia.

Georgia has an active automotive industry and strong agriculture. It ranks 1st in producing peanuts and chicken in the U.S and is a main producer of cotton, watermelon, peaches, eggs, cucumbers, sweet corn, tomato, melon, and cabbage. In movie and entertainment industry, Georgia is among the top 4 states in the U.S. Many large corporations like CNN, Coca Cola, Home Depot, UPS, Delta Air Lines, Arby's, fast food restaurant chain, Chik-fil-A, Waffle House restaurant chain, have headquarters in Georgia. Fort Benning, one of the largest military bases in the U.S, is located in the state. It's worth noting that 93% of the area covered by this base is located in Georgia, while the rest 7% is inside Alabama. Hartsfield-Jackson Atlanta International Airport, one of the largest airports universally, was one of the most crowded ones in the world for many years.

1-Savannah historical district, a part of the city which has remained the same since the Civil War age. 2- World of Coca Cola, an exhibition for history of this popular drink and company products. 3-Temple Mickve Israel, 3rd oldest Knesset in the U.S. 4-Bull Street, including its old churches and other historical buildings. 5-Georgia Aquarium, which houses more than 100 thousand aquatic animals and is one of the largest aquariums in the world. 6-Dr. Martin Luther King Jr. National Historic Site, DR. Martin Luther King was one of the famous leaders of the African American Civil Rights movement. The site includes his birthplace and tomb. 7-Chattahoochee National Forest, in the northern part of Georgia, including lakes, rivers and waterfalls, is an excellent place for boating, hiking, camping and in short, enjoying nature. 8-Jekyll Island, which is a site of big and old buildings, which was once a place for entertainment of the rich, but now has turned into a popular tourist destination. 9-Ocmulgee National Monument, pointing to 12-thousand-year history of human presence in Macon County. Also, this is a good place to learn about Native Indian culture and the Civil War. 10-Jimmy Carter National Historic Site, consisting of a personal house and farm belonging to Jimmy Carter, 39th president of the U.S. 11-Stone Mountain Park, which includes enormous rock relic depicting 3 Confederation leaders, President Jefferson Davies and 2 of his Generals, Robert.E. Lee and Stonewall Jackson. 12-Fox Theatre, built in 1920 and used as a place for showing movies, performing opera shows, ballet shows and Rock concerts. 13-Historic Oakland Cemetery, first designed and built in 1850 as a garden cemetery and during the Civil War, was resting place of soldiers killed in hostilities. 14-Bonaventure Cemetery, one of the best-known cemeteries in the U.S. The site is famous for its stone buildings and oak trees and includes 1300 tombs belonging to dead persons who were killed or died in the Civil War, Spanish-American war and other wars which the U.S took part.

These were some of the historical and natural attractions in Georgia, which helped the tourism sector in the state.

Jimmy Carter, 39th president of the U.S, Martin Luther King, leader of the American civil rights movement, Lula Carson Smith McCullers, American author and playwright, and Julia Roberts, American actress are among famous people from Georgia. Hossein Khosrow, Ali Vaziri, known as The Iron Sheik, a wrestler, and Zahra Karinshak (Sheikholeslam), politician and lawyer who became the state senator from district 48 of Georgia in 2019, are among famous Iranian Americans from Georgia.

From 1789 to now, Georgia has taken part in all of 59 U.S presidential elections except the 1864 election, because of its temporary secession from the Union during the Civil War. In these 58 contests, the Democratic Party gained 34 victories, Republicans won 10 times, Democratic-Republicans scored 8 wins, Whig Party had 3 victories, Federalists won 2 times and American Independent Party was able to gain a single victory.

To have a better inspection, we can divide the history of the presidential elections in Georgia into 3 periods: First part, from 1789 to 1860, the last election before the Civil War saw 19 elections. Democratic-Republicans gained 8 victories, Democrats won 6 times, Whigs scored 3 wins, and Federalist Party had 2 victories. Republicans had no victories, but it's not so strange as the Republican Party was established in 1854 at the end of this period. In the second period, from 1868 to 1960, 24 rounds of elections were held, and Democrats won all of them and Republicans had no victories. In the third part, from 1964 to 2020, there were 15 elections, and the Republican Party scored 10 wins, while the Democratic Party had 4 victories, and the Independent American Party was not able to gain a single victory. It's worth noting that before 1964, Republicans were not able to gain any wins, and the 1964 elections witnessed their first victory.

In 2020 Democratic Party presidential primaries in Georgia, Joe Biden defeated Bernie sanders by winning 84.5% of the votes and got the candidacy, while Sanders got 9.6% of the votes.

In 2020 Republican Party presidential primaries in Georgia, Donald Trump elected by gaining 100% of the votes.

Finally, the 2020 presidential election in Georgia witnessed a victory for the Democratic Party candidate, Joe Biden, who got 49.47% of the votes, while his Republican rival, Donald Trump, won 49.24% of the votes. All 16 electoral votes from Georgia went to Biden.

From 1789 to 2020, Georgia has sent 65 senators to the U.S Senate, 33 were Democrats, 9 were Democratic-Republicans, 7 were Republicans, 2 were Jacksonians, 2 were Whig Party members, one was a Federalist, one was a Pro-Administration Party member, and 10 were senators who changed their political affiliations during their careers. Among them, 2 were Democratic-Republicans and Jacksonians, 2 were sometimes Democratic-Republicans and sometimes Crawford Republicans, 2 were sometimes Democrats and sometimes Jacksonians, one was once a Democrat and served as Whig for a while, one was a Jacksonian and Crawford Republican, one had a record of serving as an Anti-Administration Party member and sometimes as a Democratic-Republican, and a senator switched sides among Anti-Administration and Federalist parties.

It's clear that Democrats have had an upper hand in the history of the Senate elections in Georgia. Before 1981, the Republican Party had sent only 1 senator to the U.S Senate from Georgia, but after that, Republicans gained more popularity in the state since 1981, and from 2005 to 2020, both Georgia Seats in the Senate were held by Republican senators, but in the last election in 2020, Democrats were able to regain them.

According to the statistics shown above, the number of those senators who only had membership in the Democratic Party or along this had records of membership in other parties is 36, and the same number for the Republican Party is 7, showing a clear edge for Democrats.

Currently, T. Jonathan Ossoff and Raphael G. Warnock, both Democrats, represent Georgia in the U.S Senate.

Richard B. Russell Jr, with a 38-year record of service in the Senate (1933-1971) and Walter F. George with a 35-year history of presence in the Senate (1922-1957), both Democrats, have been the longest-serving senators from Georgia.

From 1789 to 2020, 291 persons have represented Georgia in the

U.S House of representatives; of which 160 were Democrats, 40 were Republicans, 21 were Democratic-Republicans, 14 were Whig Party members, 10 were Jacksonians, 5 were Anti-Administration Party members, 3 were from Native American Party (also known as Know Nothing Party, founder of this party, Lewis Charles Levin, was the first Jewish person who entered the House), 3 independent Democrats, 2 were members of the Unionist Party, one was a Federalist, and other representatives had records of changing their political affiliations during their careers. Among these, 8 were sometimes Democratic and sometimes Jacksonians, 3 were Democratic-Republicans and Jacksonians, 3 were Democratic-Republicans, Crawford Republicans and Jacksonians, 2 were sometimes Whigs and sometimes Jacksonians, 2 were once Democrats and sometimes served as Unionist Party members, 2 were sometimes Democrat and sometimes state's Rights Democratic Party, 2 were sometimes Whigs and sometimes Democrats, one was Democrat and Republican, one served as Democratic-Republican and a member of the Anti-Administration Party, one was once a Federalist and sometimes a Democratic-Republican, one had a record of membership in the Democratic-Republican and Crawford Republican parties, one was sometimes a Jacksonian and sometimes Crawford Republican, one served as a Whig and member of the Anti-Jacksonian Party, one was once a Democrat and served as a member of the Opposition Party for a while, one served as a Democrat and Populist Party member, one switched sides among Democrats, Whigs and Unionists, and one had a history of membership in these parties: Democratic Party, Whig Party, Van Buren and Democratic Party.

As the statistics show, those representatives who only served as Democrats or had a history of membership in other parties along with this have been 179 persons. The same number for Republicans is 41, which indicates a clear superiority for Democrats in this issue in Georgia. In a 90-year period, from 1875 to 1965, none of Republicans were able to gain a seat in the House from Georgia, but the recent 20 years witnessed a major shift in this trend, and right now, 8 out of 14 Georgia seats in the House belong to the Republican Party, while Democrats have 6. As an interesting case, it could be pointed out that Carl Vinson from the Democratic Party represented Georgia in the U.S House of representatives for 51 years (1915-1965) and was one of the longest-serving representatives in the history of the House.

Brian Porter Kemp, current governor of Georgia, is serving as the 83rd governor of the state. 77 governors have served after the revolution, and those before that won't be discussed here. As said before, history of governorship in Georgia dates back to 1776.

Since 1776 to the present, 77 persons became governor of the state of Georgia. Among these, 42 were Democrats, 14 Democratic-Republicans, 5 Republicans, 1 was a Whig, 1 was a military governor, 1 was a member of both Whig and Democrat, and finally, 13 non-partisan governors. In fact, American parties had not yet been formed.

As it could be observed, those governors who remained Democrat during their entire political career, in addition to George Rockingham Gilmer who served a term as Democrat and in another term did his job as a Whig, were 43 persons, while the same Number for the Republican Party is 5. This is a clear sign of the Democrat Party superiority in the issue. In a 130-year period (from 1872 to 2003) there were no Republican governors in Georgia, but recent years have seen more popularity for the Republican Party in the state, and since 2003, all 3 elected governors of Georgia have been Republicans. Right now (2021), Brian Kemp, from the Republican Party is governor of Georgia.

James Earl Carter Jr, also known as Jimmy Carter, 39th president of the U.S, also served as a Georgia governor during his political life.

Eugene Talmadge and his son, Herman Eugene Talmadge, both served as governors of Georgia in the 20th century.

Conclusion: It could be observed that Democrats have won 34 rounds of U.S. presidential elections in Georgia (while Republicans had 10 victories) including the last contest in 2020; they also sent 36 senators to the U.S Senate from Georgia, while Republicans had only 7 elected candidates. Since 2005, the situation has changed and Republicans gained both Georgia seats in the Senate, but the Democratic Party was able to regain them recently in (2020). History of the House elections in the state also shows a clear edge for Democrats who sent 179 of their party members to the House, while Republicans had 41 representatives, but recent years and decades witnessed more popularity for Republicans in House elections in Georgia, and currently, in (2021), 8 out of 14 House representatives from Georgia are Republicans, while the Democratic Party holds 6 seats. Democrats had 43 governors in the history of Georgia, while 5 Republican Party members were able to gain governor's seat, but since 2003, all of the 3 recent governors have been Republicans. It could be said that Georgia has been a Democratic-leaning state during most of its history, but for 20 years ago, the situation changed in favor of the Republican Party. 2020 saw a strong return for Democrats who won the presidential election in the state and gained both Georgia seats in the U.S Senate and a House seat, so, if Republicans lose the next gubernatorial election in Georgia, it could be stated that the Democratic party has regained its historical popularity in Georgia.

Connecticut

Connecticut state and its capital, Hartford, are located in the northeastern part of the U.S. Along with Rhode Island, Vermont, Massachusetts, Maine and New Hampshire, Connecticut was one of 6 states known as New England and was among the initial 13 colonies which declared their independence from British colonial rule during the American Revolution and began a rebellion. On 19 April 177, the rebellion began in Lexington, Massachusetts, and after that the news reached Connecticut, 3700 persons from the colony joined George Washington's Continental Army as soldiers. In September 1781, the cities New London and Groton, Connecticut witnessed one of the largest battles of the Revolutionary War. After capturing Groton and Fort Griswold, General William Ledyard, commander of the fort was killed, and the Ledyard city was named after him. Finally, by ratification of The Constitution on 9 January 1788, Connecticut joined the U.S as its 5th state. Connecticut was a main center for arms production in the 18th and 19th centuries, and during the Civil War, through arms production, mobilization of forces and providing money and supplies played a major role in helping the Union Army. Because of its role, Connecticut was named " The Provision State" during the Civil War. Nathan Hale, a revolutionary young man from Connecticut, was captured by the British while conducting an espionage and was later executed. It's quoted that before execution, he said: "What pity is it that we can die but once to serve our country". Nathan Hale is a historical hero of the state. Hannah Bunce Watson, a lady from Connecticut, was also a patriot who helped the revolutionaries through publishing news of the Revolution in the Connecticut Courant newspaper, improving their morale. She was among the most important and effective personalities of Connecticut during the Revolutionary War. Connecticut and Rhode Island were the 2 states which didn't ratify the 18th amendment of the Constitution (on prohibition of alcoholic drinks).

According to the last census, Connecticut had a population of 3.565.287 inhabitants. 65.9% of population is white, 16.9% are Latinos, 12.2% are blacks, 5% are Asians, 0.6% are Native Americans and Alaskans, 0.1% are Hawaiians and other Pacific islanders and 2.5% are from other races and ethnicities.

Yale University, the 4th old university in the U.S and one of the top universities in the world, was founded in 1701 in Connecticut and was the first university in the country to award Ph.D. degrees in 1861. Yale University is a member of the Ivy league, and many famous people like Prescott Sheldon Bush and his son and grandson, Gorge.H.W. Bush and George.W. Bush (41st and 43rd presidents of the U.S), Bill and Hilary Clinton, and John Kerry were among alumni of this university. The University of Connecticut and Quinnipiac University are among other important universities and education institutes in the state.

Connecticut isn't an agricultural state. Vegetables, chicken, eggs and milk are major agricultural products of the state, but mainly for internal consumption. Due to a major decrease in number and area of farmlands, in 1978 a law was passed to save them., but Connecticut is well-known for producing Connecticut shade tobacco and oyster. Connecticut was a major mineral state in the past, but today only extraction of sand, gravel and some other minerals is common in the state.

Insurance and financial services have been a major part of economy in Connecticut since a long time ago, and right now help the state to gain billions of dollars of revenue each year. Connecticut was a major firearms producer during most of its history, and it is known as " a cradle of the American gun industry". Even after the shutting down of companies like Winchester, Connecticut has remained a major arms producer, and several companies like Ruger, O.F. Mossberg & Sons and General Dynamics Electric Boa (which produces submarines) are active in the state. The Famous Company of Winchester Repeating Arms was located in Connecticut and shut down in 2006.

In addition to the companies mentioned above, some large

corporations like 1. XPO LOGISTICS (providing transportation services universally), 2. AMPHENOL (producing electronic and fiber optic connectors), 3. OTIS ELEVATOR (producing and selling elevators, escalators, moving walkways, and related equipment), 4. STANLEY BLACK & DECKER (manufacturer of industrial tools and household hardware and provider of security products), 5. WESTERN CONNECTICUT HEALTH NETWORK (providing medical and health services), 6. SUBWAY restaurant chain with its own style, and 7. WEBSTER BANK have headquarters in Connecticut.

Among the tourist attractions of this state, the following can be mentioned:

1.The Mark Twain House & Museum (famous American author), 2. The State Capitol built in 1879, 3. Harriet Beecher Stowe Center, in remembrance of the famous author of the well-known novel "Uncle Tom's Cabin". Abraham Lincoln, the U.S president during the Civil War, believed she was the main inciter of the Civil War, 4. Old State House building, built in 1796 and one of the oldest buildings in the state, 5. Museum of Connecticut History, where you can see historical asset like weapons, paintings, and original manuscripts of the U.S. Constitution and Declaration of Independence, 6. Hartford Old Cemetery, which dates back to the 15th century, along with Hartford Ancient Burying Ground and Butler-McCook House with their special historical attractions, 7. Old University of Yale, with its beautiful and historical buildings and museums, 8. Lighthouse Point Park with a playground for children around it and antique carousel, 9. Haven Grove Street Cemetery, one of the first cemeteries in the world with avenues and segmentations dating back to late 16th century, surrounded by Yale University campus, 10. Mystic Seaport Museum and its naval tours, 11. Gillette Castle State Park, which was originally William Hooker Gillette's (best remembered for portraying Sherlock Holmes) house, 12. Submarine Force Museum and the USS Nautilus, including a visit to the first nuclear submarine in the world, 13. Mashantucket Pequot Museum & Research Center, an exhibition for history of Native American Indians, 14. Lake Compounce theme Park, dating back to 1864, originally the oldest playground in the U.S which has remained active until now, 15. Mohegan Sun Casino and Foxwoods Resort Casino, along with beautiful beaches, make Connecticut an attractive and charming tourist destination and help the tourism sector of the state to improve its economy.

1.George.W. Bush, 43rd president of the U.S, 2. John Mayer, singer and guitarist, 3. Meg Ryan, actress, 4. Katharine Hepburn, actress, 5. Stephenie Meyer, novelist, 6. William C. Chittick, philosopher, Islamologist, and specialist in Molavi, Ibn Arabi Mysticism (Holding a Ph.D. in Persian literature) and 7. Ralph Nader, Lebanese American politician and candidate of 4 U.S presidential elections are among famous people from Connecticut.

Generally, Connecticut has a strong economy and high GDP per capita and is among the top states in number of millionaire households.

Since 1789 (the date the first U.S presidential election was held in the state), Connecticut has taken part in all 59 elections which have been held until now (2021). In these contests, Republican Party scored 23 victories, Democrats won 21 times, Federalist Party won 8 times, Whigs gained 3 victories, Democratic-Republicans won 2 times and the National Republican Party was able to gain the electoral votes from the state in 2 elections.

To have a better inspection, it would be better to divide this history into 3 different parts: in first period, from 1789 to 1848, 16 rounds of elections were held, and the Federalist Party gained 8 victories, while Whigs were able to win 3 rounds, Democratic-Republicans emerged victorious in 2 contests, National Republicans gained 2 victories, and the Democratic party achieved a single victory. The Republican Party hadn't been established yet.

Second period, from 1852 to 1988, saw 35 elections in which Republicans won 23 times, and Democrats gained 12 victories. But, the third period, from 1992 to 2020 witnessed a decisive round of victories for the Democratic Party in Connecticut, which won all of 8 recent presidential elections in the state.

As it could be seen, during most of their history, Republicans had an upper hand in the presidential elections. They won in 23 rounds in Connecticut compared to Democrats who won in 21 rounds, but by winning all of 8 recent contests, Democrats have shown that people of the state have switched toward their party.

In the 2020 Democratic presidential primaries in Connecticut, Joe Biden gained the candidacy by winning 84.8% of the votes, while his rival Bernie Sanders gained 11.6% of the votes.

The 2020 Republican presidential primaries in Connecticut witnessed a victory for Donald Trump who was able to win 78.7% of the votes, while his closest rival, Rocky De La Fuente, gained 7.4% of the votes.

Finally, the 2020 U.S presidential elections in Connecticut saw a victory for the Democratic candidate, Joe Biden who defeated Donald Trump by gaining 59.3% of the votes, while Trump won 39.2%. All 7 electoral votes from the state were taken by Democrats.

From 1789 to 2020, 55 people from Connecticut have served in the U.S Senate, and from these, 15 were Republicans, 15 were Democrats, 6 were members of the Federalist Party, 4 were Whigs, 3 were members of the Pro-Administration Party, 2 were Anti-Jacksonians, and 2 were once Adams's Men gathering members and then Anti-Jacksonians. As mentioned before, Adams-Clay Republican, Adams's Men, Anti-Jacksonian, and National Republican all are different names for the same political party in different periods. One was a Jacksonian, one was a member of the Free-soil Party, one was a Democratic-Republican, and 5 were senators who changed their political affiliations during their careers. Among these, one was sometimes a Republican and sometimes an Opposition Party member, one was once a Democratic-Republican and sometimes a Crawford Republican Party member, one served as a member of the Pro-Administration and Federalist parties, one served as a Republican and a Liberal Republican, and finally, one switched sides among Democrats and an Independent Democratic Party.

According to the statistics, a number of those senators who served only as Republican Party members from Connecticut, in addition to those who experienced membership in other parties during their careers, were 17. The same number for Democrats is 16, showing superiority of Republicans in the issue. Recent years have been better for Democrats in the state, and out of 2 U.S Senate seats belonging to the state, Democrats have gained one of them since 1963, and the other seat has been in their hands since 1989, showing a tilt toward the Democratic Party among voters of the U.S Senate elections in Connecticut. Currently (2021) both U.S Senators representing the state, Richard Blumenthal and Chris Murphy are Democrats.

Christopher John Dodd, with a 30-year record of serving in the U.S Senate (1981-2011) and Joseph Isadore Lieberman, who represented the state in the Senate for 24 years (1989-2013) have been the longest-serving senators from Connecticut. Both of them were Democratic Party members.

Prescot Sheldon Bush, father of George.H.W. Bush, 41st president of the U.S, represented Connecticut in the U.S Senate for 11 years.

Since 1989 (the year the first U.S House of representative's election was held in Connecticut) to now (2021), 218 people from the state have entered the House. Of these, 77 were Democrats, 59 were Republicans, 29 were members of Federalist Party, 9 were Whigs, 5 were members of the Pro-Administration Party, 5 were Anti-Jacksonians, 3 were Adams's Men gathering members, one was an Adams's Men gathering member and then an Anti-Jacksonian (as said before, all these 3 names point to a single party in different periods), 5 were Democratic-Republicans, 2 were Jacksonians, one was a Free Soil Party member, one was an Adams-Clay Republican, one was a member of the Native American Party (also known as Know Nothing Party), and 20 were representatives who had different political affiliations during their careers. Among these, 5 were sometimes Democrats and sometimes Jacksonians, 3 served as Anti-Jacksonians and Whigs, 3 were once Republicans and sometimes served as members of Native American Party, 3 were sometimes Democratic-Republicans and sometimes served as Adams's Men gathering members, Adams-Clay Republicans and Anti-Jacksonians for a while, 2 had a record of membership in Pro-Administration and Federalist parties, 2 served as Democratic-Republicans and Adams-Clay Republicans, one was sometimes a Whig and sometimes a Republican, and a representative experienced membership in both Democratic-Republican and Adam's Men parties during his career.

As the statistics show, those representatives who only served as Democrats during their entire career, in addition to those who had memberships in the other parties, were 82 persons. The same number for the Republican Party is 63. So, it could be said that in the history of the US House of representative's elections in Connecticut, the Democratic Party has an upper hand. Today (2021), all 5 representatives from the state in the House are Democrats, and no Republican candidate from Connecticut has been able to gain a seat in the House for 10 years ago.

Edward Miner "Ned" Lamont Jr, from the Democratic Party, is the current governor of Connecticut, and its' 89th governor during its' history. Until the 15th governor, Connecticut was still a British colony, and here we discuss those who held this position after the Independence. Jonathan Trumbull Sr, 16th governor of Connecticut, was its' colonial governor from 1769 to 1776, but because of his efforts in helping the revolutionaries, he was among numerable colonial governors who kept their positions after the Independence. His son, Jonathan Trumbull Jr also served as the governor of Connecticut from 1797 to 1809.

Taking a look into the history of the governorship in Connecticut after the Independence, it could be seen that during 74 terms, 71 persons served as governors of Connecticut (3 governors elected 2 times in non-continuous terms). For example, Henry Waggaman Edwards served as the 27th governor of the state from 1833 to 1834, then Samuel Augustus Foot served as the 28th governor of the state from 1834 to 1835, and again, Edwards was able to gain the governor's seat as the 29th governor from 1835 to 1838. Since 1776 (the date Connecticut declared its independence) to now (2021), 71 Persons served as governors of this state. 30 were Republicans, 21 were Democrats, 7 were Whigs, 6 were members of the Federalist Party, 2 were Democratic-Republicans (or Jeffersonian Republicans), one was a member of the National Republican Party, one was a member of the Native American Party (also known as Know Nothing Party), one was an Independent candidate, and 2 governors had no political affiliation. According to these numbers, historically, Republicans had 30 governors and were superior in this issue, while Democrats had 21 governors. However, recent years have witnessed a better performance by Democrats, and since 2011, both elected governors of Connecticut have been Democrats.

Conclusion: It could be observed that Republicans have a better record in history of U.S. presidential elections in Connecticut than Democrats (23 wins vs 21 victories). While Democrats have won all 8 recent presidential elections in the state, Republicans have a better record in history of the U.S. Senate elections in Connecticut (they won 17 elections while Democrats had 16 victories), but the Democratic Party has kept both seats belonging to the state in the U.S Senate for a long time. History of the U.S. House of representatives' elections in Connecticut has been in favor of the Democratic Party, and Democrats have an upper hand (they sent 82 members of their party in Connecticut to the House, while Republicans sent 63), and all 5 current representatives from the state in the House are Democrats. Finally, the Republican Party has a better position in history of gubernatorial elections in the state (30 governors vs 21 for Democrats), but both recent governors of Connecticut have been Democrats. It could be concluded that although Connecticut has been a Republican-leaning state during most of its history, today (2021) it's a bastion of the Democratic Party.

Massachusetts

T he Historical state of Massachusetts is located in Northeastern America. Boston is the capital of the state. Massachusetts is a part of the New England area and was one of the initial 13 colonies which revolted against the British colonial rule and declared their independence in 1776. During the U.S history, Massachusetts has played an important role in culture, art, economy, and generally, the formation of the U.S. Boston Tea Party Movement, which was a protest and political movement and marked the first major public disobedience of the British colonial rule, which began on 16 December 1773 after the historical incident of Boston Tea Party in Griffin's Wharf, Boston, Massachusetts, making it a prelude to the Revolutionary war, Independence Declaration and finally, the formation of the U.S. In 1775, the first Revolutionary battles of Lexington and Concorde were fought in Lexington, Massachusetts between the American Revolutionaries and British forces. Soon, fighting spread to Concorde, Lincoln, Menotomy and Cambridge. After declaring its independence on 4 July 1776, like other initial 13 colonies, Massachusetts was governed as an autonomous area until 6 February 1788. On this day, the state ratified the U.S Constitution and joined the newborn nation as its 6th state. During the Civil War, Massachusetts was an anti-slavery state and remained in the Union, and because of its high industrial capacity, helped the Union Army through providing munitions, supplies, and mobilization of more than 160 thousand soldiers. Armory Springfield, first Federal firearms factory, was one of the first factories in the country which specialized in manufacturing weapons and acted as the main arms production facility for the Union Army, playing a major role in the Civil War.

Despite the cotton trade embargo implemented by the southern states during the Civil War, which caused the shutdown of the Massachusetts textile industry, citizens and tradesmen of the state continued to support the Union Army, and Boston newspapers covered news of the War constantly.

According to the last census, Massachusetts had a population of 6.892.503 inhabitants. 71.1% of the population is white, 12.4% are Latinos, 9% are blacks, 7.2% are Asians, 0.5% are Native Americans and Alaskans, 0.1% are Hawaiians and other Pacific islanders, and 2.6% are from other races and ethnicities. Most of the Irish-Americans in the U.S live in Massachusetts.

Massachusetts is home to many credible universities and education institutes, including the Massachusetts Institute of Technology (MIT), Harvard University (Oldest university in the U.S and a member of Ivy league), University of Massachusetts in Amherst, University of Boston, Tufts University in Medford city (where Iranian-American Billionaire and owner of E-Bay site, Pierre Omidyar and Nasser Talebzadeh, controversial Iranian-American physician graduated) have turned the state into a higher education hub, and Boston, capital of the state, because of its numerous universities, is known as a cultural capital.

Historically, Massachusetts was an Industrial state, but now, it's a hub for technology, investment, biotechnology, education, and tourism. Large scale agriculture is not a common activity in the state, but house and family agriculture are done by many inhabitants, and 79.7% of the population have their private agricultural lands. Direct selling of agricultural products is common in Massachusetts, and the state is among the top 10 states of the country in this issue. Greenhouse corps, apple, sweet corn and white mulberry are the main agricultural products of Massachusetts. The state also ranks 5th among the countries states in cranberry production. All these factors together help Massachusetts to maintain a strong economy. Boston and Cambridge cities are major centers of biotechnology.

Many large corporations have headquarters in the state, like 1. GENERAL ELECTRIC, one of the giant industrial and home products manufacturers in the world, 2. TJX (chain store for shoes, clothes and home products), 3. NATIONAL AMUSEMENTS (theater company and mass media holding company), 4. STOP & SHOP (store chain), 5. THERMO FISHER SCIENTIFIC (active in technology) , 6. Raytheon(one of the largest defense corporations in the U.S), 7. STAPLES (office retail company and electronic and printing services, in addition to selling office products and furniture) are among these corporations.

1.Freedom Trail, the trail which includes sites of some events of the American Revolutionary War, and meeting site of the revolutionaries. 2. Faneuil Hall, which witnessed popular protests, political meetings, gatherings and anti-slavery speeches. 3. Museum of Fine Arts and the Isabella Stewart Gardner Museum, Isabella Stewart Gender Museum was home of a collector and patron of the arts. Due to her own precept, his house was opened as a museum to the public. 4. Mayflower II and Plymouth Plantation reconstructed museums, this is where separatists from the Church of England, known as pilgrims, entered there in 1620 and formed the Plymouth colony. 5.Salem's Historic Houses, including judge Jonathan Corwin who was in charge of the famous witch hunt. 6. Armory Springfield, the first federal firearms factory and one of the first factories which specialized in arms production in the U.S and acted as the main provider of weapons for the Union Army. Now it's open to the public as a museum, historical site, and largest American firearms collection in the world. 7. Old Sturbridge Village, a historical village with a mill and many shops, dating back to the 1800s. 8. Minute Man National Historical Park and Lexington Green, a trail British colonial forces passed to suppress the Massachusetts Revolutionaries. 9. Historic Deerfield district, houses and art galleries located here were built during the period 1650-1900. 10. Making trips in Island Life on Martha's Vineyard, testing fresh agricultural products and enjoying a calm and charming environment. 11. Amherst and the Pioneer Valley with their museums, galleries, bookshops and historical places.12. Cape Cod beautiful beach with its lighthouse and fresh weather, an ideal place for boating, hiking and serving sea foods. 13. Harvard Square and museums, all are among tourist destinations in Massachusetts, which make the state a historical and calm area and help the tourism sector as a part of the economy in the state.

1. John Adams, John Quincy Adams, John.F. Kennedy, George H. W. Bush (also known as Bush the father), 2. Michael Rubens Bloomberg, politician, merchant and one of the founders of Bloomberg Media

Company, 3. Ralph Waldo Emerson, American philosopher and founder of Transcendentalism Literary School, 4. Edgar Allan Poe, author, poet, and one of the central figures of the Romanticism Movement in the U.S., 5. Uma Thurman, actress and model, are among people from Massachusetts. The name of the Kennedy family (among them Joseph Kennedy Sr, John.F. Kennedy, Robert.F. Kennedy, Ted Kennedy) is tied with Massachusetts. Father of the family, Joseph Kennedy Sr, was the American Ambassador to the UK and hoped to win the U.S presidency but wasn't able to achieve it. Later, his son, John, turned his father's dream into reality. Even for John, when he was a candidate for the presidency, it was said that because of his Irish origin, he had little chance.

Since 1789, (the date the first U.S presidential election was held in Massachusetts), the state has taken part in all 59 U.S presidential elections. Republicans won 21 contests, Democrats had 21 victories, Federalist Party scored 7 wins, Whigs had 5 wins, Democratic-Republicans won 3 contests and the National Republican Party was able to score 2 victories.

For a better inspection, the history of the presidential elections in Massachusetts could be divided into 3 parts. First part, from 1789 to 1852, witnessed 17 presidential elections in the state. The Federalist Party won 7 times, Whigs scored 5 victories, Democratic-Republicans gained 3 wins, and the National Republican Party had 2 victories. As it could be seen, in this part, the Democratic Party failed to win any contests in the state, while the Republican Party established first in 1854. This period saw an edge for Federalists, led by Alexander Hamilton, first United States Secretary of the Treasury and one of founding fathers of the nation. Second period, from 1856 to 1924, saw 18 elections, and the Republican Party won 17 of them, while the Democratic Party emerged victorious in a single contest. The second period was clearly in favor of the Republicans. Third part, from 1928 to 2020, which included 24 elections, saw 20 victories for the Democratic Party, while Republicans won 4 times. It's worth noting that 9 out of 20 Democratic victories in this period happened from 1988 to 2020, which shows a tilt toward the Democratic Party among the voters in the state during the recent 30 years.

In the 2020 Democratic Party presidential primaries in Massachusetts,

Joe Biden won the candidacy by gaining 33.6% of the votes, while his closest rival, Bernie Sanders, got 26.7%.

The 2020 Republican Party primaries in Massachusetts witnessed a victory for Donald Trump who got the candidacy by winning 87.7% of the votes, while his rival Bill Weld won 9.3% of the votes.

Finally, the 2020 U.S presidential election in Massachusetts witnessed a decisive victory for Democratic candidate, Joe Biden, who won 65.6% of the votes, while his Republican rival, Donald Trump, got 32.1%. Biden won all 11 electoral votes from Massachusetts.

Before entering discussions about the history of the U.S Senate elections, it should be pointed out that the National Republican Party (active 1824-1834) changed its name 3 times during its activity and ended its political life under the name mentioned above. The party established for the first time in 1824 as Adams-Clay Republican Party, changed its name to Adams's Men in 1825 and then to Anti-Jacksonian Party in 1828, and finally called itself the National Republican Party in 1830. As mentioned before, the aim of mentioning these explanations about the political parties is to clear the mind of the readers who are interested in the political history of the U.S. (specially history of elections) about different names of political parties during their life. For example, John Bailey, House representative from Massachusetts during 1823-1831, served as a member of a single party with 3 different names (Adams-Clay Republicans, Adams's Men gathering and Anti-Jacksonians).

From 1789 to 2021 , 53 persons have entered the U.S Senate as elected representatives from Massachusetts , of which 14 were members of the Republican Party , 12 were Democrats , 11 were Federalists , 5 were members of the Whig Party , 1 was a Democratic-Republican , 1 was an Adams's Men Gathering member and then Anti-Jacksonian , 1 was a member of Pro-Administration Party (actually , not a real political party; those who supported George Washington and treasury secretary , Alexander Hamilton were called by this title , and robust political parties in those days have not been shaped yet). 8 senators changed their political affiliations during their careers, of which 2 were Pro-Administration Party members and Federalists , 2 were once Federalists and sometimes Adams-Clay Federalist Party members and once served as Adam's Men Gathering members , one had a record of membership in the Adams' Men , Anti-Jacksonian and Whig parties , one served as

Anti-Jacksonian and Whig , one experienced membership in the Free Soil Republican and Liberal Republican parties. Henry Wilson entered the Senate through a coalition of Democrats, the Native American Party (also known as Know Nothing Party), Whigs and Free Soil Party in Massachusetts, but later joined the Republicans, and until 1851, none of the Republican and Democratic candidates from the state were able to enter the U.S Senate. In this year, the first Democratic candidate entered the U.S Senate. For Republican Party, that's not strange, because the party hadn't been established yet.

As the statistics show, the number of those senators who served only as Republican Party members from Massachusetts, in addition to those who experienced membership in other parties during their careers, was 16, while the same number for Democrats is 12, showing superiority of Republicans in the issue. But since 1979, sympathy toward the Democratic Party among the voters has increased, and out of 8 elected senators in this 40-year period, 7 were Democrats and one was a member of Republican Party. Current U.S senators representing the state, Elizabeth Warren and Edward John Markey, both are members of the Democratic Party.

Edward Moore Kennedy (known as Ted Kennedy), younger brother of John.F. Kennedy (former president of the U.S), with a 47-year record of presence in the U.S Senate (1962-2009) as a Democrat and Henry Cabot Lodge from the Republican Party with a 31-year history of serving in the Senate (1893-1924) were the longest-serving U.S Senators from Massachusetts. The Lodge family is among old political families from Massachusetts, and several generations of the family served as U.S Senators from Massachusetts. John Quincy Adams and John Kennedy, both U.S. presidents, had also served as U.S Senators from Massachusetts during their political careers.

From 1789 to 2021, 420 persons have represented Massachusetts in the U.S House of representatives, of which 122 were members of the Republican Party, 94 were Democrats, 52 were Federalists, 47 were Democratic-Republicans, 31 were members of the Whig Party, 5 were Pro-Administration Party members, 4 were Anti-Jacksonians, 4 were Adams's Men Gathering members and then Anti-Jacksonians, 2 were Anti-Administration Party members, 2 were sometimes Adams-Clay Republicans who later became Adams's Men Gathering members and later Anti-Jacksonians, one was an Adams-Clay Republican and then an Adams's Men gathering member, one was an Adams-Clay Republican, one was an Adams's Men Gathering member, one was a Jacksonian, one was a Free soil Party member, one was member of Native American Party (also known as Know Nothing Party), one was an Anti-Masonic Party member, one was a Union Party member, one was an Independent Democrat, one was an Independent Republican, one was an independent candidate, and the rest were representatives with different political affiliations during their careers. Of these , 9 were sometimes Whigs and sometimes Anti-Jacksonians , 8 were Republicans and Native American Party (Also known as Know Nothing Party) members , 8 were sometimes Federalists and sometimes Pro-Administration Party members , 3 had a record of presence in the Anti-Administration and Democratic-Republican parties, 2 served as Federalists and Adams-Clay Federalists , one served as a member of the Federalist and Adams-Clay Federalist and Anti-Jacksonian parties, one was sometimes a Federalist and sometimes a Democratic-Republican , one had a record of serving as a Whig and Republican , one was a Federalist and an Anti-Jacksonian , one was sometimes a Whig and sometimes a member of the Free Soil Party , one served as member of the Free Soil and Native American parties , one was sometimes an Adams-Clay Republican Party member and sometimes a Democratic-Republican , one had a record of membership in the Whig , Democratic and Jacksonian parties, one was sometimes a Federalist and sometimes a Jacksonian and served as a Federalist Jacksonian for a while , one served as member of the Whig and Constitutional Union parties , one was sometimes a Democratic-Republican , a member of Adam-Clay Republican party for a while and sometimes served as a member of the Adams's Men gathering , one was sometimes a Democratic-Republican and sometimes an Adams's Men and sometimes an Anti-Jacksonian , one was sometimes a Federalist and sometimes an Adam-Clay Republican party and sometimes a Adams's Men, one was sometimes a Republican and sometimes a Democrat , an Independent for a while and also served as a member of the Native American Party, one served as a member of the Federalist , Jacksonian , Adams-Clay Federalist and Adams's Men parties. One experienced 5 political affiliations: Federalist, Anti-Jacksonian, Adams-Clay Federalist, Anti-Masonic Party and Whig.

Most of the representatives who changed their political affiliations during their careers, served between 1789 and 1860. As the statistics show, those representatives from Massachusetts who remained Republican during their entire serving record in the House, in addition to those who experienced membership in other parties, were 132 persons, and the same number for Democratic Party is 96. This shows that historically, the Republican Party had a better performance in the U.S. House of Representative elections in the state, but since 1997, none of the Republican Party members have been able to be elected in the House elections in Massachusetts, and Democrats have won all House elections in the recent 24 years. Today (2021), all 9 representatives from the state are Democrats.

John Quincy Adams and John.F. Kennedy, both U.S presidents, have also served as U.S House representatives from Massachusetts during their political careers.

John W. McCormack, a Democrat, with a 44-year record of presence in the House and Joseph W. Martin Jr from the Republican Party, who represented Massachusetts in the House for 42 years, have been the longest-serving representatives from the state in the U.S. House of representatives.

Cyrus King (his name is taken from Cyrus the Great, famous ruler of ancient Persia)served as the House representative from Massachusetts (1813-1817), and his name would be an interesting issue for the Iranians.

John Hancock was president of the Second Continental Congress, and as president of the Congress, was the first person to sign and ratify the Declaration of Independence on 4 July 1776. He was from a rich and merchant family and spent a large amount of his capital to serve the Revolution. After his death, (220 years ago), his wealth was estimated to be about 350 thousand dollars. He served as the first governor of Massachusetts from 1780 to 1785, and some years later, was reelected as the 3rd governor of Massachusetts and served from 1787 to 1793.

From 1775 to 1780, Massachusetts was governed by a council, and in 1780, the first governor was elected. After service of several governors, again a council took the duty of governing the state from 1799 to 1800, and some years later, gubernatorial elections resumed. From 1780 until today (2021), Massachusetts has seen 66 governors, of which 31 were Republicans, 18 were Democrats, 5 were Whigs, 5 were Federalists, 5 were members of the Democratic-Republican Party, one was a National Republican, one was a Native American Party (also known as Know Nothing Party) member, and one had no political affiliation. Republicans have had the upper hand in the history of the gubernatorial elections in the state. They had 31 governors that were Republicans vs 18 for Democrats), and out of 9 elected governors in the recent 55 years, 6 were members of the Republican Party, while 3 were Democrats. Charles Duane Baker Jr, current governor of the state, is a Republican. It should be noted that Massachusetts witnessed 8 acting governors during its history, a subject that wouldn't be discussed here.

Calvin Coolidge, 30th president of the U.S, and Mitt Romney, current Senator from Utah state and 2012 U.S presidential candidate have served as governors of Massachusetts during their political careers.

Conclusion: As it could be seen, Republicans and Democrats have equal share of wins in the U.S presidential election in Massachusetts (each with 21 victories), but the Democratic Party has been able to gain all 8 recent elections in the state. Historically, Republicans have an upper hand in the U.S Senate elections in Massachusetts. They sent 16 of their members in the state to the U.S Senate, while the number for Democrats is 12, but in the recent 40 years, out of 8 U.S Senators from the state, 7 have been Democrats, and both current U.S Senators from the state are members of the Democratic Party. Republicans also have an edge in the history of the U.S. House of representatives' elections in the state (132 representatives vs 96 for Democrats), but all 9 current representatives from Massachusetts in the House are Democrats, and while Republicans had 31 governors in the history of the state (Democrats had 18) and the current governor of Massachusetts is a Republican, it's clear that, today, Massachusetts is a Democratic-leaning state.

Maryland

The historical and coastal state of Maryland and its' capital hosted the first local, general assembly of America in 1772. Annapolis is the capital of the state. The name of the state is taken from Queen Henrietta Maria (also known as Queen Mary in England). This coastal state (located by Atlantic coast) was one of the initial 13 colonies which declared their independence from the British colonial rule during the American Revolution on 4 July 1776 and began a rebellion against the colonial rule. Finally, on 28 April 1788, Maryland joined the U.S. as its 7th state. Because of the bravery shown by the soldiers from Maryland during the Revolutionary War, George Washington called them "Old Line Soldiers", and the title "Old Line State" was given to Maryland. Baltimore is among important cities of the state and witnessed several battles during both the Revolutionary and Civil Wars. During the Civil War, although Maryland supported slavery, it didn't choose to secede from the Union, and 50 thousand soldiers from the state joined the Union Army, while 22 thousand volunteers joined the Confederate States Army. According to the last census, Maryland had a population of 6.045.680 inhabitants. 50% of the population is white, 31.1% are blacks, 10.6% are Latinos, 6.7% are Asians, 0.6% are Native Americans and Alaskans, 0.1% are Hawaiians and other Pacific islanders and 2.9% are from other races and ethnicities. Johns Hopkins University, one of the most credible universities in the U.S, especially in the research field, St. John's College, 3rd oldest university in the country, which its foundation dates back to 1696, University of Maryland, College Park,

Howard Hughes Medical Institute (a major center for biological and medical research in the U.S), and Goddard space flight center, the first, oldest, and one of the most important space centers of NASA, are all among scientific and education institutes in Maryland. Also, Maryland is the cybersecurity hub, and headquarters of the NSA (National Security Agency).

Apart from the apple, the main agricultural product of the state, Maryland farmers produce watermelons, peas, sweet corn, tomatoes, cucumbers, seedlings, indoor trees, flowers, chicken, eggs, pork, beef, turkey and dairy products. Also, Maryland is a top state in fishing crabs and sea shells, and is known as the main crab producer of the country.

Electronic and computer products, processed foods, extracting iron, copper, chromium, silver, magnesium, titanium, crushed stone and coal are among other industrial and mineral products of Maryland. Maryland is a top state in producing processed food, and some of the largest factories involved in this industry are located in the state. The headquarters of some large corporations like 1. MARRIOTT (chain hotel), a universally well-known corporation, 2. LOCKHEED MARTIN, manufacturer of F-16, F-22, F-117 and F-35 fighter jets, a weapons manufacturer giant in the world, 3. PERDUE FARMS, a major food production company, 4. GEICO insurance, one of the largest in the U.S., 5. Laureate International Universities, with more than 150 university branches around the world, and 6.the SOCIAL SECURITY ADMINISTRATION company are all located in Maryland.

These industries and research centers, together help Maryland to have a strong economy. In 2020, the state was second nationwide in the nation of millionaire household per capita.

Maryland has many tourist attractions, and among them, these could be named: 1- Fort McHenry National Monument, a fort which defended Baltimore against a British invasion in 1814 and made the British attempt futile. 2- Old Town Annapolis and William Paca House, Paca was among signers of the Declaration of Independence, and also served as the 3rd governor of Maryland. 3- Hammond-Harwood House, a house which belonged to Matthias Hammond, a rich farmer and landowner. The house was built in 1774. 4-The Walters Art Museum, with a unique collection of historical assets. 5- Ocean City Boardwalk, a resort with many shops and an old carousel on the Atlantic coast.

6-Antietam National Battlefield monument, the battle took place in 17 September 1862 and was one of the bloodiest battles of the Civil War, resulting in more than 23 thousand of the dead, wounded and missing. 7-Baltimore and Ohio Railroad Museum, which contains information about the history of the railroad in the U.S. 8-Maryland State House, the oldest State House still in use in the U.S 9-U.S. Naval Academy Museum and Chapel, containing assets and memorials of the academy and famous personalities and events in the history of the Navy. 10-Chesapeake Bay Maritime Museum and the lighthouse nearby. 11-Historic London Town and Gardens, a settlement dating back to mid 17th century. 12-Chesapeake & Ohio Canal National Historical Park, along with beaches, several museums, and resorts.

Nancy Pelosi, current Speaker of the U.S House of Representatives, Michael Phelps, swimmer and one of the most successful and medal-winner athletes in the history of Olympics, Thurgood Marshall, American lawyer, activist in Civil Rights movement and the first black person who gained membership in the U.S Supreme Court, Frank Vincent Zappa, musician, electric guitarist and director, Edward Witten, American mathematician and physicist, Harriet Tubman, social activist and one of the most successful leaders of the "Underground Railroad" movement in 19th century are among famous people from Maryland. The Underground Railroad was an organization that helped black slaves flee to northern states where slavery was obsolete.

From 1780 to 2021, Maryland has taken part in all 59 U.S presidential elections. Of these contests, the Democratic party won 30 times in the state, among which 2 rounds were in 1904 and 1908, those electoral votes were split seven vs one and six vs two in favor of the Democratic Party between the Democratic Party and the Republican Party, respectively. Republicans had 12 victories, Whigs scored 4 wins, Democratic-Republicans won 3 times, Federalist Party scored 2 win and the Native American Party (also known as Know Nothing Party) emerged victorious in a single contest. 5 rounds of elections saw a split of the electoral votes between Federalists and Democratic-Republicans, and also 2 rounds between National-Republicans and Democrats.

For a better inspection, history of the U.S presidential elections in Maryland could be divided into 2 periods. First part, from 1789 to 1856, saw 18 elections. Whigs won 4 times, Democratic-Republicans gained 3 victories, Federalists had 2 wins, Democrats and the Native American party each scored a single victory and as mentioned above, 7 contests resulted in a split of the electoral votes. Second period, from 1860 to 2020, witnessed 41 presidential elections, of which Democrats won 27 contests, Republican Party scored 12 victories, and as pointed before, 2 contests (1904 and 1908) resulted in split of the electoral votes, in favor of Democrats. As the statistics show, Democrats have an edge in the issue, and also in recent decades have shown a strong performance, winning all 8 recent U.S presidential elections in Maryland.

The 2020 Democratic presidential primaries in Maryland saw a victory for Joseph Biden, who won 84.9% of the votes, while his closest rival, Bernie Sanders got 6.3% of the votes.

In the 2020 Republican presidential primaries, Donald Trump gained the candidacy through winning 88.3% of the votes, defeating Bill Weld, who won 11.7% of the votes.

Finally, the 2020 U.S Presidential elections in Maryland resulted in a win for the Democratic Party candidate, Joe Biden, who won 65.4% of the votes, while his Republican counterpart, Donald Trump, won 32.2% of the votes. All 10 electoral votes from Maryland were added to Biden's vote basket. From 1789 to 2021, 57 persons have represented Maryland in the U.S Senate. Among them, 20 were Democrats, 10 were Republicans, 5 were Federalists, 4 were Democratic-Republicans, 3 were Whig Party members, 2 were members of the Unconditional Union Party (originally Unionist Party, which changed its name during the Civil War), one was a Pro-Administration Party member, one was an Adams's Men Gathering member and then an Anti-Jacksonian (as mentioned in previous parts, these were 2 different names for the same party), and 11 were senators who changed their political affiliations during their careers , of which 2 were sometimes Pro-Administration Party members and sometimes Federalists , 2 served as Whigs and Anti-Jacksonians , one was a Whig for a while and sometimes served as a member of the Opposition Party , one served as a Federalist and an Anti-Jacksonian , one was once a Democrat and then a Republican , one was a Native American Party member who also served as a Unionist , one experienced membership in Whig , Democratic and Unconditional Union parties , one had served as a Whig , Democrat and Opposition Party member , and one switched sides among Democratic-Republicans,

Crawford Republicans, and the Opposition Party. As the statistics show, those senators who only served as Democratic Party members and represented Maryland in the U.S Senate, in addition to those who experienced membership in other political parties, were 33 persons, while the same number for Republicans is 11. This shows a better record for Democrats in the history of the U.S Senate elections in Maryland. The trend has continued in recent decades, and one of the Maryland seats in the U.S Senate has been held by Democrats since 1977, while the other seat has seen the same situation since 1987. Benjamin Louis Cardin and Christopher J. Van Hollen Jr, both Democrats, currently (2021) represent the state in the U.S Senate. Paul Sarbanes (years of service 1977-2007) and Barbara Mikulski (years of service 1987-2017), both Democratic Party members, were the longest-serving senators from Maryland; each represented the state for 30 years.

From 1789 to 2021, Maryland has sent 286 elected candidates to the U.S House of representatives. Among them, 115 were Democrats, 48 were Republicans, 25 were Democratic-Republicans, 20 were Whigs, 16 were Federalists, 9 were Jacksonians, 7 were members of Anti-Administration Party, 5 were Pro-Administration Party members, 5 were Anti-Jacksonians, 2 were Adams's Men Gathering members, one was first Anti-Jacksonians and then an Adams's Men Gathering member (as mentioned before , both names point to a single party), 3 were members of the Native American Party (also known as Know Nothing Party), 2 were Unionists, one was member of Unconditional Union Party (as said before Unionist and Unconditional Union are different names for the same party in different periods), one was a Federalist Jacksonian, one was a Crawford Republican, and 23 representatives changed their political affiliations during their careers, of which, 3 were sometimes Anti-Administration Party members and sometimes Democratic-Republicans, 2 were once Pro-Administration Party members who later joined the Federalists , 3 were Democrats who defected to Jacksonians, 2 were members of the Native American Party who joined the Unconditional Union Party, one switched between Federalists and Jacksonians, one was once an Adams-Clay Federalist and then a Federalist, one was a Whig who later became a Democrat, one was a member of an Unconditional Union Party who later defected to Republicans, one was a Whig who joined Anti-Jacksonians, one was sometimes an Adams-Clay Republican and sometimes a Jacksonian, one was a Whig who defected to the Unionist Party, one was once a Jacksonian and then a Whig, one was sometimes a Democrat and sometimes a Unionist, one was first a member of Unconditional Union Party and then joined Conservative Party, one was a Democratic-Republican who later defected to Adam's Men gathering and finally Jacksonian Republicans, one was once a Democratic-Republican who later joined Jacksonian Republicans, then Democrats and finally Jacksonians, one changed his political affiliation 4 times: first a Democrat, then a Jacksonian, then Republican, then Unionist and finally an Unconditional Union Party member. Finally, according to available sources, political affiliation of 2 House representatives from Maryland is not clear. As the statistics show, the number of those representatives who only served as Democratic Party members, in addition to those who had record of membership in other parties along their affiliation to Democrats, was 122. The same number for Republican Party is 50, showing an upper hand for Democrats in the issue.

Today (2021), Democrats of Maryland continue to maintain their superiority in the House, and 7 out of 8 seats belonging to Maryland in the House is in their hands, while Republicans only have 1, showing popularity of Democrats among voters in the history of the U.S House elections in Maryland.

After declaring independence from the British colonial rule, the first governor of Maryland was elected in 1777, and until today (2021), 62 governors have served in the state. Among them, 29 were Democrats, 8 were Federalists, 8 were Democratic-Republicans, 7 were Republicans, 4 were members of Whig Party and 3 were governors who changed their political affiliations during their careers, of which one was once a Whig and a Democrat for a while, one served as a member of the Unconditional Union and a Democrat, one had record of membership in the Native American and Constitutional Union parties and 3 governors were independent candidates.

As the statistics show, a number of the governors served as Democratic Party members during their entire terms, in addition to those who had record of membership in other political parties, was 31, and the same number for Republicans is 7, showing an upper hand for the Democratic Party in the history of gubernatorial elections in

Maryland, but the Republican Party has improved its performance in the issue during the recent years, and the current (2021) governor of the state, Lawrence Joseph Hogan Jr, is a Republican.

Conclusion: As seen before, the Democratic Party has a better record in the history of U.S. presidential elections in Maryland (30 victories, while Republicans won 12 times) and has won all 8 recent contests, and during the history of the U.S Senate elections, the situation is not much different. Democrats have sent 23 of their members to represent the state in the U.S Senate, while the same number for the Republican Party is 11, and currently (2021) both Maryland seats in the Senate are held by Democratic senators. During the history of the U.S House of representatives' elections in Maryland, Democrats had 122 elected candidates, while their Republican counterparts succeeded in sending 50 of their fellows to the House. Today (2021), 7 out of 8 House representatives from Maryland are Democrats. Finally, in the history of gubernatorial elections, the state shows an upper hand for Democrats, who had 31 candidates in the position of governor of Maryland, while the same number for the Republican Party is 7. so, it could be concluded that the Democratic Party has been the stronger side in the political history of Maryland, and currently, Maryland is a state with strong affiliation to the Democratic Party.

South Carolina

S outh Carolina state is located in southeastern America, and Columbia is its capital. The state was among13 colonies that in 4 July 1776 declared independence from British rule and formed the U.S in its initial shape. Charleston is the main city of the state, and according to the historical sources, about 40% of all black slaves who entered the U.S, were transported through this city. The state witnessed more than 200 battles and skirmishes during the Revolutionary War. Carolina was an independent area from 1776 to 1788, without existence of a central government in the U.S. But after ratification of U.S Constitution in 23 May 1788, South Carolina became 8th state of the country. And worth noting, South Carolina was first state to declare its withdrawal from the Union in 20 December 1860 through the vote of its legislative council, the move which became a prelude for beginning of the Civil War in the coming year (1861). Fort Sumter in Charleston harbor, South Carolina, was the first point attacked by Southern forces in 1861, resulting in outbreak of the American Civil War. In a show of respect to Charles I, king of England, the colony was named Carolina. The word "Carolina" is taken from the Latin word "Carlos", which in English changes shape to "Charles". According to last census, South Carolina is home to 5148714 residents, which 63.7% of them are whites, 27% blacks, 6% Latinos, 0.1% Hawaiians and other Islanders, 1.8% Asians, 0.5 native Indians and Alaskans, and 2% are from other races. University of South Carolina, one of the most active universities in research field through the U.S, Furman University, Clemson University, Wofford College, Citadel Military College of South Carolina and Medical University of South Carolina are among universities and education centers of the state.

Agriculture is the main sector of economy in South Carolina. Agriculture in the state is highly mechanized, and corns, beans, cotton, peanuts, tobacco, chicken, turkey and beef are main agricultural products of the state.

South Carolina was home to one of the oldest automotive factories in the U.S, Anderson Motor Company, which does not exist today. Today, South Carolina is a main center for manufacturing and assembling automobiles and their parts. The state ranks 1st in manufacturing car tires. In addition to automotive assembly plants and factories, one of 2 main places for assembly of Boeing-787 Dreamliner planes is located in South Carolina. Some large corporations, like 1-SONOCO (active in packaging industry) 2-INTERTECH GROUP, active in aviation industry, chemical industry and entertainment industry 3-AVX, manufacturing electronic components 4-BLUECROSS BLUESHIELD OF SOUTH CAROLINA insurance company, and 5-Denny's chain restaurant have headquarters in the state.

Among tourist destinations of South Carolina, these could be named: 1-Charleston's Historic District, which includes more than 1400 historical houses, churches and other buildings, among them Cathedral of St. John the Baptist 2-Myrtle Beach, along with hotels, shops, restaurants and amusement parks 3-South Carolina Plantations, known as oldest American-style gardens.4-Hilton Head Island, with long bicycle passages. 5-Fort Sumter and Charleston Harbor, first point attacked by the Confederate Army in 1861, the incident which marked beginning of the American Civil War. 6-Riverbanks Zoo and Garden, Columbia , including many wild living species , from giraffes to African lions 7-Middleton Place Plantation , plantation and house dating back to 16th century , with antique style and furniture 8-Drayton Hall ,oldest farmhouse dating back to 17th century which has not seen reconstruction 9-Old Slave Mart Museum , site of a slave market before the Civil War 10-Historic District in Downtown Wilmington , a district with hundreds of historical houses , dating back to 19th and early 20th century. 11-Bellamy Mansion, a historical mansion which belonged to a wealthy merchant, John Dillard Bellamy, one of the rare mansions which wasn't damaged during the Civil War. 12-Cape Fear & Brunswick

Islands Beaches, and its beautiful nature 13-beautiful and historical Airlie Gardens, dating back to 1886. 14-Poplar Grove Plantation, one of the oldest peanut plantations in the US 15-USS Yorktown and Patriots Point. These, along with other museums, beaches and historical places help the tourist sector in South Carolina to grow.

Some of famous people from South Carolina could be named here: 1- Andrew Jackson, 7th President of the U.S, who was a soldier of 1812 war with the British, was from South Carolina. Jackson became national hero of this war. But he is also known for being in possession of many slaves, getting involved in killing of Native peoples and his involvement in Indian removal act.2- Joseph Leonard Goldstein, Nobel Prize winner in Medical sciences. 3- Ronald Erwin McNair, NASA astronaut and physicist, who was killed in Challenger space shuttle accident 4- Joe Frazier, former heavy boxing world champion 5- James Brown, singer and lyricist.

Since 1789 to now, 59 presidential elections have been held in the U.S, and South Carolina has taken part in every presidential election except 1864, because of Civil War. In these 58 rounds, Federalist Party emerged winner in 2 contests, Democratic-Republicans won 8 elections, independent candidates scored 2 victories, State's Rights Democratic Party won a race, Republicans gained 17 victories and Democrats won 28 elections.

To take a better look into the subject, the period could be divided into 3 parts: in first part, from 1789 to 1876, 22 elections were held in the state, and Democratic-Republicans were the most successful party during these years and won 8 contests, while Democrats scored 7 victories, Republicans won 3 contests, Federalist Party had 2 victories, and 2 independent candidates won 2 rounds of elections.

But in second part, from 1880 to 1960, the state witnessed 21 presidential elections, and Democrats won 20 of them, while States Rights Democratic Party was able to gain a single victory.

Third part, from 1964 to 2020, has seen 15 contests in South Carolina, and except 1976, Republican Party was able to win remaining 14 elections. As it could be seen, Democrats have the upper hand in history of the U.S presidential elections in the state, and won 28 contests while Republicans had 17 victories, but in recent 60 years Republicans have been decisive winners of presidential elections in South Carolina, winning 14 out of 15 elections, including 11 recent contests since 1980, and political sphere of the state is in their favor.

In 2020, because of decisive statewide support for Donald Trump as the Republican candidate, Republican presidential primaries in South Carolina were not held.

Democratic primaries in the same year witnessed a victory for Joseph Biden, who got 48.6% of the votes, while his closest rival, Bernie Sanders took 19.8%.

Finally, 2020 presidential elections in South Carolina saw a victory for Republican candidate Donald Trump, who won 55.1% of the votes, defeating Joseph Biden who was able to gain 43.4% of the votes. Though, Trump took all 9 electoral votes of the state.

Since 1789 until now, 56 Senators from South Carolina have entered the U.S Senate, and among them there were 34 Democrats, 6 Republicans, 6 members of Democratic-Republican Party, a Jacksonian , a Nullifier Party member, a Federalist, a member of Pro-Administration Party, And 6 were Senators with multiple party affiliations , of which one was sometimes a Whig and sometimes a Nullifier Party member , one was once a Democrat and served as a Republican for a while , one experienced membership in Nullifier and Democratic parties , one served as Democratic-Republican , Crawford Republican and Jacksonian , one was sometimes a Jacksonian , sometimes a Nullifier Party member and also a Jacksonian Republican , and finally , a senator experienced membership in Pro-Administration , Anti-Administration and Democratic-Republican parties.

According to the statistics, Number of those senators who served only as members of Democratic Party from South Carolina, in addition to those who experienced membership in other parties during their careers, was 36. The same number for Republicans is 7, showing an upper hand for Democrats in the issue. But Recent years have been better for Republicans in the state, and out of 2 U.S Senate seats belonging to the state, Republican Party has gained one of them since 1964, and the other seat has been in the hands of Party members since 2005. Currently (2021), Timothy Eugene Scot and Lindsey Olin Graham represent the state in U.S Senate, both Republicans.

James Strom Thurmond from Republican Party (with a 49-year record of serving in U.S Senate,1954-2003) and Ernest. Hollings from

Democratic Party (with 39 years of presence in Senate, 1966-2005) have been longest-serving U.S senators in the history of South Carolina. Thurmond served his first 10 years as a Democrat and then Joined Republican Party. It should be noted he was one of the longest-serving senators in history of the U.S Senate.

From 1789 until 2021 , 221 persons have been elected as U.S House of representative members from South Carolina.99 of them have been Democrats, 36 were Republicans, 40 were from Democratic-Republican Party, 6 were Federalist , 5 were members of Nullifier Party , 1 was member of Whig Party , 4 were Anti-Administration Party members , 2 were Pro-Administration Party members, 4 were Jacksonians , one was Independent Republican Party member , a State's Democratic Rights Party member was able to enter the House And 22 winners had multiple party affiliations , of which 5 were sometimes Jacksonians , sometimes Democratic-Republicans and finally Jacksonian Republicans , 3 served as Democratic-Republicans and Jacksonians , 3 served as members of Nullifier Party and Jacksonians , 2 were once Democrats and once Nullifiers , 2 were sometimes Democrats and sometimes Jacksonians , 2 were once Democrats , and sometimes Jacksonians and Nullifiers , one experienced membership in Federalist , Pro-Administration , Democratic-Republican and Anti-Administration parties , one served as Jacksonian Republican and Nullifier , one was once a Whig and sometimes an Anti-Jacksonian , and finally , one had record of membership in Democratic and Republican parties .

As the statistics show, Number of those House representatives who served only as Democrats during their careers, in addition to those who experienced membership in other parties, was 106, and the same number for Republicans is 37, showing a clear edge for Democrats in the history of the U.S House of representatives in South Carolina. From 1897 to 1963 (66 years), none of Republican candidates in the state were able to enter the U.S House of representatives. But Republicans have improved their performance in recent years, and currently (2021), 6 out of 7 House seats belonging to South Carolina are held by them, while Democrats have 1.

Since 1776, South Carolina has seen service life of 87 governors. Among these, 56 were Democrats, 13 were Democratic-Republicans 9 were Republicans, 4 were members of Federalist Party, one was from

Conservative Party and 4 were without political affiliation (it should be noted that these 4 governors served before establishment of political parties in the U.S). Whole number of South Carolina governors during is history is 117, but the first 30 governors served during the British colonial rule and won't be discussed here. During the history of gubernatorial elections in South Carolina, Democrats had 56 governors while Republican Party had 9, and Before 1975, Democrats had 54 candidates who served as governors of the state, while only 3 Republican victories were scored, indicating a strong Democratic popularity. Bur after 1975 situation saw a dramatic change, and among last 8 governors, six have been Republicans and Democrats only had 2 wins. Current governor of South Carolina, Henry McMaster, is a member of Republican Party.

Conclusion: According to statistics presented above, Democratic Party won 28 presidential elections in the history of South Carolina, while Republicans won 17 times, showing an upper hand for Democrats in the issue, but Republicans have been winners in all recent 11 contests. In the history of the U.S Senate, the U.S House of Representatives, and gubernatorial elections the situation has not been much different, Democrats had 36 U.S senators, 106 House representatives and 56 governors, while Republican Party had 7 U.S senators, 37 House representatives and 9 governors. But Republicans have worked better in recent years and decades, holding one the U.S Senate seats belonging to South Carolina since 1964, and the other one since 2005, currently (2021) 6 out 7 House seats from the state is in their hands, and out of 8 recent governors, 6 have been Republican Party members (3 were elected governors since 2003). It could be concluded that South Carolina was a Democratic Party bastion through most of its history, but recent 40 years has seen a strong turn toward Republican Party among voters in the state.

New Hampshire

New Hampshire state and its capital, Concord, are located in Northeastern America. New Hampshire was one of the 13 Colonies that revolted against the British colonial rule and formed the United States of America in 4 July 1776. The state ratified the first local constitution independent of the British law among the colonies in 5 January 1776 (six months before Declaration of Independence). Finally, New Hampshire joined the new nation as its 9th state in 21 June 1788 through ratification of the Constitution. The state played a major role during the American Civil War, through mobilizing troops and providing arms, clothes and shoes to the Union Army. According to the last census, New Hampshire is home to 1359711 residents. Demographic statistics of New Hampshire shows composition of its population as this: 89.9% white, 1.8% black, Asian 3%, Native Indian 0.3%, Latino 4% and 1.8% others. Dartmouth College, one of the oldest and most credible colleges in the U.S and a member of Ivy League, University of New Hampshire, Saint Anselm College, Phillips Exeter Academy (one of the oldest high schools in the U.S along its famous library, Phillips Exeter Academy Library, the largest universally in its kind), are among universities and education centers in New Hampshire. Because of its geographical conditions and rocky topography, most of the area in the state is not suitable for agriculture, and main agricultural products of New Hampshire are Greenhouse crops, dairy, apples, cows, beef, and sweet corns. Sand and gravel (for road construction) and granite are main mineral products of the state. Computer and electronic products like phones, microchips, military communication tools and metalwork machinery, printing equipment, lens manufacturing equipment, optical tools, ball bearings and industrial tools are among other products of the state.

1- C&S WHOLESALE GROCERS (wholesale distributor of food and grocery store items) 2- ALBANY INTERNATIONAL (industrial-goods company) are among large corporations which their headquarters are located in New Hampshire.

Among tourist destinations in the state, these could be named: 1-Mt. Washington and The Cog Railway, which could be matched along a trip with the world's first mountain-climbing cog railway 2- The Flume Gorge and Franconia Notch, an 800 feet-long gorge located near Mount Liberty with a beautiful stream and amazing natural view. 3-Strawbery Banke Outdoor History Museum, the first town in Portsmouth area which was founded in 1623 4-Kancamagus Highway and White Mountain National Forest, which is not a real highway , but a trail with beautiful and attractive natural views , part of White Mountain National Forest 5-Market Square and Portsmouth's Historic Houses including historical houses and shops, some of them dating back to 16th century 6-North Conway and Mt. Washington Valley Ski Resorts , a suitable site for winter sports and entertainments 7-Hampton Beach with its white sands and entertainment facilities 8-Story Land amusement resort , a place for entertainment of children 9-Clark's Bears , a site to see shows presented by trained bears 10-Warner House , built in 1716 , which its furniture and paintings have remained untouched 11-Black Heritage Trail , a place for entering the black slaves into the U.S before the Civil War. 12-John Paul Jones House, a house which John Paul Jones, Hero of the Revolutionary War, lived there for a while 13-Fort Constitution and Portsmouth Harbor Light, which witnessed armed clashes during the Revolutionary War 14-Wentworth Coolidge Mansion, a 40-room mansion which was governor's seat building during Benning Wentworth service 15- Governor John Langdon House. These form the tourist sector of economy in the state.

1-Franklin Pierce , 14th president of the U.S , 2- Alan Bartlett Shepard, well-known astronaut of Apollo-14 space mission and the first American person to travel into space 3- Charles Carleton Coffin , one of the famous journalists during the Civil War 4- Plausawa , last known

Native American person who lived in Hancock city , New Hampshire 5-
John Stark , American military commander during the Revolutionary
War 6- Ralph Adams Cram , American architecture in 19th and 20th
centuries are among famous people from New Hampshire

Since 1788 to 2021, New Hampshire has taken part in all 59 U.S
presidential elections. In process Republican Party secured 29 victories,
while Democrats won 19 presidential elections in New Hampshire,
share of Federalist Party was 6, victories Democratic-Republicans won
4 elections, and National Republican party was able to make a victory
in the history of the state.

To have a better inspection, the history of the U.S presidential election
in New Hampshire could be divided into 2 periods. First period, from
1789 to 1852 saw 17 elections, in which Federalists gained 6 victories,
Democrats won 6 times, Democratic-Republicans scored 4 wins and
National Republican Party won a single contest. Second part, from 1856
to 2020 witnessed 42 rounds of elections in the state, and Republican
Party won 29 of them, while Democrats scored 13 victories. As it could
be observed, Republicans have an upper hand in the issue, and in a
52-year period (1856 to 1908) won all 14 U.S presidential elections in
New Hampshire, but Democratic Party has improved its performance
in recent years, and have won 5 recent elections in the state.

In 2020 Democratic primaries in the state, Bernie Sanders defeated
Pete Buttigieg, Sanders won 25.7% of the votes while his rival took
24.4%. Joe Biden ranked 5th in the state.

2020 Republican primaries in New Hampshire saw a victory for
Donald Trump who got 85.6% of the votes, while his rival, Bill Weld
won 9.1% of the votes.

And finally, in 2020 U.S Presidential elections in New Hampshire,
Democratic Party candidate Joe Biden was able to win the contest in
New Hampshire, gaining 52.7% of the votes while Republican candidate
Donald Trump took a share of 45.4%. Biden got all 4 electoral votes
from the state.

Since 1789 to 2021, 64 senators have been elected to represent New
Hampshire in the U.S Senate. 30 were Republicans, 15 were Democrats,
6 were Federalist Party members, 4 were Democratic-Republicans, 2
were Jacksonians, one was a member of Anti-Administration Party,
one was an Adams-Clay Republican, Adams's Men gathering member

and Anti-Jacksonian (as mentioned in previous part, 3 different names for a single party), And 5 were senators who changed their political affiliations during their careers. among them, one served as Democrat and Jacksonian, one had record of membership in Pro-Administration and Federalist parties, one was once a Democratic-Republican and served as an Adams-Clay Republican for a while, one was sometimes a Pro-Administration Party member, sometimes an Anti-Administration Party member and also worked as a Democratic-Republicans, and a senator switched sides among Free Soil Party, Republicans, Opposition Party and Independent Democrats.

According to the statistics shown above, Number of those senators who served only as Republican Party members from New Hampshire, in addition to those who experienced membership in other parties during their careers, was 31. The same number for Democrats is 16, showing superiority of Republicans in the issue. But Recent years have been better for Democrats in the state, and Cynthia Jeanne Shaheen, along with Margaret Coldwell Hassan, who currently (2021) represent New Hampshire in the U.S Senate, are both Democrats.

Jacob Harold Gallinger (with a 27-year history of presence in the U.S Senate, 1891-1918), and Henry Styles Bridges, who served as U.S senator from New Hampshire for 24 years (1937-1961) were longest-serving U.S senators from the state. Both of them were Republicans.

Franklin Pierce, 14th president of the U.S, once served as a U.S senator, representing New Hampshire in the U.S Senate.

From 1789 to 2021, 148 representatives from New Hampshire have been members of the U.S House of Representatives. These 148 consist of : 42 Republicans , 35 Democrats , 24 Federalists , 15 representatives from Democratic-Republican Party , 9 Jacksonians , 4 Adams's Men gathering members, an Adams-Clay Republican who later became an Adams's Men gathering member , 2 Whigs , an Anti-Administration Party member , And 14 were representatives with multiple political affiliations during their careers , of which 3 were sometimes Pro-Administration Party members and sometimes Federalists , 3 were Native American Party members (also known as Know Nothing Party) who also served as Republicans , 3 were Democratic-Republicans and Adams-Clay Republicans , 1 were once Democratic-Republicans and once Adams-Clay Federalists , one served as Federalist and Democratic-Republican

, one was sometimes a Jacksonian and sometimes a Democrat , one had record of serving as Anti-Administration Party member and Democratic-Republican , one was once a Whig , sometimes served as Free Soil Party member and once was a member of Independent , and according to our sources , a representative had no clear political affiliation.

Number of those House representatives who served only as Republicans during their careers, in addition to those who experienced membership in other parties, was 45, and the same number for Republicans is 36, showing an edge for Republicans in the history of the U.S House of representatives in New Hampshire. But Democrats have improved their performance in recent years, just like what they did in the U.S Senate elections in the state, and currently (2021), both House seats belonging to the state are held by them.

Franklin Pierce, 14th president of the U.S, who once served as a U.S senator, also served as a representative from New Hampshire in the U.S House of representatives during his political career.

Since 1776, the year Meshech Weare was elected as the first governor of New Hampshire, until now, 82 persons have served as governors of the state.49 were Republicans, 19 were Democrats, 7 were Democratic-Republicans, 3 were members of Federalist Party, one was a National Republican, one was a Whig, and one was a member of Native American Party. Meshech Weare had no political affiliation, because when he was elected, there were no political parties in the U.S, yet. Republicans have been superior in history of gubernatorial elections in New Hampshire, and Right now (2021), Chris Sununu, a Republican, is the governor of New Hampshire.

Conclusion: Republicans have an upper hand in the history of U.S presidential elections in the state (29 wins , while Democrats had 19) , while Democratic Party emerged winner in all 5 recent contests , and Republicans have the same situation in both U.S Senate and U.S House of representatives elections in the history New Hampshire (they had 31 U.S Senators and 45 House representatives , while Democrats had 16 senators and 36 representatives) , But both U.S senators and both House representatives who currently represent the state in the U.S Senate and U.S House of representatives , are Democrats. Gubernatorial elections in the state have a same history, and Republican Party was superior, which had 49 governors in the history of the state, while Democrats had 19 (current governor is a Republican, too). Statistics discussed above show that New Hampshire has been a Republican-leaning state through most of its history, but during recent years, a tilt toward Democratic Party is taking shape.

Virginia

Virginia state is located in the southeastern United States. Richmond is the capital of the state. Virginia which hosts the CIA, the Pentagon, and several major US military bases is the first and oldest British colony in North America. Virginia is known as the "mother of presidents" because it was the birthplace of most American presidents. Virginia was one of the thirteen colonies that rebelled against British colonialism and declared independence during the American Revolution. It is true that the American Revolutionary War ended in 1783 But in 1781, after the surrender of the British army in Yorktown, Virginia, a major blow was dealt to the British army, which was the prelude to the end of the war and the final victory of the revolutionaries. It eventually joined the United States on June 25, 1788, as the tenth state. During the Civil War, Virginia was one of the rebel states that called for secession and independence, but the northern part of the state wanted to stay in the Union, or the United States, so it seceded from Virginia and became known as West Virginia two years later. According to the latest census, the population of the state is 8,535,519. Its demographic context includes 61.2% whites, 19.9% blacks, 6.9% Asians, 9.8% Latinos, 0.5% Native Americans and Alaskans, 0.1% Hawaiians and people from other Pacific islands, and the rest 3.2% are from other races and ethnicities. The University of Virginia which is one of the most prestigious and oldest universities in the United States and the world, was founded in 1819 by Thomas

Jefferson, the third President of the United States; the College of William & Mary which is the oldest higher education institution in the United States after Harvard; Washington and Lee University which is one of the oldest institutions of higher learning in the United States; Virginia Polytechnic Institute and State University which are one of the most prestigious engineering universities in America; Thomas Jefferson National Accelerator Facility which is known as Jefferson Labs contains the largest free electron laser in the world. All these are among the scientific and educational centers of this state.

Virginia has a good agricultural industry and in the production of cereals, apples, grapes, tomatoes, peanuts, turkeys, dairy products and wine, it is one of the top states and the largest producer of seafood on the Atlantic coast. It is also one of the top five states in the field of tobacco production.

Technical, scientific, specialized services, repair shops, engineering and programming companies, and in general the services of a large part of the work are in this state.

In addition to computer chips, of which Virginia is a major producer, wood products, electrical equipment, furniture and transportation equipment are other products of the state. Coal is also one of the state's leading minerals.

The state hosts the headquarters of large corporations such as 1. Dollar Tree Chain Retail, 2. Hilton Hotels which has branches in most countries of the world, 3. Working at DXC Technology International IT service provider, 4. General Dynamics manufacturer of weapons and aerospace industries, 5. NORTHROP GRUMMAN manufacturer of weapons and aerospace industries, 6. BRINK'S provider of security and protection services, 7. Bechtel the largest construction company in the United States, 8. CAPITAL ONE. Also, there are a number of other such large companies.

The tourist attractions of this historic state consist of: 1. Colonial Williamsburg, live Historical Museum which consists of the old part of Williamsburg, which was also the first capital of the state of Virginia with old shops and streets, taking a walk there can be reminiscent of the walks of the founding fathers of the United States and the revolutionary debates, and it takes any tourist to the inflammatory period of the American Revolution. 2. Virginia Beach with golden sands and a variety of hotels and entertainment 3. Arlington National Cemetery which was built during the Civil War and celebrities, including John F. Kennedy, were buried there. 4. Mount Vernon which was actually the home and farm of George Washington, the first president of the United States. 5. Monticello and Charlottesville, which was the farm and personal property of Thomas Jefferson, the third president of the United States 6. Colonial National Historic Park (The pre-independence era) which consists of different parts such as: Jamestown the first entry point for British immigrants to Yorktown, where the British Army was finally defeated in the American Revolutionary War and also Manassas National Battlefield in which two civil wars took place in 1861 and 1862. 7. George Wythe House which was a signatory to the US Declaration of Independence in Virginia and trained Thomas Jefferson, John Marshall, Henry Kelly, and other men who were American leaders. 8. Chincoteague and Assateague Islands with a beautiful nature and Assateague Lighthouse, which adorns the island. 9. The American Civil War Center at Historic Tredegar which interprets the causes and consequences of the civil war from the perspective of the parties and monuments such as the Presidential Palace of US President Jefferson Davis are located there. 10. Virginia State Capitol in which Significant historical events have taken place, including the ratification of Virginia's secession and the appointment of Robert E. Lee as commander of the Southern Army in the Civil War. 11. Church Hill Historic District which is one of the oldest churches in the United States, where Patrick Henry, the famous speaker of the American Revolution, gave his famous speech "give me liberty or give me death" here. 12. Shenandoah National Park and Skyline Drive Along with many other historical, recreational and natural sites that have boosted the state's tourism industry and revenue.

1.George Washington, Thomas Jefferson, James Madison, James Monroe, William Henry Harrison, John Tyler, Zachary Taylor, Woodrow Wilson Former Presidents of the United States. 2. Patrick Henry the famous speaker of the American Revolution. 3. Robert Edward Lee, Senior Commander of the Allied or Separatist Soviet Army during the American Civil War. 4. Louise Firouz, Iranian-American woman who discovered the Caspian horse breed in northern Iran and lived in Iran for 40 years and introduced this breed to the world are among the celebrities born in this state.

Since 1789, when the first presidential election was held in the United States, Virginia state participated in the all 57 rounds except for the 1864 and 1868 elections due to the civil war. In these 57 contests, Democratic Party gained 31 victories, Republicans won 15 times, Democratic-Republicans scored 8 wins, Federalists won 2 times and Constitutional Union was able to gain a single victory.

To examine this election, we divide it into three parts. The first part is from 1789 to 1860, when the last election was held before the Civil War. 19 elections were held and the Democratic Party won eight elections, the Democratic-Republican Party won eight elections, the Federalist Party won two elections and the Constitutional Union Party won one election. The second part is after the civil war from 1872 to 1948 when 20 elections were held, and the Democratic Party won 18 elections and the Republican Party won two elections.

The third part is from 1952 to 2020 when 18 elections were held. The Republican Party won 13 rounds, and the Democratic Party won 5 rounds of electoral votes. It is noteworthy that the Democrats won the last four rounds of this election.

Statistics show Virginia Democrats winning 31 rounds ahead of the Republicans who only won 15 rounds during the state's presidential election. In addition, Democrats also won the last four rounds which shows the tendency of the people of Virginia in the presidential election to the learn towards the Democrats in recent years. In the 2020 presidential primary in Virginia, Democratic Joe Biden defeated Bernie Sanders by 23.1 percent with 53.2 percent of the vote.

The Republican Party did not hold primaries in the state because of its' strong support for the re-election of Donald Trump.

In the 2020 presidential election in the Virginia constituency, Joe Biden defeated Donald Trump with 54.1 percent of the vote and won 13 electoral votes in the state.

Finally, the 2020 presidential election in Virginia witnessed a victory for the Democratic Party candidate, Joe Biden, who got 54.1% of the votes, while his Republican rival, Donald Trump, won 44% of the votes. All 13 electoral votes from Virginia went to Biden.

From 1789 until 2021, Virginia has sent 54 senators to the U.S Senate. 20 were Democrats, 9 were Democratic-Republicans, 5 were Republicans, 3 were Anti-Administration party members, 3 were members of the Unionist Party who later changed their name to the Unconditional Union Party, 1 was a Whig Party member, 1 was a Pro-Administration party, 1 was a Jacksonian, 1 was an Anti-Jacksonian, and 10 were senators who changed their political affiliations during their careers. Among them, 2 were Readjuster party members who became Republicans, 1 was a Democratic-Republican who became a Crawford Republican, 1 was a Jacksonian and then became an Anti-Jacksonian, 1 was Democrat and then a member of Independence party, 1 was a Democratic-Republican and then a member of the Anti-Administration party, one was a Jacksonian and then a Jacksonian-Republican, one was a Democrat and then a Jacksonian, 1 was a Democrat, Jacksonian and then a Whig, and finally one was a member of the Anti-Administration party, Democratic-Republican and Crawford-Republican.

As the statistics show, the total number of senators who were only a member of the Democratic Party, plus senators who, in addition to other parties, also had a history of membership in the Democratic Party is 23 people, and there are also six Republican senators which shows the overwhelming superiority of the Democrats throughout the history of this election, and no Republican senator has won the election in the state since 2009. Mark Robert Warner and Timothy Michael Kaine are the state's two current senators who are both Democrats.

Harry Flood Byrd, a Democrat, with a 32-year record of service in the Senate (1933-1965) and John William Warner III, a Republican, with a 30-year record of service in the Senate (1979-2009), have been longest-serving senators from Virginia.

James Monroe and John Tyler, the former US presidents, have been state senators in the past.

Since 1789 to 2021, 422 persons have represented Virginia in the U.S. House of representatives, of which 161 were Democrats, 59 were Republicans, 50 were Democratic-Republicans, 21 were Federalist, 18 were Whig Party members, 14 were Jacksonians, 5 were National Republican Party, 3 were Adams men, 1 was Anti-Jacksonian and 2 were Adams men and Anti-Jacksonian. As mentioned in the previous sections, Adams and Anti-Jacksonians are the names of the same party in different eras and to show the working process of these parties, we mention them completely separate. 5 were Conservatives, 4 were members of the Unionist Party, 3 were Readjuster Party members, 3 were Anti-Administration party, 2 were Independent Democrats, 2 were Pro-Administration Party, 1 was Jackson-Republican, 1 was a member of Labor Party, 1 was a member of the Opposition Party, 64 were Representatives who changed parties during their tenure of which 12 were Anti-Administration party and Democratic-Republican party members, 10 were Democratic-Republicans and Crawford-Republicans and Jacksonians, 9 were Democrats and Jacksonians, 3 were Democratic-Republicans and Crawford-Republicans, 3 were Whigs and Democrats, 3 were Jacksonians and Anti-Jacksonians, 2 were Democrats and Independent Democrats, 2 were Democrats, Jacksonians and Conservatives, 1 was Pro-Administration party and Federalist, 1 was Federalist and Crawford Republican, 1 was Democratic-Republican and Jacksonian, 1 was Jacksonian and a National Republican party member, 1 was a Whig and a National Republican party member, 1 was a Readjuster party member and a Republican, 1 was a Jacksonian and a Crawford Republican, 1 was a Unionist Party member and Conservative, 1 was Pro-Administration and an Administration party member, 1 was Whig, Democrat and Jacksonian, 1 was Pro-Administration party member and Anti-Administration party member and Federalist, 1 was a Unionist party member and American Natives or Know Nothing party members, 1 was a Democratic-Republican, Jacksonian and a Jacksonian-Republican, 1 was a Democrat and Republican and an Independence party member, 1 was a Democratic-Republican and Crawford-Republican and Jacksonian and National-Republican party member, 1 was a Democratic-Republican and an Adams-Clay Republican and an Adams' Men and Anti-Jacksonian, 1 was a Democratic-Republican and Crawford-Republican and Adams' Men and Anti-Jacksonian and Whig, 1 was a Federalist and Adams' Men and Anti-Jacksonian and Crawford and Whig. Four representatives whose party names are unknown according to the sources we used.

As the statistics show, the total number of representatives who were only a member of the Democratic Party, plus representatives who, in addition to other parties, also had a history of membership in the Democratic Party is 179 people and 61 people were Republican representatives Which shows the superiority of the Democrats throughout the history of this election. Of the state's 11 current representatives, seven are Democrats and four are Republicans.

James Madison and John Tyler, former US presidents have represented the state in the U.S. House of Representatives.

Since Virginia declared independence in 1776, 70 people have served as governors, and the current governor of this state is the Seventy-fourth governor of this state and the reason for this numerical difference is that four of these governors held this position for two non-consecutive terms and as a result, have been recorded twice separately in history. Patrick Henry (1776-1779) was the first governor and again served as the sixth governor (1784-1786), and because it was two non-consecutive terms, he is recorded as the first and sixth governors in history. There were also 11 interim governors or acting governors that are out of our discussion because they were not elected.

Out of a total of 70 people who became governors, 36 were Democrats, 12 were Democratic-Republican, seven were Republicans, two were Whigs, two were Federalists, two were Conservatives, one was anti-Federalist, one was a Readjuster Party member, one was called Mills Edwin Godwin who won 2 rounds, once when he was a Democrat and once when he was a Republican. There were also seven governors who had no political party affiliation because American parties had not yet been formed at that time.

According to statistics, all governors who were only members of the Democratic Party and only Republicans in addition to Mills Edwin Godwin, who has served as governor in both Democratic and Republican parties, are estimated to be 37 Democrats and 8 Republicans, which shows the superiority of the Virginia Democrats throughout the history of this election. From 1874 to 1970, for nearly a century, no Republican governor held the post, and in 2022, Glenn Allen Youngkin from the Republican Party became the current governor of the state.

Former United States Presidents, Thomas Jefferson, James Monroe, and John Tyler are among the most prominent governors in the state.

Conclusion: Given that Virginia Democrats have won 31 rounds against the Republicans with 15 wins in the history of the presidential election and won electoral votes in all four recent elections, and Democrats have been superior throughout history of the Senate and the House of Representatives with 23 senators and 179 representatives vs. Republicans with 6 senators and 61 representatives and both current Senators of the state are Democrats and of the current 11 representatives,

7 are Democrats and 4 are Republicans. Moreover, the Democratic Party is superior and won 36 seats against the Republican Party with 7 seats in the history of the presidential election and, also the current governor of the state is a Democrat. Thus, it can be concluded that Virginia has been a Democratic-leaning state throughout history and it is still a state with a high percentage of Democrats.

New York

New York State, located in Northeastern America, was among the initial 13 colonies, which declared their independence from the British colonial rule and began a rebellion, leading to the American Revolutionary War. Albany City is the capital of the state. New York state played an important role during the American Revolution, and more than 1/3 of the battles of the war took place there. New York megapolis with the Times square and Manhattan district skyscrapers, Brooklyn district, famous Yellow taxies, and 11 September 2001 terrorist attacks, is a well-known city universally. Names like: the Rockefeller family, Donald Trump, Michael Bloomberg, Rudy Giuliani (Donald Trump's lawyer and Mayor of New York when 9/11 attacks happened), make people Remember New York. For a long time, New York has been a major universal cultural, political and economic center, and because of this, sometimes is called "the capital of the world". British "Stamp Act" which came into effect in 1765 made people of the New York area angry and played a role in formation of " Sons of Liberty " organization in New York (second state after Massachusetts), the group that began resisting the British colonists. New York finally joined the U.S as its 11th state on 26 July 1788. During the Civil War, despite some voices who supported seceding from the Union, New York remained Loyal to the Republic, and more than any other state, volunteers from New York served in the Union Army. According to the last census, New York state had a population of 19453561 inhabitants, of which 55.3% were whites, 19.3% were Latinos, 17.6% were blacks, 9% were Asians,

1% were Native Americans and Alaskans, 0.1% were Hawaiians and other Pacific islanders, and 2.7% were from other races and ethnicities.

Colombia University , 10th oldest university in the U.S (founded 1754 , one of the 9 universities which were established before the Independence) and one of the most credible research universities universally, Cornell University, New York University (a research university), University of Rochester, New York state university at Buffalo (mostly known as University at Buffalo, the largest state university in New York, Bellevue Hospital (oldest Federal hospital in the U.S and one of the largest in the country), and many other universities and colleges shape the research and education sector in New York .

New York state, and specially New York city, are major centers of economic, banking, financial, agricultural, technology, transportation, tourism, fashion companies, organizations and thinktanks, which help the state to maintain its strong economy. Wall Street (greatest stock exchange in the world), John.F. Kennedy airport (one of the largest airports universally, used in national and international flights, and containing 9 terminals), LaGuardia airport (one of the most crowded in the country) and Metropolitan museum are among major economic hubs in the state. New York also hosts the United Nations HQ on East Riverbank. New York is also home to New York Times newspaper, Fox Corporation and News Corp, Hearst Media Corporation, and many other media companies, and is known as "world's media capital".

First wind turbine in the world, which produced alternating electric current (designed by Nicola Tesla and manufactured by Westinghouse corporation) was installed in New York state (near Niagara waterfalls).

Because of its suitable weather and fertile soil, New York has a strong agricultural and animal husbandry sector. Apples, maple syrup, grapes, cauliflower, oil seeds and nuts, wheat, barley, different kinds of fruits, cow, beef, ducks, eggs, and dairy are among agricultural products of New York.

In addition, many large corporations have headquarters in New York. some of them could be named: 1-IBM (active in IT field). 2- DELOITTE (multinational professional services network providing tax and financial services around the world). 3-PEPSICO, also known as PEPSI, producing food, snacks, and drinks. 4-JPMORGAN CHASE, one of the 4 largest banks in the U.S. 5-CITI, financial services corporation, one of the most credible banks universally. 6-PFIZER, pharma company. 7-VERIZON COMMUNICATIONS (communication company).

New York is a in important universal tourist destination , and these are among its main attractions : 1-Saratoga National Historical Park, including many parts like the site where Battles of Saratoga was fought, the battle saw victory of American Revolutionary forces over the British Army, Schuyler House, living place of General Philip Schuyler, Revolutionary War Hero, and Saratoga Monument, in remembrance of surrender of British General, John Burgoyne ,along his forces, to General Horatio Gates, American Revolutionary commander on 17 October 1777, are located in this park. 2-Victory Woods, the last camp used by the British forces before surrender of General Burgoyne 3-Ellis Island, which hosts famous Statue of Liberty, a symbol of the U.S. Ellis Island Immigration Museum shows history of the island, once a gate for immigrants entering the U.S. 4-Times Square, one of the best-known places in the U.S. 5-Central Park , which has many parts like : Shakespeare garden or Chess & Checkers, zoo , shopping center and etc. 6-Niagara Falls State Park , including 3 waterfalls and 5 islands near Niagara Falls. 7-National Baseball Hall of Fame and Museum in Cooperstown, a place for baseball fans to learn more about history of this sport. 8- George Eastman House and the International Museum of Photography and Film, with 50 rooms filled by photos and writings taken and written by George Eastman. 9- Metropolitan Museum of Art, one of the best-known museums in the world. 10-Broadway and the Theater District, known as center of theater in the U.S. 11-9/11 Memorial and Museum, along an exhibition about the attacks. 12-Brooklyn Bridge, once a time the longest suspended bridge in the U.S. 13-Fifth Avenue, a famous shopping avenue in the U.S. Many fashion designers have their shops here. Grand Central Terminal, with its large and stunning building is located here, too. 14-New York Public Library, with its amazing architecture and decoration. 15-Wall Street, the street and areas nearby host most important financial deals and purchases in the world. 16-Sleepy Hollow and Tarrytown: Colonial-Era Villages, dating back to the British rule era. 17-Governor's Island, which contains military fortifications dating back to the Revolutionary and Civil War days. 18-Shea's Performing Arts Center, along with dozens of parks, a lake, museum, theater saloons, and historical buildings. These destinations attract 10s of millions of tourists annually, and along other industries, tourism sector helps New York to have 2nd largest economy among the U.S states.

1-Martin Van Buren, Millard Fillmore, Theodore Roosevelt, Franklin Delano Roosevelt, Donald Trump, presidents of the U.S. 2-Howard Melvin Fast, American great novelist and author. 3-Howard Zinn, historian, social critic, anti-war activist, and playwright. 4-Ferdinand Lewis Alcindor Jr (also known as Karim Abdul-Jabbar), one of the most famous basketball players during the history of NBA. 5-Thomas Cruise Mapother IV, well-known Hollywood actor. 6-Mike Tyson, famous boxer, and former world champion. 7-Larry King, veteran presenter of CNN. 8-Michael Jordan, basketball myth. 9-John Peter Petrucci, one of top guitarists universally. 10-Geraldo Rivera, journalist, presenter, and lawyer. 11-Eugene Luther Gore Vida, famous American novelist, playwright, and political activist. 12-James Montgomery Flagg, cartoonist, painter and poster designer. In 1917, he draws the famous "I want you for the U.S Army" poster, which showed Uncle Sam (symbol of America) appealing the Americans to join the military to participate in WWI. These were among well-known people from New York.

Because of having 29 electoral college votes, New York is a very important state in U.S presidential elections. Apart from the 1st U.S presidential election (which New York didn't take part, because of internal conflicts), the state has taken part in remaining 58 presidential elections held in the country until today (2021), of which Democrats won 26 times, Republican Party scored 20 victories, Democratic-Republicans won 6 contests, Federalists had 3 victories, Whigs won 2 contests, and an election in 1828 saw split of the votes among Democrats (20 votes) and National Republicans (16 votes).

Because of the sensitivity of the issue and to have a better inspection, it would be better to divide the history of U.S presidential elections in New York to 3 different periods. First part, from 1792 to 1852, saw 16 rounds of elections, and Democratic-Republicans won 6 of them, while Democrats had 4 victories, Federalists won 3 times and Whigs scored 2 victories. As mentioned before, 1828 elections witnessed a vote split between Democrats and National Republicans. Republican Party hadn't been established, yet.

Second period, from 1856 to 1984, witnessed 33 rounds of elections, in which Republicans had an upper hand (they won 20 contests), while Democrats gained 13 victories. But third period, from 1988 to 2020 has been completely in favor of Democratic Party, which won all 9 contests. As it could be seen, Democrats have an edge in history of the U.S presidential elections in New York, and recent decades witnessed decisive superiority of the party in political sphere of the state. Now (2021) New York is a major Democratic Party stronghold with its 29 electoral votes.

In 2020 Democratic presidential primaries in New York, Joe Biden won the candidacy through gaining 70.2% of the votes, while his closest rival, Bernie Sanders, won 17.6% of the votes.

Because of statewide popular support for Donald Trump, Republican Party in New York didn't hold its presidential primaries in 2020.

Finally, 2020 U.S presidential elections in New York resulted in a victory for Democratic candidate, Joe Biden, who defeated his Republican counterpart, Donald Trump. Biden won 60.9% of the votes, while Trump gained 37.7%. All 29 electoral votes from New York were taken by Biden.

Since 1789, the date first U.S Senate election were held, until now (2021), 60 persons have represented New York as U.S senators, of which 19 were Republicans, 16 were Democrats, 6 were Democratic-Republicans, 5 were members of Federalist Party, 2 were Jacksonians, one was a Whig , one was a Conservatist, and 10 were senators who changed their political affiliations, and among these 2 were sometimes Democrats and sometimes Jacksonians, one was once a Pro-Administration Party member and once served as a Federalist, one served as member of Pro-Administration and Democratic-Republican parties, one was sometimes a Whig and sometimes a member of Opposition Party, one had record of serving as Liberal Republican and Republican, one experienced membership in Democratic-Republican Party, Adams's Men gathering and Anti-Jacksonians Party, one served as Democratic-Republican, Crawford Republican and Jacksonian, one had record of membership in Pro-Administration, Federalist and Adams-Clay Federalist parties, and finally, a senator switched sides among Whigs, Opposition Party and Republicans.

According to the statistics presented above, Number of those senators who served only as Republican Party members from New York, in addition to those who experienced membership in other parties during their careers, was 21. The same number for Democrats is 18, showing an edge for Republicans in the issue. But Democrats have improved their performance in recent decades, and one of the U.S Senate seats belonging to New York is in their hands since 1977, and the other one has the same situation since 1999. Currently, both senators representing New York in the U.S Senate, Kirsten Gillibrand and Charles Ellis Schumer, are Democrats.

Jacob Koppel Javits from the Republican Party (present in the U.S. Senate 1957-1981) and Daniel Patrick Moynihan, a Democrat, (served in the U.S. Senate from 1977-2001), each with a 24-year history of service in the U.S Senate, were the longest-serving U.S. Senators from New York state.

Martin Van Buren, 8th president of the U.S and Hillary Clinton, former U.S secretary of the state, and wife to Bill Clinton, 42nd president of the U.S, were also U.S Senators from New York during their political lives.

Since 1789, the year the first U.S. House of representatives' election was held in New York, to 2021, 1457 persons have entered the U.S. House of representatives as representatives from New York. Because of the long political history of the state and its important role, a large number of political parties have emerged in the history of New York, which shows a lasting democratic sphere of the state and its' capacity for different political views. From these 1457 representatives, 552 were Democrats, 434 were Republicans, 102 were Democratic-Republicans, 93 were Whigs, 73 were Jacksonians, 53 were Federalist Party members,12 were Adams's Men Gathering members, 11 were Anti-Jacksonians, 2 were Adams-Clay Republicans, 2 were first Adams-Clay Republicans and later Adams's Men Gathering members, one was first an Adams-Clay Republican and then Anti-Jacksonian. As mentioned in previous parts, Adams-Clay Republican, Adams's Men and Anti-Jacksonian were all different names for a single party in different periods, 10 were Opposition Party members, 10 were Crawford Republicans, 8 were members of Anti-Masonic Party, 7 were members of the Native American Party (also known as Know Nothing Party), 6 were Independent Democrats, 3 were Pro-Administration Party members,

2 were Independent Republicans, 2 were Anti-Administration Party members, 2 were members of Independent, one was a member of the Anti-Lecompton Democratic Party, one was a member of the Socialist Party; one was a member of the Labor Party, and one was a member of the Free Soil Party .

Other House representatives from New York changed their political affiliations during their careers, of which: 10 were sometimes Jacksonians and sometimes Democrats, 6 were Democrats and Republicans, 5 were once Whigs and once Opposition Party members, 5 were sometimes Opposition Party members and sometimes Republicans, 4 served as Whigs and Republicans, 4 were sometimes Democratic-Republicans and sometimes Jacksonians, 4 were Anti-Masonic Party members who also served as Anti-Jacksonians, 3 were sometimes Whigs and sometimes Republicans and sometimes Opposition Party, 3 were once Whigs and sometimes served as Anti-Jacksonians, 3 were Pro-Administration Party members and Federalists, 3 served as Federalists, Adams-Clay Federalists , Adams's Men gathering members and Anti-Jacksonians, 2 were Anti-Lecompton Democrats who also had a record of membership in the Democratic Party, 2 were sometimes Republicans and sometimes Progressives, 2 served as Adams-Clay Republicans and Democratic-Republicans, 2 were sometimes Crawford Republicans and sometimes Democratic-Republicans, one had a record of serving as a member of the Labor and Republican parties, one was an Anti-Administration Party member who also served as Democratic-Republican, one experienced membership in the Federalist and Democratic-Republican parties, one served as a Democrat and a member of a Liberal Party of the New York Party, one had a record of serving as a Federalist and member of Adams's Men Gathering, one served as a Federalist and Jacksonian, one was sometimes a Whig and sometimes a Democratic-Republican, one served as a Democratic-Republican and a member of the Democratic Party, one was a Jacksonian Republican who also served as a Jacksonian, one had record of membership in Jacksonian and Crawford Republican parties, one served as a Jacksonian and member of Adams's Men gathering, one was sometimes a Whig and sometimes a Democrat, one was sometimes a Whig and sometimes an Adams-Clay Republican, one experienced membership in the Whig party and Adams's Men gathering , one was sometimes an Independent Republican and also served as a Republican, one had record of membership in Federalist, Adams's Men and Anti-Jacksonian parties, one switched sides among Democratic-Republicans, Jacksonians and Republican Jacksonians, one was sometimes a Democratic and sometimes an Jacksonian and sometimes Whig, one served as Democrat, member of Free Soil Party and Republican, one switched sides among Whigs, Anti-Jacksonians and Anti-Masonic Party, one served among Democratic-Republicans, Crawford Republicans, Jacksonians and Democrats, one served as Adams-Clay Federalist, member of Adams's Men gathering, Anti-Jacksonian and member of Anti-Masonic Party. one experienced membership in Democratic-Republican, Adams-Clay Republican, Adams's Men and Anti-Jacksonian parties, and according to our available sources, 17 representatives had no clear political affiliation.

The number of those House representatives who served only as Democrats during their careers, in addition to those who experienced membership in other parties, was 546, and the same number for Republicans is 457, showing an edge for Democrats in the history of the U.S. House of representatives' elections in New York. Currently (2021), 19 out of 27 New York representatives in the House are Democrats, and 8 are Republicans.

Millard Fillmore, 13th president of the U.S, once represented New York in the U.S House of representatives.

Emanuel Celler (with a 50-year history of presence in the U.S House representatives), Charles Bernard Rangel, who served as House representative from New York for 46 years and Daniel Alden Reed (who served for 42 years) were longest-serving members of U.S House of representatives from the state. Both of them were Republicans.

Since 1777 until 2021, 57 governors have served in New York. 24 were Democrats, 19 were Republicans, 10 were Democratic-Republicans (or Jeffersonian Republican), 3 were members of Whigs Party, and one was a Federalist.

As it could observed, Democrats have an upper hand in the issue, and since 2007, all 4 recent governors of New York have been members of Democratic Party. Kathleen Courtney Hochul, current (2021) governor of New York, is also a Democrat.

Martin Van Buren, Theodore Roosevelt, Franklin Delano Roosevelt and Stephen Grover Cleveland, presidents of the U.S, once served as governors of New York during their political careers.

Name of the Clinton Family is tied to the political history of the New York state. Col.Charles Clinton, was an English Irish military officer and politician during the colonial era. George Clinton, first governor of New York and 4th vice president of the United States, was also a member of continental congress which ratified the Declaration of Independence, and his brother, James Clinton, fought as a general during the Revolutionary War. Both of them were Charles Clinton's sons. General James Clinton was father to DeWitt Clinton, 6th governor of New York (who also had record of representing the state in the U.S Senate). George Clinton Jr and James G. Clinton were House representatives from New York. The family also had relationship with Simeon De Witt, geographer and Surveyor General of the Continental Army during the Revolutionary War.

Conclusion: Noting that Democrats have an upper hand in the history of the U.S presidential elections in the state (26 wins, while Republicans won 20 times), and Democratic Party has emerged winner in all 9 recent contests , Republicans have an edge in the U.S Senate and elections in the history of New York (they had 21 U.S Senators, while Democrats had 18), but both U.S Senate seats belonging to the states is held by Democrats (one since 1977 and the other one since 1999), that Democrats were superior in the history of the U.S House of Representatives election in New York (546 Democratic representatives vs 457 Republicans), currently (2021), 19 out of 27 House seats belong to Democrats (8 for Republicans), and finally, Democratic Party had 24 governors in the history of the state (19 were Republicans), including 3 recent governors, it could be said that historically, New York has been a Democratic Party bastion and the current situation is not much different.

North Carolina

North Carolina state, with its high mountains and stunning nature is located in southeastern America. Raleigh is the capital of this state. North Carolina was one of the initial 13 colonies which revolted against the British colonial rule. The initial 13 colonies declared their independence on 4 July 1776. These actions led to the Revolutionary War, and finally, end of the British rule. North Carolina kept its autonomy until 21 November 1789, the date U.S Constitution was ratified by the state legislators, and North Carolina joined the U.S as its 12th state. The state was a member of Confederation (southern states) during the Civil War, which tried to secede from the Union. Charlotte and Asheville are among important cities of the state. According to the last census, North Carolina had a population of 10488084 inhabitants, of which 62.6% were whites, 22.2% were blacks, 9.8% were Latinos, 3.2% were Asians, 1.6% were Native Americans and Alaskans, 0.1% were Hawaiians and other Pacific islanders, and the rest 2.3% were from other races and ethnicities. North Carolina hosts largest research park in the U.S, Research Triangle Park. The name is taken because of its proximity to 3 research universities, North Carolina State University, Duke University and North Carolina University at Chapel Hill. University of North Carolina at Chapel Hill (one of the oldest universities in the U.S), Duke University (transformed from a small school in 1838 to a credible university today), Wake Forest University, Davidson College, North Carolina State University (the largest in the state) and National Institute of Environmental Health Sciences are among universities and education centers in North Carolina.

North Carolina has a rich agriculture sector, and watermelons, strawberry, peaches, peanuts, tomatoes, corn, soybean, cotton, grapes, chicken, fishes, eggs and beef are among its main products. The state also ranks among top states in producing Christmas trees, sweet potatoes, tobacco and turkey.

Chemicals, cleaning agents, medical drugs, electronic communication and computer devices, car and truck parts, and aerospace industry products are among other goods produced and made in North Carolina.

Some large corporations like: 1-LOWE'S (American retail company specializing in home improvement). 2-BANK OF AMERICA (one of the largest banks in the U.S). 3- FAMILY DOLLAR (variety store chain). 4- FOOD LION (grocery store chain). 5-Mack Trucks, Truck manufacturer with global reputation. 6- Trust Financial (bank holding) have headquarters in North Carolina.

Among tourist attractions of the state, these could be named: 1- The Biltmore Estate, largest private mansion in the U.S with 250 rooms, containing artworks, antiques and stunning architecture. 2- Biltmore Village, a place which once settled George Washington Vanderbilt II's staff (rich merchant and owner of Baltimore estate). 3- Billy Graham Library, living place of Billy Graham, famous Evangelical priest since he was 9 years old. Containing some of the family furniture and memorials. 4- Blue Ridge Parkway, a road with beautiful nature and enjoyable for walking and driving. 5-Chimney Rock State Park, with a stunning and untouched nature. 6-Battleship North Carolina, one of the 10 military vessels which joined the U.S Navy on 9 April 1941 and later fought in WWII, largest warship of its kind in those years. 7- Cape Hatteras beach, along its historical lighthouse. 8- Carolina Beach, with its calm and friendly inhabitants. 9-Smoky Mountains National Park, due to its permanent morning fog, rich wildlife and stunning nature, 800 miles distance from famous Apache mountains in Tennessee border, is one the best-known national parks globally, and attracts tourists more than any other national park in the U.S. 10-Smith-McDowell House Museum, which once hosted some commanders of the Civil War. 11- North Carolina Museum of Natural Sciences .12- Topsail Island, with its numerous forests and amazing beaches, which shape a stunning nature. These destinations, along with museums and many historical buildings, form the tourist sector of North Carolina.

1-Andrew Jackson and James Knox Polk, presidents of the U.S. 2-Charles Eldon Brady Jr, American astronaut who remained in the Space for 16 days in 1996, traveling on the STS-78 space shuttle. 3-Ava Lavinia Gardner, actress. 4-Charlie Rose, veteran journalist and professional TV anchor. 5-Roberta Flack, singer and artist. 6-William Franklin Graham Jr, prominent evangelical Christian are among famous people from North Carolina.

Apart from the 1789 and 1864 U.S presidential elections (in 1789 election, North Carolina hadn't ratified the U.S Constitution yet and wasn't able to take part, and 1864 elections weren't held in the state because of the Civil War), the state has taken part in remaining 57 U.S presidential elections until today (2021), of which Democratic Party scored 30 victories, Republican Party gained 15 victories, Democratic-Republicans won 5 contests, Whigs won 3 contests, Federalists had a single victory and 3 elections saw split of the votes among Democratic-Republicans and Federalists. It's worth noting that one of the Republican victories was 1968 election in which they gained 12 out of 13 electoral votes from the state, and the remaining electoral vote was won by American Independent Party.

To have a better inspection, the history of U.S presidential elections in North Carolina could be divided into 3 different parts. The first part, from 1792 to 1860 (the last election before the Civil War) witnessed 18 presidential elections, and Democrats won 6 of them, Democratic-Republicans gained 5 victories, Whig Party scored 3 gains, Federalist Party had a single win, and 3 rounds of elections saw split of electoral votes among Democratic-Republican and Federalist parties, and a contest resulted a split of electoral votes between a Republican candidate and a member of American Independent Party.

Second period, from 1868 to 1964, saw 25 rounds of elections, and Democrats won 22 of them, while Republican Party gained 3 wins.

In the third period, from 1968 to 2020, 14 rounds of U.S presidential elections were held in the state, and Republicans won 12 of them, while Democratic Party was able to win 2 times.

As It's clear, Republican Party hadn't been established in the first period, but even in the second part, Republicans were not able to win any U.S presidential election in North Carolina. Founders of Republican Party were anti-slavery, and voters in North Carolina (which took part in the Civil war as a member of Confederation) had no tendency toward Republicans for many decades. For nearly 100 years, from 1868 to 1968, Republican Party only won 3 U.S presidential elections in the state. But 3rd part saw a different trend, and Republicans won 12 out of 14 elections (including 3 recent contests), while Democrats had 2 victories.

2020 Republican Party primaries in North Carolina, witnessed a victory for Donald Trump, who got the candidacy by winning 93.5% of the votes, while 2.5% of the votes belonged to the voters who had written "No preference".

In 2020 Democratic Party presidential primaries in North Carolina, Joe Biden won the candidacy by gaining 43% of the votes, while his closest rival, Bernie Sanders, got 24.1%.

Finally, 2020 U.S presidential election in North Carolina witnessed a victory for Republican candidate, Donald Trump, who won 49.9% of the votes, while his Democratic rival, Joe Biden, got 48.6%. Trump won all 15 electoral votes from North Carolina.

From 1789 (the date first U.S Senate election was held in North Carolina) to 2021, 55 elected candidates from the state have served in the U.S Senate, of which 27 were Democrats, 10 were Republicans, 6 were Democratic-Republicans, 2 were Whigs, one was a member of Populist Party, one was a Pro-Administration Party member and one was a Jacksonian. Other elected senators changed their political affiliations during their careers, of which , one served as member of Pro-Administration and Anti-Administration parties, one switched sides among Democratic-Republicans and Anti-Administration Party, 2 were Sometimes Democrats and sometimes Jacksonians, one had record of membership in Jacksonian and Crawford Republican parties, one experienced membership in Democratic-Republican, Crawford Republican and Jacksonian parties , and a senator switched sides among Whigs, Jacksonians and Anti-Jacksonians .

As it could be observed, Number of those senators who served only as Democratic Party members from North Carolina, in addition to those who experienced membership in other parties during their careers, was 29. The same number for Republicans is 10, showing superiority of

Democrats in the issue. Before 1873, only 2 Republican candidates were able to enter the U.S Senate as U.S senators from the state, and from 1873 to 1973 (100 years), out of 20 elected senators, 18 were Democrats, one was a Republican and one was a member of Populist Party. But in recent 4 decades (specially from 1973), popularity of Republican Party in the issue has increased, and 7 out of 12 U.S Senators elected in North Carolina have been Republicans, while 5 were members of Democratic Party. Actually, before 1973, only 3 Republicans served as U.S senators representing North Carolina.

Currently (2021), Richard Mauze Burr and Thomas Roland Tillis, both Republicans, represent the state in the U.S Senate.

Furnifold McLendel Simmons (with a 30-year record of presence in the U.S Senate, 1901-1931) from Democratic Party and Jesse Alexander Helms Jr (with a 30-year record of service, 1973-2003), a Republican, have been longest-serving U.S senators in history of North Carolina.

From 1790 (the year first U.S House of representatives' election was held in the state) to 2021, 339 elected candidates have entered the U.S House of representatives as representatives from North Carolina. 142 were Democrats, 63 were Republicans, 41 were Democratic-Republicans, 13 were Federalist Party members, 13 were Whigs, 7 were Jacksonians, 6 were members of People's Party, 6 were Anti-Administration Party members, 3 were Crawford Republicans, 2 were Anti-Jacksonians , 2 were members of Native American Party (also known as Know Nothing Party), 2 were members of Pro-Administration Party, one was a member of Opposition Party, one was a member of Independent, one was a member of Greenback Party, one was an Independent Democrat, And 35 representatives changed political affiliations during their careers, of which 4 were sometimes Democrats and sometimes Jacksonians, 3 served as Anti-Administration Party members and Democratic-Republicans, 2 were had record of membership in Pro-Administration and Federalist parties, 2 served as Whigs and Democrats, 2 were sometimes Democratic-Republicans and once served as Jacksonians, 2 were once Democratic-Republicans and also worked as Crawford Republicans, 2 experienced membership in Whig and Anti-Jacksonian parties, 2 served as members of Democratic-Republican, Crawford Republican and Jacksonian parties , 2 were Whigs, Jacksonians and Anti-Jacksonians, one switched sides among

Federalists and Adams-Clay Federalists, one served as Democrat and Democratic-Republican, one had membership in Federalist and Jacksonian parties, one served as Crawford Republican and Jacksonian, one experienced membership in Adam's Men and Jacksonian parties, one switched sides among Jacksonians and Anti-Jacksonians, one had record of membership in Opposition and Democratic parties, one served as member of Native American and Opposition parties, one was sometimes a Whig and sometimes a member of Conservative Party, one served as Whig and member of Native American Party, one was once a Democratic-Republican and sometimes served as member of Crawford Republican and Adams's Men parties, one switched sides among Democratic-Republicans, Jacksonian Republicans, Jacksonians and Democrats, one served as Democratic-Republican, Crawford Republican, Jacksonian and Democrat. A representative experienced membership in Democratic-Republican, Crawford Republican, Adams's Men, Anti-Jacksonian and Whig parties.

As the statistics show, Number of those House representatives who served only as Democrats during their careers, in addition to those who experienced membership in other parties, was 152, and the same number for Republicans is 63, showing an edge for Democrats in the history of the U.S House of representatives' elections in North Carolina. But in recent decades, Republican Party has improved its performance in the issue, gaining more popularity among the voters, and currently (2021), 8 out of 13 House representatives who have seats from North Carolina, are Republicans, while the rest 5 seats are held by Democratic Party members.

Robert Lee Doughton, a Democrat, who represented North Carolina in the House for 42 years, was the longest-serving House representative from the state, and also one of the longest-serving House representatives in the History of the U.S.

Since 1776 (the year North Carolina declared its independence from the British Colonial Rule), 69 persons have served as governors of North Carolina, and It is worth noting that Roy Asberry Cooper III, current governor of the state, is actually 75th governor of North Carolina. the 6-number difference here is due to that 6 governors gained the seat in 2 non-continuous terms. for instance, Richard Caswell served from 1776 to 1780 as the first governor, and later was able to gain the seat as the 5th governor from 1785 to 1787.

Among these 69 governors, 37 were Democrats, 12 were Democratic-Republicans, 7 were members of Republican Party, 5 were Whigs, 3 were Federalists, one was a member of Anti-Federalist Party, and 4 were independent candidates without political affiliations.

As it could be seen, this shows a clear upper hand for Democrats in the issue. From 1877 to 1973, from 25 elected governors, only one Republican candidate was able to gain the governor's seat in North Carolina, and even Democratic-Republicans had better results than Republicans. From 1901 to 1973, no Republican candidate was able to win any gubernatorial election in North Carolina, and Democrats won all of the contests. Even in more recent years, from 1993 to 2020, only one out of 5 North Carolina governors was a Republican.

Roy Cooper, current governor of the state, is a Democrat.

Conclusion: Noting that Democrats have won 30 U.S presidential elections in North Carolina (Republicans won 15 including 3 recent contests), It's clear they had an upper hand in the history of the U.S presidential elections in the state. Democrats had 29 U.S senators and 152 House representatives in the history of the state (the numbers for Republican Party are 10 and 63), but both current senators representing North Carolina in the U.S Senate are Republicans and 8 out of 13 House seats belonging to the state are being held by them (5 for Democrats), and Democrats have 37 governors in the history of the state (vs 7 Republicans), including the current governor ,so it could be concluded that North Carolina has been a Democratic Party bastion during most of its history, but currently, sympathy toward Republicans among the voters in the state is stronger.

Rhode Island

Historical state of Rhode Island (birthplace of famous historian and expert on Iranian art, Artur Upham Pope) is located in northeastern America. Providence city is the capital of the state. The state is located on the Atlantic coast, and is famous for its numerous historical and colorful mansions and beautiful beaches. Rhode Island was the first colony to hold the Continental Congress in 1774. Along with 12 other colonies, Rhode Island began a rebellion against the British colonial Rule and declared its independence on 4 July 1776. Finally, Rhode Island joined the newborn nation as its 13th state after ratification of the U.S Constitution on 29 May 1790. Rhode Island is the smallest U.S state (area) and is located in the New England area. Along with Connecticut, the state didn't ratify the 18th Amendment of the U.S constitution (prohibition of alcoholic drinks). Also, as a colony, Rhode Island was the first to ban slavery in 1652, but the law wasn't enforced that much, and in 1750, the colony had the largest share of slave population in New England area and played a major role in slave trade. But during the Revolutionary War, Rhode Island legislators ratified a law which stated that freedom of any slave who would take part in the War as a soldier will be granted. Rhode Island 1st Regiment, which took part in the War, was a military unit with black majority (some call it as the first black-majority military unit in the history of the U.S). During the Civil War, Rhode Island remained loyal to the Union and used all of its capacities to help the Union Army. According to the last census, Rhode Island had a population of 1059361 inhabitants, of which 71.4% were whites, 16.3% were Latinos, 8.5% were blacks, 3.7% were Asians, 1.1% were Native Americans and Alaskans, 0.2% were Hawaiians and other Pacific Islanders, and the rest were from other races and ethnicities.

Brown University (one of the oldest and most credible universities in the U.S, and a member of Ivy League), where people like John Davison Rockefeller Jr, former American billionaire and Dara Khosrow Shahi, chief executive officer of Uber (Taxi service company) have been graduated, University of Rhode Island, Bryant University, US Naval War College and Rhode Island School of Design are among scientific and education centers in Rhode Island.

Agriculture and animal husbandry are not much common activities in the state, and cow, beef, corns, potatoes, milk and some other products are main agricultural products of the state, with limited production. Rhode Island once was an industrial state, and a main center of textile, shipbuilding and jewelry industries in the U.S, and was called " the jewelry capital of the world ". During the colonial era, Rhode Island was famous for its rich fishing industry, but reckless fishing and pollution resulted in decrease of fish, oyster and lobster population, but recent arrangements by Federal government has slightly improved the situation. Electronic devices, transportation, jewelry, biotechnology, cyber data analysis and data analysis shape large parts of industry in the state.

Rhode Island is host to headquarters of many large corporations, among them: 1-CVS HEALTH (retail pharmacy chain). 2- TEXTRON (active in aviation industry, medical equipment etc....). 3- CITIZENS FINANCIAL GROUP one of 15 largest banks in the U.S. 4- UNITED NATURAL FOODS (natural and organic food company). 5- FM GLOBAL, insurance company.

Among tourist destinations in Rhode Island, these could be named: 1- The Breakers mansion, containing 70 rooms, which belonged to Vanderbilt family. 2- Cliff Walk, Newport, a beautiful passage for walking on the coast. 3- Water Fire monument, which actually is a festival, being held occasionally several years. Fires are being set in rivers during the festival, musicians and shoppers from different areas take part. 4- The Elms mansion, once house of Edward Julius Bergwind, founder of Bergwind-White Coal Mining Company. 5- RISD Museum of Art, which contains a collection of historical clothes and textiles, from ancient times to contemporary era, from ancient Egypt to modern designs by famous fashion designers in 20th century. 6- Ocean Drive historical district. Many historical buildings of Newport city are located here. 7- Colt State Park, which actually was private farm of Samuel Colt (famous landowner and arms manufacturer). 8- Block Island and Mohegan Bluffs, with a beautiful beach and high rocks, which remembers of old America seen in the movies. 9- Blithewold mansion, a 45-room house, which belonged to Augustus Van Wickle. 10- Benefit Street and John Brown House, with old houses and old architecture. Most known house in the street belonged to a John Brown, a merchant 11- Herreshoff Marine Museum and its sailing boat shows. 12- Bristol Old City, containing many historical buildings like St. Stephen's church. 13- Touro Synagogue, oldest synagogue in the U.S, and the only remaining one from colonial period. 14- Brown University, one of the oldest universities in the country .15- Bellevue Avenue Mansions, largest and best-known mansions of Newport are located here. Along these attractions, many beautiful beaches, colorful historical buildings and museums shape the tourism sector in the state.

1-Professor Arthur Pope, famous historian and expert on Iranian art, who lived in Iran for many years and according to his own testament, was buried near Zayandehrud riverbank, Isfahan, Iran. 2- H. P. Lovecraf, author of Cthulhu Mythos stories (meaning mythical fantasy world). 3- William Edwards Blackmon, famous American soccer player. 4-Wendy Carlos, musician, are among famous people from Rhode Island.

After joining to the U.S, first U.S presidential election in Rhode Island was held in 1792. Since that year, Rhode Island has taken part in all 58 U.S presidential elections held in the country. Of these contests, Democratic party won 23 times in the state, Republicans had 21 victories, Federalist Party scored 5 wins, Democratic-Republicans won 4 times, Whigs scored 3 wins, and National Republican Party emerged victorious in 2 contests.

To put it under scrutiny, history of the U.S presidential elections in Rhode Island could be divided into 3 periods. First part, from 1792 to 1852, saw 16 rounds of elections. Federalist won 5 times, Democratic-Republicans gained 4 victories, Whigs had 3 wins, and Democrats and National Republican Party each scored 2 victories. (Republican Party hadn't been established yet).

Second period, from 1856 to 1924, witnessed 18 presidential elections, of which Republican Party won 17 contests, and Democrats only gained a single win.

In the third part, from 1928 to 2020. 24 rounds of elections were held and Democrats won 20 of them (including 9 recent contests), and Republicans scored 4 wins. The last Republican victory was in 1984 election.

2020 Democratic presidential primaries in Rhode Island saw a victory for Joseph Biden, who won 61.6% of the votes, while his closest rival, Bernie Sanders got 30.3% of the votes.

In 2020 Republican presidential primary in Rhode Island, Donald Trump gained the candidacy through winning 94.3% of the votes, defeating Bill Weld, who won 3% of the votes.

Finally, 2020 U.S Presidential elections in Rhode Island resulted in a win for Democratic Party candidate, Joe Biden, who won 59.4% of the votes, while his Republican counterpart, Donald Trump, won 38.6% of the votes. All 4 electoral votes from Rhode Island were added to Biden's vote basket.

From 1790 to 2021, 48 persons have represented Rhode Island in the U.S Senate. Among them 14 were Republicans, 10 were Democrats, 6 were Democratic-Republicans, 5 were Federalists, 4 were Whig Party members, one was a member of Anti-Administration Party, one was a member of Law and Order Party, And 7 senators changed their political affiliations during their careers, of which 2 were sometimes Pro-Administration Party members and sometimes Federalists, one served as Whig and Republican, one switched sides among Republicans and Liberal Republican Party, one experienced membership in Democratic-Republican and Crawford Republican parties, one was sometimes a member of Adams's Men gathering and also served in Anti-Jacksonian and Whig parties, and a senator experienced membership in Democratic-Republican, Crawford Republican, Anti-Jacksonian and Whig parties.

According to the statistics presented above, Number of those senators who served only as Republican Party members from Rhode Island, in addition to those who experienced membership in other parties during their careers, was 16. The same number for Democrats is 10, showing an upper hand for Republicans in the issue. But recent decades witnessed a better performance for Democrats in Rhode Island, and one of the U.S Senate seats has been in their hands since 1937, while the other seat has the same situation since 2007.

Currently, both senators representing Virginia in the U.S Senate, John Francis Reed and Sheldon Whitehouse, are Democrats.

Claiborne de Borda Pell (with 36 years of presence in the U.S Senate, 1961-1997) from Democratic Party and Henry Bowen Anthony (with a 25-year record of service, 1859-1884), a Republican, have been longest-serving U.S Senators in history of Rhode Island.

From 1790 (the year first U.S House of representatives election was held in Rhode Island) to 2021, 72 elected candidates have entered the U.S House of representatives as representatives from Rhode Island.24 were Republicans, 19 were Democrats, 7 were Federalist Party members, 5 were Whigs, 4 were Democratic-Republicans, 2 were members of Unconditional Union Party, one was a member of Law and Order Party, one was a member of Adams's Men gathering and Anti-Jacksonian Party, And 9 representatives changed political affiliation during their careers , of which 2 were sometimes Democratic-Republicans and sometimes Crawford Republicans, one served as Whig and Republican, one switched sides among Federalists and Democratic-Republicans, one served as Federalist and member of Pro-Administration Party, one was sometimes a Whig and once served as member of Law and Order Party , one had record of membership in Democratic and Native American (also known as Know Nothing Party) parties, and a representative experienced membership in Adams's Men, Anti-Jacksonian and Anti-Masonic parties.

As the statistics show, Number of those House representatives who served only as Republicans from Rhode Island during their careers, in addition to those who experienced membership in other parties, was 26, and the same number for Democrats is 20, showing an edge for Republicans in the history of the U.S House of representatives in Rhode Island. But It's worth noting that service years of these 20 Democratic representatives was longer than their Republican counterparts. Recent years have seen an improvement in Performance of Democrats in the issue, and since 1995, both U.S House seats belonging to Rhode Island have been held by Democrats.

Nicholas Cooke, was last governor of Rhode Island during the colonial period (gained the seat in 1775) and after the Revolution, remained in his post until 1778. Since that, 71 persons have served as governors of Rhode Island, and it should be noted that current governor, Daniel McKee, is the 76th governor in the history of the state. the 5 numbers difference here is due to that 3 governors gained the seat in several non-continuous terms. For example, James Fenner Henry first served from 1807 to 1811 as 7th governor of Rhode Island, and once again was able to gain the seat for 7 years (1824-1831) as the 11th governor of the state, and his last turn as the 17th governor of the state lasted 2 years (1843-1845).

Among 71 elected governors, 30 were Republicans, 22 were Democrats, 7 were members of Whig Party, 3 were members of Country Party (a political party which was active only several years in Rhode Island after the Civil War), 2 were Democratic-Republicans, one was a National Republican, one was a Federalist, and a governor changed his political affiliation during his career and served once as Democratic-Republican and later as a member of Law-and-Order Party. According to available sources used here, 4 governors had no clear political affiliations.

As it could be seen, Republicans have an upper hand in the history of gubernatorial elections in Rhode Island (they had 30 governors while Democrats had 22). But all 3 recent governors of Rhode Island (including the current governor, Daniel McKee, who has been serving since 2011) have been Democrats.

Conclusion: Noting that Democrats have won 23 U.S presidential elections in Rhode Island (Republicans won 21) including 9 recent contests, Republicans had 16 U.S senators in the history of the state ((Democrats had 10 , but since a long time they have the upper hand in the U.S Senate elections in the state), Republicans 26 U.S House representatives from the state (Democrats had 20, but with longer years of service, since 1995 both House seats have been held by Democrats, and finally Republicans had 30 governors in the history of Rhode Island, while their Democratic counterparts had 22 and improved their performance in gubernatorial elections in the state during recent years (all 3 recent governors were members of Democratic Party), it could be concluded that while Rhode Island has been a Republican stronghold during most of its history, It has turned into a Democratic Party bastion in recent decades.

Vermont

Vermont state, well-known for its snowy winters, is a located in northeastern America and is a part of New England area. Montpelier is the capital of the state. Vermont is known for its highest degree of safety and security and numerous ski resorts. Before the Declaration of Independence, Vermont was a part of New York colony, but after the Declaration, Vermont seceded from New York and became a separate state. Finally, the state joined the U.S as its 14th state on 4 March 1791, after ratification of the Constitution (first state after the initial 13 states). The battle of Hubbardton, one of the main battles during the Revolutionary War, was fought in Vermont. In 1777, Vermont voted to abolish adult slavery and during the Civil War, through mobilizing troops, providing clothes, shoes, food and arms helped the Union Army. According to the last census, Vermont had a population of 623989, of which 92.6% were whites, 2% were Latinos, 1.9% were Asians, 1.4% were blacks, 0.4% were Native Americans and Alaskans, and 2% were from other races and ethnicities. University of Vermont (one of the oldest universities in the U.S, its foundation dates back to 1791), Middlebury College (well-known for its progressive sphere, the college was first to grant a bachelor degree to an African-American, Alexander Twiligh, in 1823), Bennington College and Saint Michael's College, are among universities and education centers in the state. Greenhouse crops, potatoes, eggs, apple, honey, Alfalfa, vegetables, Christmas trees, timber, cows, beef, turkey, pork and salmon fish are among agricultural products of Vermont. Dairy products are other important agricultural products of the state, nearly half of the consumed milk in New England area comes from Vermont, and Vermont is among the top states in producing cheese and ice cream. Vermont is the largest producer of maple syrup in the country. Wooden furniture, clothes (especially winter socks), Teddy bears, and glass products are among other products of Vermont. Rock-of-Age's quarry (granite quarry) is the deepest granite quarry in the world.

BEN & JERRY'S (famous dairy and ice cream producer) and NATIONAL LIFE GROUP life insurance are among large corporations which their headquarters are located in the state.

Looking at tourist destinations in Vermont, these names could be pointed out: 1-Bennington Battle Monument and Museum, site of a battle of the Revolutionary war which was fought in 1777 2-Lake Champlain, with its untamed nature, a good place for boating, swimming and fishing. 3-Shelburne Museum, containing historical assets, from steamships, lighthouse and old trains to an old printing press shop and many other assets. 4-Hielden mansion, house of Robert Todd Lincoln, son of Abraham Lincoln, president of the U.S 5-Mount Mansfield and Smugglers Notch, a beautiful mountainous trail for hiking. There is a tele cabin for those want to reach the summon of the mountain. 6-Brattleboro Farmers' Market, an area with famous small and beautiful farms, where tourists can buy vegetables, fresh fruits, different kinds of high-quality breads, farm cheese, local honey, maple syrup along with jewelry and handicraft products. Peddlers will sell you natural foods, and you can serve it in unique peaceful sphere of Vermont. 7-Marsh-Billings-Rockefeller National Historic Park, including a house made by prominent Vermont lawyer, Charles Marsh, in 1805. Several years later, Frederick H. Billings, a lawyer and merchant, bought the house and established a managed forest and a progressive dairy farm in the area nearby. Later owners of this estate were Mary French Rockefeller (granddaughter of Billings) and her wife, Laurance Rockefeller (grand son of John Davison Rockefeller Sr, founder of Standard Oil company), made it public and the estate was registered as national site 8- Rock of Ages Quarry and Hope Cemetery, well-known as the deepest granite quarry in the world, located near Barre city, which its old cemetery is well-known for granite monuments and tombstones. 9- Church Street

Marketplace in Burlington city, a small street with historical buildings and houses, full of cafes and restaurants, peddlers and local musicians. 10- The Hill and University of Vermont, founded in 1791, one of the oldest universities in the U.S. 11- Ben & Jerry's ice cream factory. Visitors can watch the procedure of ice cream production along a guide during a 30-minutes trip inside the factory. 12-House of Ethan Allen Homestead, one of the Revolutionary War heroes. 13- Stowe Mountain Resort and Magic Mountain, along with many other historical buildings, museums, stunning forests and ski resorts, shape the tourism sector in the state.

Chester A. Arthur, U.S president who signed the Chinese Exclusion Act on 6 May 1882 (forbidding entrance of Chinese workers to the U.S), and Calvin Coolidge, also another president of the U.S, and U.S senator Bernie Sanders were/are among famous people from Vermont.

Since 1792, 58 U. S presidential elections have been held in Vermont. Republicans won 33 rounds, Democratic Party scored 9 victories, Democratic-Republicans had 6 victories, Whigs won 5 contests, Federalists won 3 times, National Republican Party was able to gain a single victory and Anti-Masonic Party won an election. These results show changes in political sphere in Vermont during different periods. from 1792 to 1852, 16 contests were held in the state, in which Democratic-Republicans won 6 elections, Whigs gained 5 victories, Federalist Party scored 3 victories, National Republican and Anti-Masonic parties each gained a single win. Democrats and Republicans had no victories in this period, which is not strange about Republicans, because their party was established in 1854.

From 1856 to 1988, Vermont saw 34 rounds of U.S presidential elections, and except a single contest (1964), in which Democrats gained their sole victory in the period, Republican Party won remaining 33 elections in the state. But since 1992, a dramatic change happened, and Democrats have won all 8 recent contests in Vermont.

As the statistics show, Vermont voters were staunch Republicans during most of the history, but during recent 30 years they radically changed their political affiliations towards Democratic Party.

In 2020 Democratic presidential primaries in Vermont, Bernie Sanders won the candidacy through winning 50.8% of the votes, while his closest rival, Joe Biden, took 22%.

In 2020 Republican Party presidential primaries in Vermont, Donald Trump emerged winner through gaining 88.7% of the votes, defeating Bill Weld who got 10.4%.

2020 U.S presidential election in Vermont witnessed a victory for Democratic Party candidate, Joe Biden, who got 66.1% of the votes, while Republican candidate, Donald Trump got 30.7%. All 3 electoral votes from Vermont were added to the Biden's vote basket.

From 1791 (the date first U.S Senate election was held in Vermont) to 2021, the state has sent 40 senators to the U.S Senate. 19 were Republicans, 3 were Federalists, 3 were Democratic-Republicans, 3 were Whigs, one was a member of Independent Party, one was a member of Free-Soil Part, one was a Democrat, and 9 were senators who changed their political affiliations during their careers. Among them, 2 served as Whigs and Anti-Jacksonians, 2 were sometimes Anti-Administration Party members and sometimes Democratic-Republicans, one switched sides among Republican and Independent parties, one served as Adams-Clay Republican and Democratic-Republican, one was sometimes a Whig and sometimes a Republican, one was once a Democratic-Republican and once as member of Adams's Men and Jacksonian parties, and a senator experienced membership in Democratic-Republican, Adams-Clay Republican, Adams's Men and Anti-Jacksonian parties. As it was mentioned in previous parts, Adams-Clay Republican, Adams's Men and Anti-Jacksonian all were different names for a single party in different Periods.

As the statistics show, Number of those senators who served only as Republican Party members from Vermont, in addition to those who experienced membership in other parties during their careers, was 21. The same number for Democrats is only one, and this surprising statistic show decisive superiority of Republicans in the issue. But Democrats have worked better in recent decades, and one of the U.S Senate seats belonging to Vermont is in their hands since 1975, while senator Bernie sanders, independent with Democratic affiliations, has been holding the other seat for a long time.

Currently, Patrick Joseph Leahy, a Democrat, and Bernie Sanders, independent with Democratic affiliation, represent Vermont in the U.S House of representatives.

Patrick Leahy (with a 46-year record of presence in the U. S Senate, since 1975) from Democratic Party and Justin S. Morrill (with a 31-year record of service, 1867-1898), a Republican, have been longest-serving U.S senators in history of Vermont.

Ernest W. Gibson and Ernest W. Gibson, Jr were the only father and sons which both represented Vermont as U.S Senators.

Vermont state has one seat in the U.S House of representatives, and the number is due to its population. So, number of persons who represented the state in the House was much lower than other old states. From 1791 (the year first U.S House of representatives' election was held in the state) to 2021, 96 elected candidates have entered the U.S House of representatives as representatives from Vermont. 30 were Republicans, 16 were Democratic-Republicans, 12 were Federalist Party members, 8 were Whigs, 7 were Democrats, 3 were members of Anti-Masonic Party, One was an Adam-Clay Republican, one was an Anti-Jacksonian, one experienced membership in Adams's Men and Anti-Jacksonian parties and one served as member of Adams-Clay and Adam's Men parties, one was a member of Anti-Administration Party, one was a member of Greenback Party, one was a member of Independent, And 13 representatives changed their political affiliations during their careers, of which 4 were sometimes Whigs and sometimes Anti-Jacksonians, 3 served as Whigs and members of Opposition Party, one switched sides among Whig and of Anti-Masonic parties, one had record of membership in Democratic-Republican and Jacksonian parties, one served as Democratic-Republican, Adams-Clay Republican and member of Adam's Men gathering, one was a sometimes a Democratic-Republican and once served as Adams-Clay Republican and Whig, one switched sides among Democratic-Republicans, Adam's Men gathering and Whig Party, and a representative experienced membership in Democratic-Republican, Jacksonian, Adams-Clay Republican and Adams's Men parties.

As the statistics show, Number of those House representatives who served only as Republicans during their careers, in addition to those who experienced membership in other parties, was 30, and the same number for Democrats is 7, showing a clear edge for Republicans in the history of the U.S House of representatives' elections in Vermont. But since 1990s, the situation changed dramatically, the last Republican representative ended his career in 1990. Bernie Sanders served as representative from Vermont from 1991 to 2007, and from 2007 to now (2021) Peter Welch, a Democrat, has represented the state in the House.

Philip Brian Scott, current governor of the state, who is a Republican, is actually 82nd governor of Vermont, but those persons who gained the seat numbered 77. It should be noted that the 5-number difference here is due to that 5 governors gained the seat in 2 non-continuous terms. for instance, Erastus Fairbanks served from 1852 to 1853 as the 21st governor, and later was able to gain the seat as the 26th governor from 1860 to 1861.

Thomas Chittenden served 2 terms as governor of the Vermont Republic, and during his career, Vermont joined the U.S as its 14th state after ratification of the constitution. Chittenden remained the governor of the state for another term. From 1791 to 2021, 77 persons served as governors of Vermont. Among these, 51 were Republicans, 7 were Whigs, 6 were Democrats, 6 were Democratic-Republicans, 2 were members of Federalist Party, one was an Anti-Jacksonian, one was a member of Anti-Masonic Party, one was a member of Independent Party, and 2 were governors who first served as Whigs and later joined Republicans.

As it could be seen, Number of those governors who served only as Republicans during their careers, in addition to those who experienced membership in other parties, was 53, and the same number for Democrats is 6, showing a clear edge for Republicans in the history of the gubernatorial elections in Vermont, and current governor of the state is a Republican, too.

Conclusion: Noting that Republicans have won 33 U.S presidential elections in Vermont (Democrats won 9 including 8 recent contests), It's clear they had an upper hand in the history of the U.S presidential elections in the state. Republicans had 21 U.S senators and 30 House representatives in the history of the state (the numbers for Democratic Party are 1 and 7), but current senators representing Vermont in the U.S Senate are a Democrat and a Democratic-affiliated independent and the only House seat belonging to the state is being held Democrats, and Republicans had 53 governors in the history of the state (vs 6 Democrats), including the current governor, so it could be concluded that Vermont has been a Republican Party bastion during most of its history, but currently, Democrats are much more popular among the voters in the state .

Kentucky

Kentucky state and its capital, Frankfort, are located in southern part of the U. S. Kentucky, with its famous grasslands is birthplace of Abraham Lincoln, well-known president of the U.S and Jefferson Davis, president of the southern Confederation during the Civil War. Kentucky was first a Part of Virginia colony, but seceded from it after the Declaration of Independence, and finally joined the U.S as its 15th state on 1 June 1792. During the Civil War, people of Kentucky were divided between Union and Confederation supporters. For example: John Jordan Crittenden, was the former U.S senator and current representative in the House during the same period who supported a compromise on the slavery issue to prevent the partition of the U.S. One of his sons, George Bibb Crittenden was first a member of the U.S Army, but later Joined the Confederate Army, and 2 other sons, Thomas and Eugene served in the Union Army. One of his grand sons, John Crittenden Coleman, served in the Confederate Army while his other grandson, John Crittenden Watson was a member of the Union Army. Kentucky General Assembly declared the state as neutral, and Union supporters who had gained 2/3 of state councils in the last elections tried to save Kentucky from being involved in the War. But several months after beginning of the War, on 4 September 1861, Confederate Army invaded Kentucky, occupied some parts of the state and the Union army moved into Kentucky as a response. Finally, the Union Army emerged victorious, and Kentucky remained a part of the U.S.

Today (2021), Kentucky has a population of 4467673 inhabitants. Demographic composition of the state can be seen in these numbers: 84.1% of the population is white, 8.5% are blacks, 3.9% are Latinos, 1.6% are Asians, 0.3% Native Indians and Alaskans, 0.1% are Hawaiians and people from other Pacific islands, and the rest 2 % are from other races and ethnicities.

University of Kentucky (now a research university) was first founded in 1865 by John Bryan Bowman as the Kentucky Agriculture and Mechanic College. When was founded in 1798, University of Louisville was the first city-owned university in the U.S. Bellarmine University (the first education in the U.S which had students from both sexes and different races) are among universities and education centers in Kentucky.

Coal is a major source of income for Kentucky, and the state ranks 3 in the U.S in coal mining. Cow, beef, wheat, corns, soybean and tobacco are main agricultural products of Kentucky. Lexington city is known as the horse capital of the world. Oil, natural gas, limestone, aircraft parts, boats, air conditioners, elevators, compressors, printers, medical products, industrial colors and chemicals are other products of the state.

Some large corporations have headquarters in Kentucky, including: 1- YUM! BRANDS (fast food chain restaurant). 2- TEXAS ROADHOUSE (Texas-themed American steakhouse chain restaurant that specializes in steaks). 3- HUMANA (health insurance). 4- GRUPO ANTOLIN (one of the largest manufacturers in the car interiors market internationally and a worldwide supplier of headliner substrates). 5- LEXMARK (manufactures laser printers and imaging products). 6- PAPA JOHN'S PIZZA (pizza restaurant franchise).

Among tourist attractions in Kentucky, these could be named: 1- Kentucky Derby, one of the most famous horseback riding races in the U.S, held on first Sunday of May, annually. 2- Louisville Slugger Museum & Factory, manufacturing baseball equipment. 3- Daniel Boone National Forest, with rocks, necks and valleys shaped by rivers. Daniel Boone was a pioneer and later national hero who gained his fame because of exploring Kentucky and encouraging people to migrate there out of 13 initial colonies. 4- Abraham Lincoln Birthplace National Historic Park, which once was his ancestral farm. Lincoln was born there and lived several decades. 5- Mammoth Cave National Park, one of the largest known caves in the world. Large natural limestone columns in front of the cave resemble ancient temples. 6- Kentucky Horse Park, an exhibition of many horse breeds, from big to small, and from racehorses to retired ones. 7- Muhammad Ali Center, which was founded to pursue humanitarian desires and activities of former international boxing champion, Muhammad Ali Clay. 8- Lost River Cave, and the boating tour in this cave. 9- Shaker Village of Pleasant Hill and Pleasant Hill historical district, and the buildings in the village, with handmade furniture and daily life tools dating back to 1800s, showing simple life of the members of Shaker religious sect. 10- Mary Todd Lincoln House, father's house of Mary Todd, Abraham Lincoln's wife. 11- Farmington mansion, childhood home of Joshua Fry Speed, closest friend of Abraham Lincoln 12- Thomas Edison House, which this great innovator lived there for a while 13- Frazier History Museum. In addition to history of Kentucky, historical assets like Josiah Bartlett's sword (one of the signers of the Declaration of Independence), the bow which allegedly belonged to Geronimo, Native American chieftain and well-known Apache warrior, pistols which belonged to General George Armstrong, cavalry commander during the Civil War and Indian War could be seen here. 14- Cumberland Gap National Historical Park. Along these, many other museums, old mansions, cemeteries and beautiful forests shape the tourism sector in the state.

1-Abraham Lincoln, 16th president of the U.S. 2- Jefferson Davis, president of the southern Confederation. 3-Muhammad Ali Clay, legendary Boxing champion 4- Loretta Lynn, singer and lyricist, are among famous people from Kentucky. Colonel Harland David Sanders (founder of KFC chain restaurant, who was not born in Kentucky, but lived in Kentucky most of his life and began his business there) are among famous people from Kentucky.

Since 1792 (the date first U.S presidential election was held in Kentucky), the state has taken part in 58 U.S presidential elections. Democrats had 26 victories, Republicans won 16 contests, Democratic-Republicans gained 8 wins, Whigs had 5 victories, Federalist Party scored a single win, National Republican Party was able to score a victor and Constitutional Union Party won a single contest.

For a better inspection, history of presidential elections in Kentucky could be divided into 3 parts. First part, from 1792 to 1860, witnessed

18 presidential elections in the state., Democratic-Republicans gained 8 wins, Whigs scored 5 wins, Democrats gained 2 contests and each of Federalist, National Republican and Constitutional Union parties gained a single victory. Republicans had no share in this period, and this part could be called as the Democratic-Republican Party area.

Second period, from 1864 to 1952, saw 23 elections, and Democratic Party won 20 of them, while Republicans emerged victorious in 3 contests (one of these contests, 1896 election, saw a split of electoral votes in which Republicans took 12 out of 13 votes and the remaining vote was won by Democrats). This period could be pointed as the Democratic Party era.

In the third period, from 1956 to 2020, 17 elections were held in the state, and Republican Party won 13 of them, while Democrats scored 4 wins. All 6 recent elections were Republican victories, and this period was clearly in favor of Republican Party.

As it could be observed, historically, Democrats have an upper hand in the issue (they had 26 victories, vs 16 Republican wins), but Republican Party has gained more popularity in recent decades, resulting in winning all of 6 recent U.S presidential elections in the state.

2020 Republican Party primaries in Kentucky, witnessed a victory for Donald Trump, who got the candidacy by winning 86.6% of the votes, and "uncommitted" votes who were counted 13.4% ranked 2nd.

In 2020 Democratic Party presidential primaries in Kentucky, Joe Biden won the candidacy by gaining 67.9% of the votes, while his closest rival, Bernie Sanders, got 12.1%.

Finally, 2020 U.S presidential election in Kentucky witnessed a decisive victory for Republican candidate, Donald Trump who won 62.1% of the votes, while his Democratic rival, Joe Biden, got 36.2%. Trump won all 8 electoral votes from Kentucky.

From 1792 to 2021 , 66 elected candidates from Kentucky have served in the U.S Senate, of which 30 were Democrats, 12 were Republicans, 8 were members of Democratic-Republican Party, 4 were Whigs, 2 were Federalists, one was an Jacksonian, one was a member of Anti-Administration party, one was a member of Native American Party (also known as Know Nothing Party) And 7 senators changed their political affiliations during their careers, of which one was sometimes a Democratic-Republican and sometimes a member of

Anti-Administration Party, one served as Democratic-Republican and Jacksonian, one switched sides among Democratic-Republicans and Adams-Clay Republicans, one had record of membership in Democratic and Unionist parties, one served as Democratic-Republican, Whig and Anti-Jacksonian, one experienced membership in Democratic-Republican, Jacksonian and Jacksonian Republican parties, and a senator switched sides among Democratic-Republicans, Whigs , Anti-Jacksonians and Native American Party.

According to the statistics presented above, Number of those senators who served only as Democratic Party members from Kentucky, in addition to those who experienced membership in other parties during their careers, was 31. The same number for Republicans is 12, showing clear superiority of Democrats in the issue. But Republicans have improved their performance in 2 recent decades, and one of the U.S Senate seats belonging to Kentucky has been held by them since 1985, while the other seat has the same situation since 1999. Mitch McConnell and Rand Paul, both Republicans, currently (2021) represent the state in the U.S Senate.

Mitch McConnell, with a 36-year record of presence in the U.S Senate(1985-present) as a Republican and Wendell H. Ford from Democratic Party with 25-year history of serving in the Senate (1974-1999) were longest-serving U.S Senators from Kentucky.

From 1792 (the date first U.S House of representatives election was held in Kentucky) to 2020, 343 persons have represented the state in the U.S House of representatives, of which 143 were members of Democratic Party, 61 were Republicans, 36 were members of Whig Party, 33 were Democratic-Republicans, 12 were Jacksonians, 7 were members of Unconditional Union Party, 4 were Unionists, (Unconditional Union and Unionist both were different names for a single party), 5 were Anti-Jacksonians, 2 were Adams-Clay Republicans, one was a member of Adams's Men gathering, one was first a member of Adams's Men gathering and later an Adams-Clay Republican, and a representative served as member of Adams's Men gathering, Adams-Clay Republican Party and Anti-Jacksonian Party (3 different names of a single party in different periods), 4 were members of Native American Party (also known as Know Nothing Party), 2 were members of Opposition Party, one was an Independent Democrat (not an official member of

Democratic Party, but politically affiliated to it), 28 were representatives with different political affiliations during their careers. Of these, 3 were sometimes Democratic-Republicans and sometimes Adams-Clay Republicans and Adams's Men gathering members , 2 served as Whigs and Anti-Jacksonians, 2 had record of membership in Whig and Native American parties, 2 were sometimes Whigs and sometimes Opposition Party members, 2 served as Democratic-Republicans and members of Anti-Administration Party, 2 were once Republicans and once members of Unconditional Union Party, 2 served ad Whigs, Adams's Men gathering members and Anti-Jacksonians, one switched sides among Democrats who and Unionist Party, one was sometimes a Unionist and once a member of Opposition Party, one had record of membership in Jacksonian and Anti-Jacksonian parties, one served as Democratic-Republican and Anti-Jacksonian, One experienced membership in Democratic-Republican and Jacksonian Republican parties, one switched sides among Democratic-Republicans, Jacksonians and Jacksonian-Republicans, one served as Democratic-Republican, member of Adams's Men gathering, and Anti-Jacksonian, one was sometimes a Democrat, once a Unionist and sometimes a Whig, a representative switched sides among Jacksonian, Jacksonian Republican and Unionist parties and according to available sources, 2 representatives have no clear political affiliation.

As the statistics show, those representatives from Kentucky who remained Democrat during their entire serving record in the House, in addition to those who experienced membership in other parties, were 147 persons, and the same number for Republican Party is 62. This shows that historically, Democratic Party had a better performance in the U.S House of representative elections in the state. But Republicans have worked better in recent years, and currently (2021), 5 out of 6 representatives from the state are Republicans (vs one Democrat. (

William Huston Natcher, a Democrat, with a 41-year record of presence in the House (1953-1994) and Harold Dallas Rogers, from Republican Party, who has been representing Kentucky in the House for 40 years (1981-present), have been longest-serving representatives from the state in the U.S House of representatives, and among numerated House representatives with more than 40 years of service in the U.S House of representatives.

It's worth noting that Andy Beshear current governor of Kentucky and a Democrat, is the 63rd governor in the history of the state. But during the history of Kentucky, 59 persons served as governors. the 4 numbers difference here is due to that 4 governors gained the seat in 2 non-continuous terms. For example, Albert Benjamin Chandler first served from 1935 to 1939 as 44th governor of Kentucky, and once again was able to gain the seat for 4 years (1955-1959) as the 49th governor of the state.

Since 1792 (the year Kentucky joined the U.S as its 15th state), 59 governors have served in the state. Among them, 32 were Democrats, 9 were Republicans, 8 were Whigs, 8 were Democratic-Republicans (also known as Jeffersonian Republicans), one was a Jacksonian, and one was a member of Native American Party. During the history of gubernatorial elections in Kentucky, Democrats had an upper hand (32 governors, vs 9 Republican governors), while Republicans have done better in recent years, and 2 out of 4 recent governors of the state were members of Republican Party, but current governor of Kentucky, Andy Beshear, is a Democrat.

Conclusion: As seen before, Democratic Party has a better record in the history of U.S. presidential elections in Kentucky (26 victories, while Republicans won 16 times) but Republicans emerged victorious in 6 recent contests. Democrats, by having 31 U.S senators,147 House representatives and 32 governors in the history of the state (the numbers for Republican Party are 12, 62 and 9), have a better record, but both U.S Senate seats have been in hands of Republicans since a long time, and currently (2021), 5 out of 6 House representatives from Kentucky are Republicans (vs 1 Democrat). Current governor of Kentucky is a Democrat. So, it could be said while Democratic Party had the upper hand during the most of political history of the state, today, Kentucky is a Republican-leaning state.

Tennessee

Tennessee state, and its capital, Nashville, are known as the Country Music Capital of the World. With its stunning natural views, industrial products, and rich agriculture, Tennessee is a well-known southern state. Memphis is the most important city in the state. Actually, Tennessee was a part of Territory South of the River Ohio (known as southwest territory). Tennessee was the land which North Carolina state handed to the Federal government in April 1790, as a compensation for its debt, and finally joined the U.S as its 16th state on 1 June 1796, the last state to do the same in 18th century. During the Civil War, the western part of Tennessee, which had an agricultural economy supported the Confederation, but the eastern part remained loyal to the Union, and 31 thousand soldiers from the eastern part joined the Union Army. Despite the tendency of Isham Green Harris, governor of the state on the eve of the Civil War, in a referendum on 9 February 1861, people of Tennessee voted to remain in the Union. After several months, in a reaction to secession of South Carolina (the first state which declared its secession from the Union), president Lincoln appealed for 75 thousand soldiers, and Tennessee played a part in mobilization of this force. After this, another referendum was held in the state on 8 June 1861, and this time, majority of voters chose to secede from the Union (as the last state to join the Confederation), Tennessee returned to the U.S after the War. According to the last census, Tennessee had a population of 6829174 inhabitants. 73.5% of the population was white, 17.1% were blacks, 5.7% were Latinos, 2% were Asians, 0.5% were Native Americans and

Alaskans, 0.1% were Hawaiians and other Pacific islanders and 2% were from other races and ethnicities.

Vanderbilt University (private and research university, its foundation dates back to 1873), University of Tennessee (one of the oldest universities in the U.S , established in 1794), Belmont University, Tennessee Technological University, University of Memphis, Oak Ridge National Laboratory (largest Federal laboratory researching on Energy sciences, specializing in applied and basic experiments aiming to solve energy problems, home to Spallation Neutron Source, largest Neutron source global , and the main laboratory taking part in Manhattan Project, which resulted in production of the first nuclear bomb) are among universities and scientific centers in Tennessee.

Nearly 40% of the lands in the state are agricultural farms, and this has helped Tennessee to be a top agricultural producer. Cow, beef, chicken, wheat, tomatoes, alfalfa, tobacco, corns, cotton and dairy products, are main agricultural and animal husbandry products of the state. Tennessee is also among top states in producing soybean, timber, processed food and alcoholic drinks. Tennessee is the main automotive industry hub in southern America, and manufacturing boats, aircraft parts, transportation equipment, film industry, coal extraction, and Electric power industry are major parts of industrial sector in Tennessee. The state is home to headquarters of some large corporations like 1- FEDEX (shipping & delivery services company). 2- DOLLAR GENERAL (chain of variety stores). 3- AUTOZONE (retailer of aftermarket automotive parts and accessories). 4- HCA HEALTHCARE (for-profit operator of healthcare facilities). 5-TENNESSEE VALLEY AUTHORIT (federally- owned electric utility corporation, one of the largest in the U.S). 6- Envision Healthcare (healthcare company and national hospital-based physician group). 7- Pilot Corporation (oil company). 8- Regal Cinemas (movie theater chain).

Among tourist attraction pf Tennessee state, these could be named: 1- The Great Smoky Mountains National Park, with large forests containing wild boars. 2- Graceland and the Elvis Presley Memphis Complex, former house of Elvis Presley, legendary American singer, actor and musician, which was known as "The King of Rock and Roll". 3- Home of the Blues: Memphis. A famous street in Memphis city, home to Gospel blues music band. 4- Andrew Jackson's Hermitage, private farm and residence of Andrew Jackson, 7th president of the U.S. 5- Chattanooga and the Tennessee Valley Railroad. Visitors can experience a trip with a steam locomotive through a passage which was a main logistical route during the Civil War. 6- Nashville Music Festivals, with their unique attractions. 7- The Titanic Museum, containing more than 400 assets from the famous sunk ship. 8- Museum of Appalachia, an open-air museum, showing lifestyle of native people of Appalachia mountain. 9- The General Jackson Showboat, and tourist tour with this boat, resembling 19th century boats. 10- The Belle Meade Plantation, dating back to 1845. The plantation witnessed a skirmish between Confederate and Union Army forces during the Civil War, hole signs of the firefight are still visible on the walls. 11- Fort Nashborough, established by early immigrants to Tennessee, the building has been reconstructed recently. 12- Dollywood amusement park, a place for concerts, festivals and steam locomotive tours. 13- Country Music Hall of Fame and Museum in Nashville city. 14- Tennessee's Civil War Heritage. These, along other historical buildings, museums and music festivals shape the tourism sector in the state.

1- Quentin Jerome Tarantino, American director, actor, playwright, and Academy Award winner. 2- Yusef Abdul Lateef, musician and instrumentalist, Grammy Award winner, famous for innovating in the blending of jazz with Eastern music. 3- Davy Crockett, national hero and military commander, he opposed Indian Removal Act proposed by President Andrew Jackson. 4-Morgan Freeman, famous actor and Academy Award winner. 5- Tamara Jernigan, researcher and astronaut, are among famous people from Tennessee.

Since 1796 (the year Tennessee joined the U.S), Tennessee has taken part in 56 out of 57 U.S. presidential elections (because of the Civil War, the 1864 election didn't take place in the state). The Democrats won 25 rounds, the Republican Party scored 17 victories, Democratic-Republicans had 8 victories, Whigs scored 5 victories and Constitutional Union Party was able to gain a single victory. It's worth noting that one of the Democratic Party wins (1948) witnessed a split of electoral votes: Democrats took 11 out of 12 while States' Rights Democratic gained one electoral vote.

To have a better inspection, the history of U.S presidential elections in

Tennessee could be divided into 3 different parts. The first period, from 1796 to 1860 (the last election held before the Civil War), witnessed 17 contests, in which Democratic-Republicans won 8 elections, Whigs gained 5 victories, Democratic Party scored 3 victories, and Constitutional Union Party won an election.

Second period, from 1868 to 1948, saw 21 rounds of elections, and Democrats won 18 of them, while Republican Party scored 3 wins. (1948 election discussed above).

In the third period, from 1952 to 2020, 18 rounds of U.S presidential elections were held in Tennessee, and Republicans won 14 of them, while Democratic Party was able to win 4 times. It's worth noting that Republicans emerged winner in all 6 recent elections.

In 2020 Republican presidential primaries in Tennessee, Donald Trump gained the candidacy through winning 96.5% of the votes, defeating Joe Walsh, who won 1% of the votes.

In 2020 Democratic presidential primaries in Tennessee, Joe Biden won the candidacy through winning 41.7% of the votes, while his closest rival, Bernie Sanders, took 25%.

2020 U.S presidential election in Tennessee witnessed a victory for Republican Party candidate, Donald Trump, who got 60.7% of the votes, while Democratic Party candidate, Joe Biden got 37.5%. All 11 electoral votes from Tennessee added to the Trump's vote basket.

From 1796 (the year the first U.S. Senate election was held in the state) to 2021, 60 persons have represented Tennessee in the U.S. Senate. 32 of them were Democrats, 10 were Democratic-Republicans, 10 were Republicans, 2 were Whigs, And 6 were senators who changed their political affiliation during their careers , of which one served as a Democrat and Unionist, one was sometimes a Whig and sometimes a member of the Opposition Party, one switched sides among Democrats and Jacksonians, one was once a Republican and sometimes a member of the Unionist Party, one had record of membership in Whig, Jacksonian and Anti-Jacksonian parties, and a senator switched sides among Whig, Opposition and Native American (also known as Know Nothing Party) parties.

According to the statistics presented above, the number of those senators who served only as Democratic Party members from Tennessee, in addition to those who experienced membership in other parties during their careers, was 34. The same number for Republicans is 11, showing clear superiority of Democrats in the issue. Before 1967, only 3 Republican candidates from the state entered the U.S Senate. But, in recent decades, popularity of the Republican Party among the U.S Senate elections voters in the state has increased, and since 1995, both U.S, Senate seats belonging to Tennessee have been held by Republicans. Currently, both senators representing Tennessee in the U.S Senate, William Francis Hagerty IV and Marsha Blackburn, are Republicans. James Ralph Sasser (with 18 years of presence in the U.S. Senate, 1977-1995) from Democratic Party and Howard Henry Baker Jr (with an 18-year record of service, 1967-1985), a Republican, have been the longest-serving U.S. Senators in the history of Tennessee.

Andrew Jackson and Andrew Johnson, both U.S presidents, and Al Gore (vice president in the Bill Clinton administration, and the Democratic Party candidate in the controversial 2000 election), once represented Tennessee in the U.S. Senate during their political lives.

From 1796 to 2021, 274 elected candidates have entered the U.S. House of representatives as representatives from Tennessee. 113 were Democrats, 63 were Republicans, 25 were Democratic-Republicans, 20 were Whigs, 9 were Jacksonians, 3 were members of the Opposition Party, 3 were Unionists, 2 were members of the Native American Party (also known as Know Nothing Party), one was a member of the Unconditional Union Party, one was an Independent Democrat, one was a Jacksonian Republican, and 33 representatives changed political affiliation during their careers, of which 6 were sometimes Jacksonians and sometimes Anti-Jacksonians, 5 served as Jacksonians and Jacksonian Republicans, 4 had record of membership in Whig and Anti-Jacksonian parties, 2 were sometimes Democrats and sometimes Jacksonians, 2 were sometimes Whigs and sometimes Jacksonians, 2 switched sides among Whigs and Native American Party, 2 were sometimes Whigs and sometimes Unionists, one experienced membership in Opposition and Unionist parties, one served as Whig and Democrat, one experienced membership in Republicans and Unionist parties, one experienced membership in Democratic-Republicans and Jacksonian Republican parties, one served as member of Republican and Unconditional Union parties, one switched sides among Jacksonian, Democratic-Republican and Jacksonian Republican parties, one experienced membership in

Whig, Opposition and Native American parties, a representative switched sides among Whigs, Jacksonians, Jacksonian Republicans and Anti-Jacksonians, one served as Republican, member of Opposition Party and member of Unconditional Union Party, and a representative experienced membership in Republican, Opposition, Native American, Unionist and Unconditional Union parties.

As the statistics show, Number of those House representatives who served only as Democrats from Tennessee during their careers, in addition to those who experienced membership in other parties, was 116, and the same number for Republicans is 67, showing a clear edge for Democrats in the history of the U.S House of representatives in the state. But Republican have worked better in recent approximate 15 years, and out of 9 current representatives from the state in the U.S House of representatives, 7 are Republicans and 2 are Democrats.

Andrew Jackson, James Knox Polk and Andrew Johnson, U.S presidents, and Al Gore (vice president in Bill Clinton administration), all represented Tennessee in the U.S House of representatives during their political lives.

Since 1776, 50 persons have served as governors of Tennessee, among them, 28 were Democrats, 10 were Republicans, 5 were members of the Democratic-Republican Party, 4 were Whigs, 1 was a member of the Farmer-Labor Party, and 2 governors changed their political affiliations during their careers, of which one served as a Democrat and Democratic-Republican, and Andrew Johnson first served as a Democrat in a term and served as the military governor of Tennessee in another term.

As it could be seen, the number of those governors who served only as Democrats from Tennessee during their careers, in addition to those who experienced membership in other parties, was 30, and the same number for Republicans is 10, showing a clear edge for Democrats on this issue. But, republicans have improved their performance in recent years, and since 2011, both governors of Tennessee have been Republicans, including Bill Lee, the current governor of the state.

It's worth noting that Robert Looney Caruthers, a Democrat, was elected as governor of Tennessee in 1863, but President Lincoln replaced him with Andrew Johnson as the military governor of the state.

Andrew Jackson and James Knox Polk, both U.S presidents, had a record of serving as governors of Tennessee during their careers.

Conclusion: Noting that Democratic Party has won 25 U.S. presidential elections in the history of Tennessee (Republicans won 17 contests including 6 recent elections), and Democrats had 34 U.S. senators and 116 House representatives and 30 governors (the numbers for the Republican Party are 11, 67 and 10), they have been historically superior in the political sphere of the state, but both current U.S senators from Tennessee are members of the Republican Party, 7 out of 9 House representatives are Republicans while 2 are Democrats, and since 2011 both recent governors of the state have been members of the Republican party, so it could be said although Democrats had an upper hand during most of the political history of the state, today (2021), Tennessee is a Republican party stronghold.

Ohio

O hio state and its capital, Columbus, are located in midwestern
America. Ohio was home to the Wright brothers, innovators of
the first operational airplane, and because of that, it is known
as the birthplace of aviation. Cincinnati is the main city of the state.
Ohio was first a part of the Northwest Territory, owned by the U.S.
government and joined the U.S as its' 17th state on 1 March 1803. During
the Civil War, the majority of Ohio inhabitants supported the Union,
but a group named Copperheads (also known as Peace Democrats)
supported solving the problems through dialogue, opposed the War and
encouraged people to avoid serving in the Union Army, deserting the
Army and other kinds of conspiracies. Ohio played an important role in
mobilizing troops and providing equipment to the Union Army during
the Civil War, and through mobilizing 320 thousand soldiers, ranked
3rd in the issue after New York and Pennsylvania. John Clem and
Joseph Fissel (Clem was only 2 weeks older than Fissel), both 11 years
old, were the youngest soldiers from Ohio who joined the Union Army.
In 1970, Kent State University, in the state, witnessed one of the most
violent suppressions during the Vietnam War era. The National guard
opened fire against anti-war students, resulting in 4 deaths and dozens
of wounded. According to the last census, Ohio had a population of
11,689,100 inhabitants, of which 78.4% were whites, 13.1% were blacks,
4% were Latinos, 2.5% were Asians, 0.3% were Native Americans and
Alaskans, 0.1% were Hawaiians and other Pacific islanders, and 2.4%
were from other races and ethnicities. Case Western Reserve University
(one of the globally well-known research universities), Ohio State

University-Columbus, Miami University-Oxford (Miami University hosts over 50 fraternity and sorority chapters, and is known as the Mother of Fraternities), Ohio University (the oldest university in the state , dating back to 1804), Kent State University and Transportation Research Center (one of the largest independent automotive laboratories in the U.S) along with the National Highway Traffic Safety Administration, and the only Federal traffic lab are among scientific and education centers in the state.

Ohio has a strong agriculture and animal husbandry sector. From soybean, corn, green bean, to strawberries, sunflower seed, blueberries, honey, cows and beef are among main the agricultural and livestock products in Ohio. Ohio ranks 1st in producing Swiss cheese and 2nd in producing eggs in the U.S. In addition to steel and solar panels to generate electric power (of which Ohio is among the largest manufacturers in the U.S), insurance services, automotive and other motorized vehicles manufacturing, biosciences, biotechnology (Ohio is one of the top states in the field); health and medical services are also among the top industries in Ohio. Ohio has one of the most diverse economies among the U.S. states and is among the top 10 states in the size of economy. Some large corporations like:1-KROGER (American retail company). 2-Procter & Gamble (multinational consumer goods corporation, producing washing and cleaning components). 3-GOODYEAR (Tire & Rubber Company). 4-CARDINAL HEALTH (American multinational health care services company). 5-Wendy's (chain restaurant) and 6-Jeep automotive manufacturing company have headquarters in Ohio.

1-Rock & Roll Hall of Fame, a museum about history of Rock music, artists, producers and other participants who played role in promoting this style of music. 2- Cedar Point Amusement Park, containing a playground with different kinds of entertainments, waterparks, and a Wave Swinger. 3-Hocking Hills State Park, with its unmated nature and walking passages, hiking, boating, caves, camping facilities and cottages. 4- Amish Country . Believers of this religious sect don't use modern technology, industrial and modern innovations like: electrical power, insurances and universal healthcare services. They don't join the Army, don't ride cars and use to ride horses and horse carriages; one can enjoy visiting this village far from daily tumults. 5-Stan Hywet

Hall & Gardens, house of Franklin Augustus Seiberling, founder of Goodyear Tire company. 6-Cincinnati Music Hall, with its splendid building, founded in 1878. 7- Great American Ball Park, site of baseball contests hosted by Cincinnati Reds baseball team. 8- Irwin M. Krohn Conservatory, containing 3500 plant species from different parts of the world. 9-Great Lakes Science Center, and a tour with William G. Mather steamship. Visitors can increase their information about living in ships and large lakes here 10-West Side Market Cleveland, an old market dating back to 1912. 11-The Lake View Cemetery, with its beautiful trees, dating back to 1869. Famous people like Abraham Garfield, 20th president of the U.S, John Davies Rockefeller, and Eliot Ness, famous federal officer (who had a major role in overthrowing of Al Capon, well-known mafia boss, and enforcing Prohibition law in Chicago), all are buried here. 12-Playhouse Square, with 9 old theater salons, built during 1920 decade with their unique historical attractions. 13-Dayton Aviation Heritage National Historical Park, which contains Wright Brothers' original bicycle shop and their Wright Flyer III airplane (the plane they did their first flight using it), and Paul Laurence Dunbar house, poet, writer and Nobel prize winner and other parts. 14-SunWatch Indian Village Archaeological Park, a historical site, which is thought to belong to ancient Native American inhabitants, with reconstructed rural houses, It's estimated that settlement in the area dates back to 2000 years ago. 15-National Museum of the US Air Force, which contains planes used by U.S presidents like F.D.Roosevelt, Harry Truman and Dwight Eisenhower 16-The Carillon Historical Park, with historical buildings, information and assets dating back to 1700s (life in the 1700s in the Early Settlement Area), and a tour with a train, with oldest wagons remained in the world in James F. Dicke Family Transportation Center, along with many museums, historical buildings and parks shape the tourist sector in Ohio.

1-Ulysses Simon Grant, Rutherford Birchard Hayes, James Abram Garfield, Benjamin Harrison, William McKinley, William Howard Taft, Warren Gamaliel Harding, presidents of the U.S. 2- Orville Wright, one of the 2 brothers who built the first operational airplane in the world 3-Steven Allan Spielberg, winner of 3 Academy Awards, and one of the most successful directors in the history of Hollywood. 4-William Clark Gable, famous American actor. His role as Rhett Butler in "Gone with the wind" was one of the masterpieces in the history of cinema. 5-Neil Alden Armstrong, American astronaut and first man to walk on the moon. 6-Philip Cortelyou Johnson, famous American architect. 7-Arthur Holly Compton, American physicist and Nobel prize winner. 8-Paul Leonard Newman, actor, Academy Awards winner and director. 9-LeBron Raymone James Sr, one of the most famous basketball players in the history of NBA, are among famous people from Ohio.

Since 1804 (the date the first U.S. presidential election was held in Ohio) to 2020, Ohio has taken part in 55 U.S presidential elections. Of these contests, the Republican Party won 30 times in the state, Democrats had 16 victories, Democratic-Republicans won 6 times and Whigs scored 3 victories (1892 election saw a split of electoral votes, Republicans won 22 and the remaining vote was taken by the Democratic Party).

To have a better inspection, the history of the U.S. presidential elections in Ohio could be divided into 3 different parts. The first period, from 1804 to 1852, witnessed 13 contests, in which the Democratic-Republicans gained 6 victories, Democratic Party scored 4 victories, and Whigs were able to win 3 contests.

Second period, from 1856 to 1908, saw 14 rounds of elections, and Republicans won all of them. As mentioned above, only in 1892 election Democrats were able to gain an electoral vote.

In the third period, from 1912 to 2020, 28 rounds of U.S. presidential elections were held in Ohio, and in every 2 or 3 rounds, a cycle of winning and losing between Republicans and Democrats was shaped.

For instance, Republican Party emerged the winner in the 2000 and 2004 elections, while Democrats won 2008 and 2012 contests, and again, Republicans scored victories in 2016 and 2020 elections. This period saw 16 Republican wins and 12 Democratic Party victories.

In the 2020 Republican Party presidential primaries in Ohio, Donald Trump was elected by gaining 100% of the votes without any rivals.

In the 2020 Democratic presidential primaries in Ohio, Joe Biden won the candidacy through winning 72.3% of the votes, while his closest rival, Bernie Sanders, took 16.7%.

Finally, the 2020 U.S presidential election in Ohio witnessed a victory for Republican Party candidate, Donald Trump, who got 53.3% of the votes, while Democratic candidate, Joe Biden got 45.2%. All 18 electoral votes from Ohio were added to the Trump's vote basket.

From 1803 (the year Ohio joined the U.S) to 2021, the state has sent 56 senators to the U.S. Senate. 20 were Republicans, 18 were Democrats, 9 were Democratic-Republicans , 1 was a Whig, 1 was a member of Adams's Men gathering, one experienced membership in Adams's Men gathering and Anti-Jacksonian party (both names point to a single party in different periods), and 6 senators changed their political affiliations during their careers, of which one served as an Anti-Jacksonian and Whig, one switched sides among Free Soil and Republican parties, a senator worked as member of Democratic and Jacksonian parties, one was sometimes a Democratic-Republican and once an Adams-Clay Republican, one experienced membership in Whig, Opposition Republican parties, and a senator switched sides among Democratic-Republicans, Crawford Republicans, Adams's Men gathering and Anti-Jacksonians.

As it could be observed, the number of those senators who served only as Republican Party members from Ohio, in addition to those who experienced membership in other parties during their careers, was 22. The same number for Democrats is 19, showing slight superiority of Republicans in the issue, but recent years have witnessed a more tense competition among these parties, and currently (2021) Sherrod Brown, a Democrat, along with Rob Portman from the Republican Party, represent Ohio in the U.S Senate.

John Sherman (with a 32-year record of presence in the U.S Senate, 1861-1877 and 1881-1897) from Republican Party and John Herschel Glenn Jr (with a 25-year record of service, 1974-1999), a Democrat, have been longest-serving U.S senators in history of Ohio.

William Henry Harrison and Warren Gamaliel Harding, both presidents of the U.S, also served as U.S senators from Ohio during their political lives.

Since 1803, to 2021, 657 elected candidates have entered the U.S House of representatives as representatives from Ohio. 276 were Republicans, 260 were Democrats, 37 were Whigs, 12 were Jacksonians, 12 were Democratic-Republicans, 5 were Opposition Party members, 4 were members of Adams's Men gathering, 3 were Anti-Jacksonians, one was an Adams-Clay Republican, one was first an Adams-Clay Republican and then a member of Adams's Men gathering, one began as an Adams-Caly Republican, then became a member of Adams's Men gathering , and finally turned to be an Anti-Jacksonian (as mentioned in previous parts , all 3 names point to a single party in different periods, finally the name changed to National Republican Party), one was an Independent Democrat, one was an Independent Republican, one was a member of Unionist Party, one was a member of Anti-Masonic Part, one was a Jacksonian Republican, one was a member of the Independent Party, and 36 representatives changed political affiliation during their careers, of which 6 were sometimes members of the Opposition Party and sometimes Republicans, 4 served as Democrats and Jacksonians, 3 were once members of Whig Party and sometimes served as Republicans, 3 switched sides among Whigs and Opposition Party, 3 representatives switched sides among Democratic-Republicans, Adams-Clay Republicans and Adams's Men gathering, 2 served as members of Whig party Free Soil Party, 2 were once Whigs, once Republicans and sometimes as members of Opposition Party, 2 experienced membership in Adams-Clay Republican, Adams's Men, Anti-Jacksonians and Whig parties, one served as Democrat and Republican, one experienced membership in Democratic-Republican and Crawford Republican parties, one switched sides among Democratic-Republicans and Whigs, one was once a Jacksonian and sometimes served as a Whig , one was a Democratic-Republican who also served as an Adams-Clay Republican, one served as Democratic-Republican, member of Adams's Men gathering and Anti-Jacksonian, one had record of membership in Jacksonian and Anti-Jacksonian parties, a representative switched sides among Democrats, Republicans and Opposition Party, one served as member of Opposition, Free Soil and Republican parties, one experienced membership in Whig, Democratic, Republican and Opposition Parties, one had record of membership in Democratic-Republican, Adams-Clay Republican, Anti-Jacksonian and Whig parties, and according to the sources available to us, 3 had no clear political affiliations.

As the statistics show, Number of those House representatives who served only as Republicans during their careers, in addition to those who experienced membership in other parties, was 291, and the same number for Democrats is 267, showing an edge for Republicans in the history of the U.S House of representatives' elections in Ohio. currently

(2021), 12 out of 16 House representatives who have seats from Ohio, are Republicans, while 3 seats are held by Democratic Party members and a seat is empty.

William Henry Harrison, Rutherford Birchard Hayes, James Abram Garfield and William McKinley, presidents of the U.S, had records of presence in the House as representatives from Ohio.

Richard Michael DeWine, current governor of Ohio (a Republican), is the 70th governor in the history of the state, but the number of those persons who acted as governor of Ohio was 65. The 5-number difference here is due to that 5 governors gained the seat in 2 non-continuous terms. for instance, Wilson Shannon served from 1838 to 1840 as the 14th governor, and later was able to gain the seat as the 16th governor from 1842 to 1844.

Among these 65 governors, 26 were Republicans, 20 were Democrats, 10 were Democratic-Republicans, 5 were Whigs, 3 were members of Unconditional Union Party and one was a member of National Republican Party. This shows an upper hand for Republicans in the issue. Also, since 2011 both governors of Ohio have been members of Republican Party. As mentioned before, current (2021) governor of Ohio, Richard Michael DeWine, is a Republican.

Rutherford Birchard Hayes and William McKinley, presidents of the U.S, once served a governor of Ohio during their political careers.

Conclusion : Noting that Republicans have won 30 U.S presidential elections in Ohio (Democrats won 16 contests) including 2 recent contests , and had 22 U.S senators, 291 House representatives and 26 governors in the history of the state (the numbers for Democratic Party are 19 , 267 and 20) and 12 out of 16 House seats belonging to the state are being held by them (3 for Democrats) , and the current governor of the state and one of the senators representing the state in the U.S senate are Republicans, it could be said the Ohio has been a Republican state through most of its history, and today, situation is the same.

Louisiana

Louisiana state and its capital, Baton Rouge, are located in southern America. The lands including Nowadays Louisiana were bought from the French government in the famous deal called the "Louisiana purchase" in 1803 and was administrated as the Territory of Orleans for some years. In 1811 and before joining the U.S, the state witnessed one of the most violent slave rebellions which ended tragically. The rebellion was suppressed and heads of rebellious slaves were displayed on pikes to warn the other slaves. Finally, on 30 April 1812, the Territory of Orleans joined the U.S. as its 18th state and renamed as Louisiana. On 24 December 1814, the Treaty of Ghent was signed between the representatives from the US and the UK, (Ghent city was a part of the United Netherlands at the date; today, it is located in Belgium) to end the war which had begun in 1812. Because of the long distance, news of the peace treaty reached the U.S. after nearly a month, and in this period, the naval Battle of New Orleans was fought between American and British forces on 8 January 1815. Finally, Americans, led by Andrew Jackson (later became 7th president of the U.S) managed to defeat the British forces. Coincidence of this victory with spreading of the news of Ghent treaty resulted in the strengthening of solidarity and common identity among residents of the young nation.

Because of its' vast cotton and sugar cane farms, Louisiana was a main center of slavery in the southern part of the U.S. and on the eve of the Civil War, 331,726 slaves (46.8% of the population of the state) were present on its' soil. By the beginning of the War, Louisiana declared secession from the Union, and between 50 thousand to 60 thousand soldiers from the state joined the Confederate Army. "Louisiana Tigers" was the title of a battalion of the Confederation Army, which consisted of soldiers from this state, who gained fame because of their bravery during the War. The story of African-Americans of Louisiana during the Civil War witnessed many ups and downs. On 29 May 1861, the first regiment, consisting of African Americans called the 1st Louisiana Native Guard, was formed and joined the Confederate Army, but soon, Louisiana legislators banned participation of color-skinned people in the Confederate Army, and this unit was dissolved on 15 February 1862. 40 days later, on 24 March, the unit was re-established again by orders from Thomas Overton Moore, governor of Louisiana, but after the capture of the New Orleans city by the Union Army, this regiment was dissolved forever, and a regiment with the same name was formed in the Union Army, consisting of freed slaves from the state and the remaining members of the old Confederate Army regiment. This was among the first military units formed by African-Americans in the Union Army. More than 24 thousand African-Americans from Louisiana fought for the Union during the Civil War period. Lewis Morrison was the sole Jewish black officer who served first in the Confederate Army and later joined the Union forces.

According to the last census, Louisiana had a population of 4,648,794 inhabitants. The demographic composition of the state can be seen in these numbers: 58.4% of the population is white, 32.8% are blacks, 3.3% are Latinos, 1.8% are Asians, 0.8% Native Indians and Alaskans, 0.1% are Hawaiians and people from other Pacific islands, and the rest 1.8% are from other races and ethnicities.

Tulane University, Louisiana State University—Baton Rouge (also known as LSU), Loyola University New Orleans, Centenary College (oldest higher-education institute in Louisiana, dating back to 1825) and Xavier University of Louisiana are among universities and education centers in the state. Rice, cotton, soybean, corn, sugar cane, cows and beef are among the main agricultural and livestock products of the state. The geographical location of Louisiana (a gulf coast state, adjacent to Gulf of Mexico) helps the state to produce nearly 25% of all sea food consumed annually in the U.S. Louisiana has large oil and natural gas resources, and with its 17 refineries, has nearly one-fifth of the refinery capacity in the U.S. In 2020, about 55% of the whole U.S. natural gas exports originated from Louisiana, and these capacities helps the state to be a major center for chemical and petrochemical industries.

Aluminum, coal, gravel, sand, clay, timber products and transportation equipment are among industrial products of Louisiana.

1-CENTURYLINK (telecommunications company). 2-ACADIA HEALTHCARE (medical services company). 3-ODYSSEA MARINE (providing marine transportation services to oil and natural gas companies). 4-ENTERGY (active in electrical power generation and distribution) are among large companies which have headquarters in Louisiana. 1-New Orleans' French Quarter, oldest and best-known district in New Orleans city, dating back to 300 years ago, with many restaurants and different entertainments. 2-Mardi Gras, which is being held in New Orleans annually, largest festival in the city. 3-Melrose Plantation, once belonged to Marie Thérèse and Claude Thomas Pierre Metoyer, freed slaves. 4-Old State Capitol, built between 1847 and 1852, when the capital of the state moved from New Orleans to Baton Rouge. 5-Historical Laura Plantation and its large exhibition, a place for learning about daily life of slaves. 6-Holly Beach, with its golden sands, on the Gulf of Mexico coast. 7-St. Martin Catholic Church, built in 1765 in St. Martinsville, but current building was built in 1836 8-Jean Lafitte National Historical Park and Preserve, site of the Battle of Chalmette between British and American forces in 1815 9-USS Kidd Veterans Memorial, actually a destroyer named after Admiral Isaac C. Kidd, who was killed in the vessel U.S.S Arizona in 1941 Peral Harbor attack. These, along many other historical places, museums and beaches shape the tourism sector in Louisiana. 1-William Felton Russell , also known as Bill Russel , legendary basketball player , first African-American coach and first black person to enter NBA hall of fame 2-Donna Brazil, Democratic Party strategist 3- Louis Armstrong , one of the best-known Jazz musicians and among most prominent trumpeters in history 4-Joe "King" Oliver , musician and orchestra leader , a pioneer of Jazz music 5-Michael Ellis DeBakey, prominent heart surgeon and surgeon of MohammadReza Pahlavi, last King of Iran, are among famous people from Louisiana.

Since 1812 (the year Louisiana joined the U.S as a state) to 2020, 53 U.S. presidential elections have been held in the country, and Louisiana took part in all of them except two contests; one of them because of the Civil War (1864 election) and the other case was 1872, in which the contest result was rejected because of irregularities. Of these contests, the Democratic party won 30 times in the state, Republicans had 13 victories, Democratic-Republicans won 4 times, Whigs scored 2 wins, and American Independent and States' Rights Democratic parties each scored a single win. For a better inspection, history of the U.S presidential elections in Louisiana could be divided into 3 periods. First part, from 1812 to 1872, saw 16 elections, and the state took part in 14 of them. Democrats won 8 times, Democratic-Republicans gained 4 victories and Whigs had 2 wins. As mentioned before, Louisiana was not a part of the U.S when 1864 election was held, and 1872 election in the state was rejected because of irregularities. Second period, from 1876 to 1944, witnessed 18 presidential elections, of which Democrats won 17 contests, and the Republican Party scored a single victory.

In the third period, from 1948, 19 elections were held in the state, and republicans won 12 of them (including the recent 6 competitions), while Democrats had 5 victories, the American Independent Party scored a win and States' Rights Democratic Party managed to gain a contest.

In the 2020 Republican presidential primaries in Louisiana, Donald Trump gained the candidacy through winning 95.9% of the votes, defeating Bill Weld, who won 1.6% of the votes. 2020 Democratic presidential primaries in Louisiana saw a victory for Joseph Biden, who won 79.5% of the votes, while his closest rival, Bernie Sanders got 7.4% of the votes. Finally, the 2020 U.S. Presidential elections in Louisiana resulted in a win for the Republican Party candidate, Donald Trump, who won 58.5% of the votes, while his Democratic counterpart, Joe Biden, won 39.9% of the votes. All 8 electoral votes from Louisiana were added to Trump's vote basket.

Since 1812 (the year the state joined the U.S) to 2020, Louisiana has sent 50 senators to the U.

Senate. 27 were Democrats, 6 were Republicans, 5 were Democratic-Republicans, 2 were Whigs, one was a National Republican, one was an Anti-Jacksonian, one was first an Adams-Clay Republican and then a member of Adams's Men gathering, and one experienced membership in Adams-Clay Republican, Adams's Men and Anti-Jacksonian parties (all 3 names point to a single party in different periods). a senator was a member of the Jacksonian Party, and 5 senators changed their political affiliations during their careers, of which 2 were once Jacksonians and sometimes served as Democrats, one was sometimes a Democratic-Republican and sometimes an Adams-Clay Republican, one switched sides among Whigs, Democrats and the Opposition Party, one switched sides among Democratic-Republican, Adams-Clay Republican and Whig Party.

According to the statistics shown above, the number of those senators who only had membership in the Democratic Party or along this that had records of membership in other parties is 30, and the same number for the Republican Party is 6, showing a clear edge for Democrats. But Republicans have improved their performance in this issue in recent years, and currently (2021), John Neely Kennedy and William Morgan Cassidy, both Republicans, represent Louisiana in the U.S. Senate. Russell Billiu Long, with a 39-year record of service in the Senate (1948-1987) and Allen Joseph Ellender with 35 years' history of presence in the Senate (1937-1972), both Democrats, have been longest-serving senators from Louisiana.

From 1812 to 2020 , 170 persons have represented Louisiana in the U.S House of representatives, of which 107 were Democrats, 35 were Republicans, 8 were Whig Party members, 3 were Democratic-Republicans, 2 were from Native American Party (also known as Know Nothing Party, 2 were Jacksonians, 2 were Liberal Republicans, 1 was a member of Unconditional Union Party, one was an Adams-Clay Republican and member of Adams's Men gathering, one was first Adams-Clay Republican, and then became member of Adams's Men gathering and Anti-Jacksonians, And 7 representatives had records of changing their political affiliations during their careers. Among these, 2 were sometimes Whigs and sometimes Anti-Jacksonians, 2 served as Democrats and Republicans, one switched sides among the Democratic and Progressive parties, one was sometimes a Republican and sometimes a member of the Unconditional Union Party, and a representative switched sides among Democrats and Jacksonians. According to our available sources, a representative had no clear political affiliation.

As the statistics show, those representatives who only served as Democrats or had a history of membership in other parties, have been 111 persons. The same number for Republicans is 38, which indicates a clear superiority for Democrats in this issue in Louisiana. Recent years have witnessed a shift in this trend, and right now, 5 out of 6 Louisiana seats in the House belongs to the Republican Party, while the other seat is empty. Since 1812, 56 governors have served in the state. 34 were Democrats, 10 were Republicans, 6 were Democratic-Republicans, 2 were National Republicans, one was a Whig, there was a military governor appointed by the federal government during the Civil War, and 2 governors changed their political affiliations during their careers, had record of membership in Democratic and Republican parties, and one experienced membership in the National Republican and Whig parties. As it could be observed, those governors who only served as Democrats or had a history of membership in other parties along this, have been 35 persons. The same number for Republicans is 11, which shows an upper hand for Democrats in this issue in Louisiana. Recent decades saw a close competition among parties, but current governor, John Bel Edwards, is also a Democrat. Pinckney Benton Stewart Pinchback, 24th governor of Louisiana, was the first African American in the U.S. to occupy such a position. He was born from a black mother and white father.

Conclusion: Noting that Democrats have won 30 rounds of U.S. presidential elections in Louisiana (while Republicans had 13 victories ,including 6 recent contests), they also sent 30 senators to the U.S. Senate from the state,111 of their party members to the House, and had 35 governors in the history of Louisiana, while 6 Republican Party members were able to enter the U.S. senate from the state, 38 have represented Louisiana in the House, and 11 governors were Republicans, It's clear that the Democratic Party has been superior in the political history of the state, but Republicans have worked better in recent decades, and currently, both U.S. Senate seats and 5 out of 6 House seats are in their hands, while the current governor is a Democrat. It could be said that Louisiana has been a Democratic-leaning state during most of its history, but currently the political sphere of the state is in the favor of the Republican Party.

Indiana

Indiana state is located in Midwestern America. Indianapolis is the capital of the state. Approved by the Congress and President John Adams, president of the U.S, the Indiana territory was established in 1800, and on 11 December 1816 joined the U.S as its 19th state. During the Civil War, Indiana remained in the Union, and through mobilizing troops and providing supplies, helped to save the sovereignty of the U.S. Indiana had a strong agriculture and a large population and played a major role in strengthening the Union Army during the War. Indiana was 2nd in soldier number per capita among the Union states, and among the 6 populated states, this rank was 1. Actually, Indiana was the first western state which mobilized forces in support of the Union. According to the last census, Indiana had a population of 673,2219 inhabitants, of which 78.4% were whites, 9.9% were blacks, 7.3% were Latinos, 2.6% were Asians, 0.4% were Native Americans and Alaskans, 0.1% Hawaiians and other Pacific Islanders and 2.2% were from other races and ethnicities. The University of Notre Dame (where Condoleezza Rice, former secretary of the state of the U.S. graduated), Purdue University--West Lafayette (established in 1869 by a rich merchant, John Purdue , and Neil Armstrong, fist astronaut to walk on the moon graduated from this university), Indiana University—Bloomington, Valparaiso University, Indiana University-Purdue University—Indianapolis (famous for its annual food and handicraft festival) are among universities and education centers in Indiana. Indiana is one of the largest producers of mint, soybean and corn among the U.S. states. Dairy products, tomatoes, pumpkins, lambs, duck, turkey and pork are among other agricultural and livestock products of the state.

Indiana ranks 1st in steel production among the U.S. states and is among top states in automotive industry. Also, the state is a major center for medical and pharma industries. Warsaw city, Indiana, is known as "Orthopedic Capital of the World". The state is globally known for manufacturing Recreational Vehicles. Office furniture and kitchen tools are among other industrial products of Indiana.

Indiana has large coal and limestone resources, and 24 coal power plants operate in the state. Generally, Indiana has a rich and diverse economy.

The state hosts headquarters of some large corporations, including: 1- CUMMINS (specializes in diesel and alternative fuel engines and generators). 2- ELI LILLY AND COMPANY (pharmaceutical company). 3- BERRY GLOBAL (manufacturer and marketer of plastic packaging products). 4- ZIMMER BIOMET (medical device company). 5-Anthem insurance company.

Among tourist attractions of the state, these could be named :1-Eiteljorg Museum of American Indian and Western Art, containing assets from western American cultures. 2-Studebaker National Museum South Bend, which was actually headquarters of Studebaker automotive company, and now has tuned to a museum. 3- Indiana Dunes National Lakeshore, a good place for boating and fishing. 4- Lanier Mansion State Historic Site, construction completed in 1844. The mansion belonged to James Franklin Doughty Lanier, a wealthy merchant of Indiana. 5- RV/MH Hall of Fame Museum, a collection of RV/MH vehicles. 6- Wylie House Museum, once house of Dr. Andrew Wylie, first president of Indiana University. 7- Tibetan Mongolian Buddhist Cultural Center, which aims to promote Mongolian and Tibetan Buddhist culture in the US 8- The Children's Museum of Indianapolis, largest children's museum in the world. 9- Indianapolis Motor Speedway, hosting best-known automobile races in the U.S. 10- Benjamin Harrison Presidential Site, containing Benjamin Harrison's (former president of the US) house. 11- Basilica of the Sacred Heart, with its stunning internal architecture. These, along many other museums, beaches and national parks, shape the tourism sector in Indiana.

1-Mike Pence, vice to Donald Trump, 45th president of the US 2-Kurt Vonnegut, American author. 3-Larry Joe Bird, basketball champion. 4-Sydney Irwin Pollack, actor, producer, director and Academy

Awards winner. 5-David Michael Letterman, TV presenter. 6-Howard Winchester Hawks, director, producer and playwright. 7-Ferid Murad, Nobel prize winner in medical sciences. 8-Wilbur Wright, one of two brothers who together built the first operational airplane in the world and Michael Jackson, are among famous people from Indiana.

Since 1816 (the year Indiana joined the U.S) TO 2020, the state has taken part in all 52 U.S presidential elections held in the U.S, of which Republican Party scored 33 victories, Democrats gained 14 victories, Democratic-Republicans won 3 contests and Whigs won 2 elections. To have a better inspection, the history of U.S presidential elections in Indiana could be divided into 2 different parts. The first period, from 1816 to 1856, witnessed 11 contests, in which Democrats won 6 elections, Democratic-Republicans gained 3 victories and Whigs scored 2 wins. But second period, from 1860 to 2020, saw 41 rounds of elections, and Republicans won 33 of them, while Democratic Party gained 8 wins. This shows that Indiana has been a Republican-leaning state during most of its history. For example, between 1940 and 2020, Republicans won 19 out of 21 U.S presidential elections held in the state, and Democrats emerged victorious in only 2 contests (1964 and 2008). Republicans have worked better in both general history of the state and recent years, including 3 recent contests which were gained by them.2020 Republican Party primaries in Indiana, witnessed a victory for Donald Trump, who got the candidacy by winning 91.9% of the votes, while his rival, Bill Weld, got 8.1%.

In 2020 Democratic Party presidential primaries in Indiana, Joe Biden won the candidacy by gaining 76.7% of the votes, while his closest rival, Bernie Sanders, got 13.4%.

Finally, 2020 U.S presidential election in Indiana witnessed a victory for Republican candidate, Donald Trump, who won 57% of the votes, while his Democratic rival, Joe Biden, got 41%. Trump won all 11 electoral votes from Indiana. From 1816 (the date the first U.S. Senate election was held in Indiana) to 2021, 47 elected candidates from the state have served in the U.S. Senate, of which 21 were Democrats, 18 were Republicans, 2 were Whigs, 2 were Anti-Jacksonians, one was a member of Unconditional Union Party, and 3 senators changed their political affiliation during their careers, of which one served as Democratic-Republican and Adams-Clay Republican, one was sometimes a

Democrat and sometimes a Jacksonian, and a senator experienced membership in Democratic-Republican, Crawford Republican, and Anti-Jacksonian parties. As it could be observed, the number of those senators who served only as Democratic Party members from Indiana, in addition to those who experienced membership in other parties during their careers, was 22. The same number for Republicans is 18, showing superiority of Democrats in the issue, but in reality, Republicans served in the U.S. Senate for more years.

The Republican Party has been more successful in recent years in Indiana, and currently (2021) Michael K. Braun and Todd Christopher Young, who represent the state in the U.S Senate are both Republicans. Richard Green Lugar (with a 36-year record of presence in the U.S. Senate, 1977-2013) from Republican Party and Daniel Wolsey Voorhees (with a 20-year record of service, 1877-1897), a Democrat, have been longest-serving U.S senators in the history of Indiana.

Benjamin Harrison, 23rd president of the U.S, once represented Indiana in the U.S. Senate.

From 1816 (the year the first U.S. House of representatives' election was held in the state) to 2021, 326 elected candidates have entered the U.S House of representatives as representatives from Indiana. 146 were Democrats, 138 were Republicans, 14 were Whigs, 4 were members of Opposition Party, 3 were Jacksonians, 2 were Democratic-Republicans, one was a member of Independent Party, one was a member of Greenback Party, one was an Anti-Jacksonian And 16 representatives changed political affiliation during their careers, of which 3 were sometimes Democrats and sometimes Jacksonians, one served as member of Anti-Monopoly Party and Democratic Party, one experienced membership in Unconditional Union and Republican parties, one was sometimes a Whig and sometimes an Anti-Jacksonian, one had record of membership in Whig and Republican parties, one was once a member of Opposition Party and once served as a Republican, one switched sides among Whig and Opposition parties, one had record of membership in Free Soil and Republican parties, one was sometimes a Democrat and sometimes a member of Opposition Party, one served as Jacksonian and Anti-Jacksonian, one worked as Democrat and member of Anti-Lecompton Democratic Party, one experienced membership in Jacksonian Adams's Men and Anti-Jacksonian parties, one switched sides among Whig, Opposition and Republican parties and a representative served as Democratic-Republican, Jacksonian, Adams's Men and Anti-Jacksonian.

As the statistics show, the number of those House representatives who served only as Democrats during their careers, in addition to those who experienced membership in other parties, was 152, and the same number for Republicans is 143, showing an edge for Democrats in the history of the U.S House of -representatives' elections in Indiana. But just like the results for the U.S Senate, Republican representatives served in the House for a longer period and more years. Currently (2021), 7 out of 9 House representatives who have seats from Indiana, are Republicans, while the rest 2 seats are held by Democratic Party members.Mike Pence, former vice president of the U.S once represented Indiana in the U.S. House of representatives. Eric Joseph Holcomb, current governor of the state and a Republican, is actually the 51st governor of Indiana, while during its history, 49 persons served as governors of the state. the 2-number difference here is due to that 2 governors gained the seat in 2 non-continuous terms. for instance, Henry Frederick Schricker served from 1941 to 1945 as the 36th governor of Indiana, and later was able to gain the seat as the 36th governor from 1949 to 1953 as the 38th governor of the state. Since 1816, 49 persons have served as governor of Indiana, and among these 49 governors, 23 were Republicans, 19 were Democrats, 4 were members of the Democratic-Republican Party and 3 were Whigs. According to the statistics presented, Republicans have had an upper hand in the history of gubernatorial elections in the state (they had 23 governors while Democrats had 19), and as mentioned before, the current governor is also a Republican. Mike Pence, vice to Donald Trump, former president of the U.S, served as the 50th governor of Indiana from 2013 to 2017.

Conclusion : Noting that Republicans have won 33 U.S. presidential elections in Indiana (Democrats won 14) including 3 recent contests, and had 18 U.S. senators and 143 House representatives in the history of the state (with longer years of service than their Democratic counterparts), while the numbers for Democratic Party are 22 and 152 with shorter years of service, and both current senators representing Indiana in the U.S Senate are Republicans and 7 out of 9 House seats belonging to the state are being held by them (2 for Democrats), and Republicans had

23 governors in the history of the state (vs 19 Democrats), including the current governor, so it could be concluded that Indiana has been a Republican Party bastion during most of its history and currently (2021), the situation is not much different.

Mississippi

Mississippi state is located in southern America, and its capital city is Jackson. The state was initially the western half of the Mississippi territory and joined the U. S. as its' 20th state in 10 December 1817. The eastern part of the Mississippi territory later formed Alabama state. On the eve of Civil War, nearly 55% of the population in the state was slave. Mississippi had vast cotton farms, and the slaves played a major role in the economy of the state through their work on these farms. During the Civil War, Mississippi was the 2nd state to declare its' secession from the Union (after South Carolina), and more than 80 thousand white men from the state joined the Confederate Army. On the other hand, about 500 white men and 17 thousand slaves and freed slaves fought for the Union Army. Strategic location of the state, along Mississippi river, made the state a major site for many battles during the Civil War. In later years of the War, a group called Knight's Company, led by Newton Knight was formed in Mississippi. Most of the group members were Confederate Army deserters, and the group engaged in resistance against the Confederation government. The Civil War ended, but ratification of the state constitution in 1890 kept the blacks in Mississippi as 2nd class citizens, and racial separation in schools continued for decades. The U.S Supreme Court announced that racial separation violates the constitution in 1954, and this resulted in eruption of riots in the state. Followed up by Robert Kennedy, former United States Attorney General, on 1 October 1962, James Meredith, as the first African-American, entered a university in Mississippi under federal protection, and finally, in 1969, by orders from a federal court, racial separation in schools in the state came to an end.

According to the last census, the population of the state was 2,976,149 residents. Demographics of Mississippi show its population consisted of 56.4% whites, 37.8% blacks, 3.4% Latinos ,0.6% native Indians and Alaskans, 1.1% Asians, 0.1% Hawaiians and other Islanders, and 1.3% are from other races. University of Mississippi (its foundation dates back to 1848), Mississippi State University, William Carey University and Millsaps College are among scientific and education centers in the state. Mississippi is among top states in producing timber.   A large part of the economy in the state is in the agriculture sector, and cotton, soybean, corn, wheat, rice, peanuts, sweet potatoes, cows, fish and chicken (the state is among top chicken producers in the country), are among main agricultural products of the state. Wire and street lighting equipment, generators, vehicle parts, textiles, natural gas and oil in small volumes, coal, clay, sand, gravel, limestone and bauxite (mineral Aluminum) are among industrial products of the state. Casinos shape another important economic sector in Mississippi, but generally, Mississippi is not a rich state. Some large corporations like: 1- SANDERSON FARMS (largest poultry producer in the United States). 2- THE YATES COMPANIES (construction company). 3- CAL-MAINE FOODS (large egg producer). 4- BANCORPSOUTH and HANCOCK WHITNEY bank holdings have headquarters in Mississippi.

Among tourist attractions in the state, these could be named: 1- Gulf Islands National Seashore, with its white sands and stunning nature. 2- Beauvoir, a house which once was residence of Jefferson Davies, president of the Confederation, dating back to 1852. 3- Tupelo Automobile Museum, a collection of unique old cars. 4- Elvis Presley Birthplace & Museum, which actually is the birthplace of Elvis Presley. 5- Stanton Hall, a large mansion built by Frederick Stanton, cotton merchant, in 1857. Stanton built the mansion with Irish style in memory of his Irish ancestors. 6-splendid Longwood mansion, with a large Byzantine-style dome, and one of the largest Octagonal buildings in the state, built by Dr. Haller Nutt, major cotton producer in 1858. 7- Natchez City Cemetery, dating back to 1822. 8- Emerald Mound cultural site, a place for religious customs of Native inhabitants. 9- Natchez Museum of African American History and Culture, which provides interesting and good information about the history of African-Americans in Mississippi. 10- Historic Jefferson College, some famous people like Jefferson Davies studied here. 11- Mississippi Petrified Forest, a stunning forest containing whale fossils and dinosaur footprints and other pre-history creatures. 12- The Mississippi State Capitol and Old Capitol Museum, in use between 1839 to 1903, and witnessed many historical and controversial decisions. 13- Mississippi Museum of Natural Sciences, these along many other destinations, shape the tourism sector in Mississippi. 1-Elvis Aaron Presley, famous American singer and actor. 2-William Cuthbert Faulkner, author and Nobel laureate in Literature. 3- James Meredith, first African-American to enter university in the state. 4- Britney Jean Spears, singer and actress. 5- Riley. B. King, Known as B.B. King, famous electric guitarist in Blues genre and winner of 17 Grammy prizes (also known as King of the Blues). 6-Opera Gail Winfrey, well-known producer, actress, Oscar prize winner and one of best-known and popular hosts around the world and 7- Newton Knight are among famous people from Mississippi.

From 1820 to 2020, 51 presidential elections have been held in the U.S, and except 2 elections of 1864 & 1868 (because of Civil War and reconstruction), Mississippi has taken part in all other 49 contests. In these 49 elections, Democrats won 30 races, Republicans had 14 wins, The Democratic-Republican party scored 2 victories, Democratic State's Rights Party had a victory, and the American Independent Party was able to gain a win.

To put the subject under a better review, it would be better to divide this history into 2 periods: before and after 1960. In the first part, from 1820 to 1960, 34 rounds of elections were held and Democrats won 29 of them, Democratic-Republican Party gained 2 victories, Whigs scored a win, Republicans gained a contest and State's Democratic Rights Party was able to win a single election. As It's observable during these 140 years, Republicans only won a single presidential election in the state.

But in the second period, from 1964 to 2020, a major shift took place, and out of 15 contests, Republicans gained 13 victories, Democrats only had a single victory and State's Democratic Rights Party won a contest. Among 13 Republican gains, 11 have been scored in 11 recent elections (1980-2020), which shows strong popularity of the Republican Party among Mississippi voters and their control over presidential elections in the state.

In the 2020 Republican primaries in Mississippi, Donald Trump won the candidacy by taking 98.6% of votes, while his rival Bill Weld got 0.9%. Democratic Primaries in the same year in Mississippi witnessed a decisive victory for Joe Biden. He gained 81.8% of votes while Bernie Sanders was only able to win 14.8%. Finally, the 2020 presidential election in Mississippi saw a victory for the Republican candidate Donald Trump, who won 57.5% of votes, vs 41% for Biden. All 6 electoral votes of Mississippi were gained by Trump. In the history of U.S. Senate elections in Mississippi from 1817 to 2021, 45 candidates have been elected. 26 of them were Democrats, 9 were Republicans, 3 were Jacksonians, 2 were Whigs, one was a Democratic-Republican and 4 senators changed their political affiliation several times, of which one served as a Democratic-Republican and a Jacksonian Republican, one was a Jacksonian who also served as an Anti-Jacksonian, one experienced membership in Jacksonian, Democratic-Republican and Jacksonian Republican parties, and a Senator switched sides among Jacksonian, Anti-Jacksonian and Whig parties.

As the statistics show, Democrats are superior in the history of the U.S. Senate elections in Mississippi (they had 26 U.S. senators while Republicans had 9), and from 1881 to 1978, nearly a century, all 16 U.S. senators who represented the state were members of Democratic Party. But since 1978, votes in the state began switching in favor of Republicans and until now (43 years), all 4 recent U.S senators from the state have been Republicans. Roger Frederick Wicker and Cindy Hyde-Smith, both Republicans, currently (2021) represent Mississippi in the U.S Senate.

John Cornelius Stennis from Democratic party served as Senator from the state for 42 years (1947-1989), while Republican William Thad Cochran had a 40-year record (1978-2018). These were longest-serving Senators in history of Mississippi. Jefferson Davies, president of the Confederation (rebel states in the south), once acted as U.S senator from Mississippi. Through its history, and from 1819 (the date the first U.S. House of representatives' election was held in the state) to 2021, Mississippi has sent 125 elected candidates to U.S House of representatives. Among these, 84 were Democrats, 23 were Republicans, 4 were Jacksonians, 3 were Whigs, 3 were members of Unionist Party, one was an Independent Republican, one was a member of Native American Party, one was a member of Anti-Jacksonians and 5 representatives had multiple political affiliations, of which 2 were Democrats for a while and Jacksonian for the rest, one served as Democrat and Republican, one switched sides among Democratic and Independent ,and one experienced membership in Jacksonian, Democratic-Republican and Jacksonian Republican parties.

Looking at the statistics shown above, it could be seen that the Number of those House representatives who served only as Democrats from Mississippi during their careers, in addition to those who experienced membership in other parties, was 88, and the same number for Republicans is 24, showing an edge for Democrats in the history of the U.S House of representatives' elections in Mississippi. For 80 years, from 1883 to 1963 Democrats were sole winners of House elections in the state. But after 1965, situation moved in direction of balance between these two parties, and finally changed radically in favor of Republican Party. Currently (2021), 3 out of 4 House representatives who have seats from Mississippi, are Republicans, while just one seats are held by Democratic Party.

Jamie Lloyd Whitten (with a 54-year record of presence in the U.S Senate, since 1941-1995) and William Meyers Colmer (with a 40-year record of service, 1933-1973), both Democrats, have been the longest-serving U.S. senators in the history of Mississippi.

Jefferson Davies, president of the Confederation (rebel states in the south), had a record of representing Mississippi in the U.S. House of representatives.Jonathon Tate Reeves, from the Republican Party, is the current and 65th governor of Mississippi, but the number of persons who served as governors in the state was 54. It should be noted that the 11-number difference here is due to that 11 governors gained the seat in 2 non-continuous terms. For instance, Hugh Lawson White served from 1936 to 1940 as the 45th governor of Mississippi and later was able to gain the seat as the 51st governor from 1952 to 1956. Since 1817, Mississippi has seen 54 governors. 45 were Democrats, 6 were Republicans and 2 governors changed their political affiliations during their careers, of which one served as Democrat and Whig, and a governor served a term as a military governor appointed by the federal government and in another term was a member of the Republican Party. According to our available sources, a governor had no clear political affiliation.

As it could be seen, the number of those governors who served only as Democrats during their careers, in addition to those who experienced membership in other parties, was 46, and the same number for Republicans is 7, showing a clear edge for Democrats in the history of the gubernatorial elections in Mississippi, but Republicans have improved their performance in recent years and since 2004 all 3 recent governors have been members of the Republican Party.

Conclusion: Noting that Democrats have won 30 U.S. presidential elections in Mississippi (Republicans won 14 including 11 recent contests), Democrats had 26 U.S. senators and 88 House representatives and 46 governors in the history of the state (the numbers for Republican Party are 9, 24 and 7), but both current senators representing Mississippi in the U.S Senate are a Republicans and 3 out of 4 current representatives in the U.S House of representatives are Republicans (vs 1 Democrat), and all 3 recent governors of Mississippi have been Republicans, it could be said that Mississippi has been a Democratic Party bastion during most of its' history, but this trend has radically changed in recent decades, and now (2021), Mississippi is a staunch Republican state.

Illinois

Illinois state and its' capital, Springfield, are located in the American Midwest. The nowadays state of Illinois was initially a part of the Indiana territory, and in 1809, seceded from this territory, shaping the Illinois territory. Finally, on 3 December 1818 and after ratification of the Constitution, Illinois territory joined the U.S. as its 21st state. Chicago is the best-known city in the state, known for its high buildings and numerous scientific and entertainment centers. Famous boss of Chicago Outfit mafia, Al Capon, was a resident of Chicago for many years. During the Civil War, the state mobilized more than 250 thousand soldiers in support of the Union and provided large amounts of supplies to the Union Army for defending the sovereignty of the country and to secure the freedom of all slaves in the U.S. In October 1871, Chicago witnessed a huge fire which lasted 2 days and killed nearly 300 inhabitants alone, causing a 200-million-dollar damage. On 1 May 1886, workers across different cities of the U.S. took part in street protests, declaring their strike for an eight-hour work day. The number of protesters in Chicago was more than 90 thousand. Protests continued for several days, and riots between protesters and the police broke out; then, an explosion resulted in several casualties. Some laborers who were detained and later charged with responsibility for the explosion case were sentenced to life in prison and the death penalty. The news about the Chicago protests spread all over the world, and after some years of holding memorials for 1 May, the day got the title of "Universal Labor Day". According to the last census, Illinois had a population of 12,671,821 inhabitants, of which 60.8% were whites, 17.5% were Latinos, 14.6% were blacks, 5.9% were Asians, 0.6% were Native Americans and Alaskans, 0.1% Hawaiians and other Pacific Islanders, and 2.1% were from other races and ethnicities. The

University of Chicago (where Barrack Obama , 44th president of the U.S. taught law science there for 12 years) , Northwestern University , University of Illinois at Urbana—Champaign (home to National Center for Supercomputing Applications, people like Steve Chen , founder of YouTube website graduated here) and Illinois Institute of Technology , all among top universities in the U.S ,along with Argonne National Laboratory (known as ANL) and Fermi National Accelerator Laboratory (known as Fermi Lab) are among education and scientific centers in the state. Corn, soybean, alfalfa, wheat, apple, melons, watermelons, peaches, pork, cow, beef, dairy products, candy, sausage and spices are among agricultural and livestock products of Illinois. Construction equipment, agricultural vehicles, tools, chemical and pharma products are among industrial products of the state. Generally, Illinois has a strong and diverse economy, and some large corporations, like: 1- BOEING, aviation industry giant 2- CATERPILLAR, manufacturer of road construction vehicles 3- JOHN DEERE (which manufactures agricultural, construction, forestry machinery and diesel engines) 4- MCDONALD'S restaurant chain with global fame 5- BAXTER INTERNATIONAL, pharma corporation 6- ALLSTATE insurance 7- WALGREENS chain drugstore and United Airlines have headquarters here.

Among tourist destinations in Illinois, these could be named : 1- Willis Tower Skydeck , and its roof , which a part of it is made of glass 2- Millennium Park & Cloud Gate , with a steel statue 3- Magnificent Mile in Chicago , a place for walking and shopping , surrounded by skyscrapers 4- Navy Pier , along with museums, restaurants, shopping centers , show and theater salons 6- Cahokia Mounds State Historic Site , largest pre-historic Native American settlement north of Mexico , which contains many hills 7- Dana-Thomas House , which belonged to a rich widow , Susan Lawrence Dana , with stunning architecture , dating back to 1902 8- Ulysses S. Grant Home State Historic Site in Galena , which actually was house of Ulysses.S.Grant , 18th president of the U.S 9- Midway Village Museum, one of the most popular parts in this museum is the "Many Faces, One Community" , which portrays stories of migrations that resulted in the establishment of Rockford City. 10-Tinker Swiss Cottage Museum and Gardens, once the house of Robert Hall Tinker, mayor of Rockford, built between 1865 to 1870

11-Abraham Lincoln Presidential Library and Museum. These, along many other museums and historical places shape the tourism sector in Illinois. 1-Ronald Reagan , 40th president of the U.S 2-Hillary Clinton , former secretary of the state of the U.S. 3-Walt Disney , FOUNDER OF Walt Disney company , globally-known media and entertainment company 4-Ernest Hemingway , prominent American author and Nobel prize winner in literature 5-Donald Rumsfeld , former secretary of defense of the U.S 6-CM Punk , professional martial art performer 7-Robert Andrews Millikan , physicist and Nobel prize winner 8-Miles Davis , prominent musician 9-Harrison Ford and Gillian Anderson , Hollywood actors , are among famous people from Illinois.

Since 1820 (the year the first U.S. presidential election in the state was held) to 2020 Illinois has taken part in 51 U.S. presidential elections. In these 51 contests, the Democratic Party gained 25 victories, Republicans won 24 times and Democratic-Republicans scored 2 wins.

To have a better inspection, we can divide the history of the presidential elections in Illinois to 2 periods: First part, from 1820 to 1928, saw 28 elections. Republicans won 16 times, Democrats gained 10 victories, and Democratic-Republicans won 2 time.

In the second period, 23 rounds of elections were held, and Democrats won 15 of them (including 8 recent elections), and the Republican party was able to score 8 victories.

As the statistics show, while Democrats have 1 more victory than Republicans, they have been winners of all 8 recent contests, which shows strong popularity of the Democratic Party in the state in recent decades.

In the 2020 Democratic Party presidential primaries in Illinois, Joe Biden defeated Bernie sanders by winning 59% of the votes and got the candidacy, while Sanders got 36.1% of the votes.

In the 2020 Republican Party presidential primaries in Illinois, Donald Trump elected by gaining 96% of the votes, while his rival, Roque De La Fuente, got 4% of the votes.

Finally, the 2020 presidential election in Illinois witnessed a victory for the Democratic Party candidate, Joe Biden, who got 57.5% of the votes, while his Republican rival, Donald Trump, won 40.6% of the votes. All the 20 electoral votes from Illinois went to Biden's vote basket.

From 1818 (the date first U.S Senate election was held in the state) to 2021, Illinois has sent 51 senators to the U.S. Senate, 22 were Democrats, 21 were Republicans, 2 were Jacksonians, one was a member of Independent Party And 5 were senators who changed their political affiliations during their careers. Among them, one was a Democrat and Republican, one switched sides among Jacksonians and Crawford Republicans, one was sometimes a Democrat and sometimes a Jacksonian, one was once a Democratic-Republican and also served as member of Adams-Clay Republican and a senator switched sides among the Democratic-Republicans, Crawford Republicans and finally Adams's Men Gathering.

According to the statistics shown above, the number of those senators who only had membership in the Democratic Party, or along this had records of membership in other parties, is 24, and the same number for Republican Party is 22, showing an edge for Democrats

Richard Joseph Durbin and Ladda Tammy Duckworth, both Democrats, currently (2021) represent Illinois in the U.S Senate. Shelby Moore Cullom, a Republican with a 30-year record of service in the Senate (1883-1913) and Richard Joseph Durbin with a 24 years' history of presence in the Senate (1997-present), a Democrat, have been longest-serving senators from Illinois.

Barrack Obama, 44th president of the U.S, once represented Illinois in the U.S Senate.

From 1819 (the date the first U.S. House of representatives election was held in the state) to 2021, 476 persons have represented Illinois in the U.S. House of representatives, of which 229 were Republicans 220 were Democrats, 4 were Whig Party members, 2 were member of Progressive Party, 2 were Jacksonians, 2 were members of Independent, one was a member of Greenback Party, one was an Independent Democrat, and 15 representatives had records of changing their political affiliations during their careers. Among these, 4 were sometimes Democrats and sometimes Republicans, 2 were once Whigs and once Republicans, 2 were Democrats and Jacksonians, one was once a Republican and sometimes served as a Progressive, one was sometimes a Whig and sometimes a Democrat, one served as Democrat and Independent Democrat, one switched sides among Jacksonians, Democrats and also served as an Independent Democrat, one experienced membership in Whig and Opposition and an Independent, a representative switched sides among Whig , Opposition , Independent and Republican parties, and one experienced membership in the Democratic-Republican, Adams-Clay Republican, and Adams's Men Gathering parties.

As the statistics show, those representatives who only served as Republicans or had history of membership in other parties along this have been 236 persons. The same number for Democrats is 229, which indicates superiority of Republicans in this issue in Illinois, but recent decades and years witnessed better performance of Democrats in the House elections in Illinois, and Currently (2021), 13 out of 18 representatives from Illinois in the House are Democrats, while Republicans have 5 seats. Abraham Lincoln, 16th president of the U.S, had record of representing Illinois in the U.S. House of representatives during his political career. Joseph Gurney Cannon (Republican), with a 46-year record of service in the U.S. House of representatives, Adolph Joachim Sabbath with a 45 years history of presence , a Democrat , Charles Melvin Price (Democrat , 43-year record) and Sidney Richard Yates (Democrat, 48-year history of service in the House) , have been longest-serving House representatives in history of Illinois.Since 1818, 43 governors have served in the state. 22 were Republicans,18 were Democrats and 3 were Democratic-Republicans. These numbers show an upper hand for Republicans in the issue (although the competition has been tense), but the current governor of Illinois, J. B. Pritzker, is a Democrat.

Conclusion: It could be observed that Democrats have won 25 rounds of U.S. presidential elections in Illinois (while Republicans had 24 victories), including the 8 recent contests in 2020, They also sent 24 senators to the U.S Senate from Illinois, while Republicans had 22 elected candidates, and both current U.S Senators from Illinois are Democrats. Republicans have been superior in the History of the U.S. House elections in Illinois, they had 236 representatives while the Democratic Party had 229, but 13 out of 18 current seats belonging to the state in the House are held by Democrats (vs 5 for Republicans), and the situation in the history of gubernatorial elections in Illinois is not much different: while Republicans had more governors (22 vs 18 Democrats), the current governor is a member of the Democratic Party. This shows a close competition among these 2 parties in the history of the state, but Illinois has been a Democratic stronghold in recent years and decades.

Alabama

Alabama state and it's capital, Montgomery, are located in southeastern America. Mobile City, Alabama is one of the most crowded harbors in the U.S. The state was initially a part of the Alabama territory and joined the U.S. as its 22nd state on 14 December 1819 through ratification of the Constitution. Before the Civil War, because of its vast cotton farms and role of slaves in cotton farming, Alabama insisted on keeping slavery. By the beginning of the War, Alabama declared its secession from the U.S. and joined the Confederation. Montgomery city was chosen as the first capital of the Confederation, and 122 thousand soldiers from the state served in the Confederate Army during the War. Alabama acted as an arms production center for the Confederation during the War. After the War, pro-slavery whites took over the state congress in Alabama, and in 1875 ratified laws which along racial segregation, weakened the position of black people as citizens. Following this and many years later, on 1 December 1955, the famous Montgomery Bus incident took place, in which Rosa Parks, African-American tailor, had to give her seat in the bus to the white person who had entered the bus according to the law, but she didn't do that and was arrested by the police. Protests and a boycott campaign against Montgomery Bus Services began led by Martin Luther King, leader of the Civil Rights movement. Protests continued for a while, and several African-American lawyers got the issue to courts, and finally, on 5 June 1965, a federal court declared the racial segregation in busses inconsistent with the Constitution and voted to abolish this law. In November 1965, the Supreme Court of the U.S. approved this declaration, and after 20 December 1965, the new law went into action.

According to the last census, Alabama had a population of 4,903,185 inhabitants. Demographic composition of the state can be seen in these numbers: 65.3% of the population is white, 26.8% are blacks, 4.6% are Latinos, 1.5% are Asians, 0.7% Native Indians and Alaskans, 0.1% are Hawaiians and people from other Pacific islands, and the rest 1.8% are from other races and ethnicities. Auburn University (where people like Tim Cook, chief executive officer of Apple company graduated), Sanford University, University of Alabama, University of Alabama at Birmingham and Cummings Research Park (one of the largest research parks in the world) are among education and scientific centers in Alabama. Along with, cows, beef, chicken, eggs and cotton, which are main agricultural and livestock products of the state, Alabama produces peanuts, soybean, grains, corn, apple, peaches, nectarine, blueberries, grape, strawberries, fish, shrimp, oyster, and lobster. Different vehicles, trucks, aircraft engines, Military and space travel-related equipment, iron, steel, heat and air-conditioning equipment, electronic and computer equipment, textiles, paper, cardboard, tissue, paper bags, wooden, chemical and plastic products, pharma drugs and specially cancer-related drugs are among industrial products of Alabama.

Extraction of Oil and natural gas, limestone, coal and iron core shape another part of the economy in the state. Some large corporations like : 1- ENCOMPASS HEALTH (one of the United States' largest providers of post-acute healthcare services) 2- BE&K (global engineering and construction company) 3- VULCAN MATERIALS (engaged in the production, distribution and sale of construction materials) 4- B.L. Harbert International (construction company) 5- DRUMMOND (involved in the mining and processing of coal and coal products as well as oil and real estate) 6- REGIONS BANK (bank holding) have headquarters in Alabama.

Among tourist destination in the state, these could be named: 1- Birmingham Civil Rights Institute and the Civil Rights Historic District. Sixteenth Street Baptist Church, which was targeted by the Klu Klux Clan sect through bombing is located here, too. 2- USS Alabama Battleship Memorial Park, a site to visit this vessel which ended its service 60 years after the ending of WWII, along other submarines and military aircraft. The site is a memorial dedicated to all Americans who participated in the War. 3- U.S. Space and Rocket Center, a large collection of space vehicles from different parts of the world 4- Montgomery Civil Rights Landmarks, including Dexter Avenue Baptist Church 5- Mobile Bay, an area with beautiful beaches and islands 6- National Voting Rights Museum and Institute, which is located in the site of bloody catastrophe called "Bloody Sunday" (the day African-Americans who were protesting for suffrage right faced a violent suppression in 1965) 7- Barber Vintage Motorsports Museum, containing more than 1400 vehicles, from early and rare models to modern motorcycles 8- Sloss Furnaces National Historic Landmark, where production of iron core began there in 1882 9- Birmingham Botanical Gardens , a beautiful 62 acre wide area 10- Civil Rights Memorials of Montgomery. These are parts of tourism sector in Alabama.1- Rosa Parks, African-American tailor, who had to give up her seat in the bus to the white person who had entered the bus according to the law. but she didn't and was arrested by the police. Protests and a boycott campaign against the Montgomery Bus Services began after this. 2-Jeff Sessions, former U.S Attorney General 3- John Lewis, politician and leader in civil rights movement which aimed to end the racial segregation in the U.S 4- Broderick Dornell Smiley, comedian, TV presenter, actor and radio personality, well known for his prank phone calls 5- DeMarcus Amir Cousins, famous American basketball player 6- Courteney Bass Cox, actor, producer and director, are among famous people from Alabama.

Since 1819 (the date Alabama joined the U.S. as a state), the state has taken part in 50 out of 51 presidential elections held in the U.S. (because of the Civil War, 1864 election didn't take place in the state). Democrats won 31 rounds, the Republican Party scored 15 victories, Democratic-Republicans had 2 victories, American Independent Party was able to gain a single victory and States' Rights Democratic emerged a winner in a single contest.

To have a better inspection, the history of U.S. presidential elections in Alabama could be divided into 3 different parts. The first period, from 1820 to 1860 (the last election held before the Civil War), witnessed 11 contests, in which Democrats won 9 elections and Democratic-Republicans gained 2 victories.

Second period, from 1868 to 1960, saw 24 rounds of elections, and Democrats won 21 of them, while Republican Party scored 2 wins and States' Rights, the Democratic Party won electoral votes from the state in a single contest. Actually, in these 2 periods, Democrats gained 30 victories, while the Republican party only won 2 times, so this period could be called the Democratic Party period. Most of the southern states, after the Civil War and the reconstruction era were strongholds of Democratic Party until the 1950s. In the third period, from 1964 to 2016, the tide turned, and the Republicans won 13 out of 15 elections held in Alabama (11 of them continuously since 1980) and Democrats and the American Independent Party each gained a single victory. Lastly, the Democratic Party victory was in 1976.

According to the numbers seen above, by winning 31 rounds of elections (vs 15 for Republicans), Democrats have been superior in the history of U.S. presidential elections in Alabama, but all 11 recent contests have been Republican victories, showing strong state-wide support for Republicans in Alabama during recent decades.

In the 2020 Republican Party presidential primaries in Alabama, Donald Trump elected by gaining 96.2% of the votes, defeating Bill Weld who got 1.5%.

In the 2020 Democratic presidential primaries in Alabama, Joe Biden won the candidacy through winning 63.3% of the votes, while his closest rival, Bernie Sanders, took 16.5%.

Finally, the 2020 U.S presidential election in Alabama witnessed a victory for Republican Party candidate, Donald Trump, who got 62% of the votes, while Democratic candidate, Joe Biden got 36.6%. All 9 electoral votes from Alabama were added to the Trump's vote basket.

From 1819 to 2021, the state has sent 43 senators to the U.S Senate. 29 were Democrats, 6 were Republicans, 2 were Jacksonians, 1 was a Democratic-Republican And 5 senators changed their political affiliations during their careers , of which one served as Democrat and Republican , one was once a Democrat and once a Jacksonians , one switched sides among Democratic-Republicans and Jacksonians , one began experienced membership in Jacksonian and Anti-Jacksonian parties and a senator experienced membership in Democratic-Republican, Jacksonian and Democratic parties. As it could be observed, the number of those senators who served only as Democratic Party members from Alabama, in addition to those who experienced membership in other parties during their careers, was 32. The same number for Republicans is 7, showing clear superiority of Democrats in the issue, but recent years have witnessed a tenser competition among these parties, and currently (2021) Richard Craig Shelby and Thomas Hawley Tuberville, both members of the Republican Party, represent Alabama in the U.S. Senate.

Richard Craig Shelby (with a 34-year record of presence in the U.S Senate, since 1987 to present ,2021, first 7 years as a Democrat and then as a Republican) and John Jackson Sparkman (with a 33-year record of service, 1964-1979), a Democrat, have been longest-serving U.S senators in history of Alabama. Since 1819 (the year the first U.S House of representatives' election was held in the state), to 2021, 188 elected candidates have entered the U.S House of representatives as representatives from Alabama. 124 were Democrats , 38 were Republicans , 6 were Whigs, 4 were Jacksonians, 2 were People's Party , one was a Liberal Republican , one was a member of Democratic-Republican Party , one was a member of Native American Party (also known as Know Nothing Party), one was a member of Greenback Party , And 10 representatives changed their political affiliations during their careers , of which 3 were Democrats and Jacksonians , 2 served as Jacksonians and Jacksonian Republicans , one switched sides among Whigs and Jacksonians , one experience membership in Whig and Republican parties , one served as Democratic-Republican and Jacksonian , one served as member of Whig and Anti-Jacksonian parties, and a representative switched sides among Unionist , Democratic and Native American parties.

As the statistics show, Number of those House representatives who served only as Democrats during their careers, in addition to those who experienced membership in other parties, was 128, and the same number for Republicans is 39, showing an edge for Democrats in the history of the U.S House of representatives' elections in Alabama. But Republicans have worked better in recent decades, and currently (2021), 6 out of 7 House representatives who have seats from Alabama, are Republicans, while 1 seat is held by Democratic Party.

Since 1819 to 2021, 55 governors have served in Alabama. Among these 55 governors, 39 were Democrats, 6 were Republicans, 3 were Democratic-Republicans, 2 were Jacksonians, 2 were members of Whig Party, one was an Independent, one was a military governor appointed by the federal government and a governor began as a Democrat and then defected to Republican Party. As these numbers show, the number of those governors who served only as Democrats during their careers, in addition to those who experienced membership in other parties, was 40, and the same number for Republicans is 7, showing a surprising edge for Democrats in the history of the gubernatorial elections in Alabama. Before 1987, only 2 Republicans were able to gain the seat. But Republicans have gained more popularity among gubernatorial elections voters in recent decades in Alabama, and since 2003, all 3 recent governors have been Republicans.

Conclusion: Noting that Democrats have won 31 U.S. presidential elections in Alabama (Republicans won 15 contests including all 11 recent contests), and had 32 U.S. senators, 128 House representatives and 40 governors in the history of the state (the numbers for Republican Party are 7, 39 and 7), they have been superior in most of the political history of Alabama, but currently (2021), both U.S senators and 6 out of 7 House representatives representing the state are Republicans (only a House representative is Democrat) and all 3 recent governors of the state have been Republicans, so it could be said while Alabama has been a Democratic bastion through most of its history, now (2021), the political sphere of the state is in full favor of the Republican Party.

Maine

Main state and its capital, Augusta, are located in northeastern America. With its' beautiful rocky beaches and vast forests, Maine is a part of the cultural and geographical New England area. Until 1820, Maine was a part of Massachusetts state, then seceded from the state through the Missouri Compromise and finally, on 15 March 1820, joined the U.S. as its 23rd state. During the Civil War, Maine remained loyal to the Union, and through mobilizing more than 80 thousand soldiers and manufacturing arms, ships and providing other supplies, played an important role in helping the Union Army. The Battle of Portland Harbor was fought near the Portland waters during the Civil War. Maine has a population of 1,344,212 inhabitants, of which 93% are whites, 1.8% are Latinos, 1.7% are blacks, 1.3% are Asians, 0.7% are Native Americans and Hawaiians and 1.8% are from other races and ethnicities. The University of Maine (Wednesday is the last week of the spring term in this university is called "Maine Day", all classes are closed and everyone helps in cleaning the university), the University of New England, Bowdoin College (dating back to 1794) and Colby College are among scientific and education centers in Maine. The soil in Maine is not much fertile for agriculture, but Maine is a top state in producing blueberries and maple syrup, and potato is among the main products of the state. In producing and breeding cows, beef, sheep, milk, eggs, fish and oyster, Maine is a successful state, and fishing lobster and salmon fish, generally fishing, is a common business in the state. In a near past, Main was an industrial state, and for example, had an active shoe production industry. But in recent decades and after relocation of many industries to cheaper destinations in other countries, economy of

Maine has moved towards services, insurance, real estate business and health and medical services.

But this doesn't mean that Maine has lost all of its industry sector. Today, Maine is a center for producing and manufacturing paper, timber and wooden products, aviation industry products, electronic device parts, medical equipment and shipbuilding. Extraction and producing granite, slate, cement, sand, gravel, clay and coal is another part of industry sector in Maine. Most durable industries in Maine are those which relate to forests. Some large corporations like: 1-L.L. BEAN (privately held retail company) 2-IDEXX (engaged in the development, manufacture, and distribution of products and services for the companion animal veterinary, livestock and poultry, water testing, and dairy markets) 3-HANNAFORD SUPERMARKETS (supermarket chain) 4-Bath Iron Works (shipbuilding company) have headquarters in Maine.

Among tourist destinations in the state , these could be named : 1-Acadia National Park, a beautiful and rocky coastline which has surrounded a wide area with many lakes, rivers and forests 2-The Old Port and Portland Head Lighthouse, along with fishing boats , crowded decks , seafood restaurants and entertainment ships 3-Pemaquid Point Light , dating back to 1835 4-Old Orchard Beach , a beach resort with an old Carousel and kiosks selling food and snacks 5-Nubble Lighthouse , in middle of a meadow , on top of rocky terrain 6-Victoria Mansion , a beautiful mansion with Italian architecture style dating back to mid 19th century 7-Monhegan Island , with a great view , a good place for fishing . No cars or asphalt road here. 8-Children's Museum & Theatre of Maine, with different entertainments and amusing games 9-Maine Narrow Gauge Railroad Co and Museum with its train trip 10-Wadsworth Longfellow House built in 1786 by General Peleg Wadsworth, grandfather to Henry Wadsworth Longfellow, American poet and first person to translate Dante Algieri's "Divine Comedy" to English. He also grew up in this house 11- York Corner Schoolhouse, one of the oldest schools from the 18th century in the New England area 12-Maine Coast. These, along many other beautiful beaches, historical lighthouses, and stunning islands, shape the tourism sector in the state. 1-Henry Wadsworth Longfellow, American poet and first person to translate Dante Algieri's "Divine Comedy" to English 2- Stephen Edwin

King, author of more than 200 literary works, most of them in the horror genre, which are among the best-selling in the world 3- Louise Bogan, female poet who was appointed the fourth Poet Laureate to the Library of Congress in 1945, the first woman to gain the title. 4- Henry Gannett, American geographer who is described as the "Father of the Quadrangle" which is the basis for topographical maps in the United States, are among famous people from Maine.

Maine and Nebraska are 2 states that don't follow the " winner-take-all electoral vote" allocation in the U.S presidential elections, but according to "by Congressional District Method", these states are divided into federal districts in accordance to the number of House representatives. Maine has 2 representatives and is divided into 2 federal districts. The state has 4 electoral votes. For example, a candidate wins a federal district through gaining 250 thousand votes, and another candidate wins another district by 270 thousand votes; every candidate takes an electoral vote by now, but the remaining 2 electoral votes are gained by the second candidate who has won more votes generally in the state (the second candidate who got 270 thousand votes). Since 1820 (the year Maine joined the U.S. as its 23rd state) to 2020, Maine has taken part in 51 U.S. presidential elections, of which the Republican Party scored 31 victories, the Democratic Party gained 16 victories, Democratic-Republicans won 2 contests, Whigs won an election and the National Republican Party was able to gain a single contest.

To have a better inspection, the history of U.S. presidential elections in Maine could be divided into 3 different parts. The first period, from 1820 to 1852, witnessed 9 contests, in which Democrats won 5 elections, Democratic-Republicans gained 2 victories, Whigs scored a single win, and the National Republicans scored a single victory.

Second period, from 1856 to 1960, saw 27 rounds of elections, and Republicans won 26 of them, while the Democratic Party gained a single win. In the third period, from 1964 to 2020, 15 rounds of the U.S. presidential elections were held in the state, and the Democrats won 10 of them, including 8 recent contests (in 2016 and 2020 elections, Democrats gained 3 out of 4 electoral votes in the state, while the Republican Party got 1), while Republican Party was able to win 5 times. In the 2020 Democratic Party presidential primaries in Maine, Joe Biden won the candidacy by gaining 34.1% of the votes, while his closest rival, Bernie Sanders, got 32.9%.

In the same year, Republican Party primaries were not held in Maine and because of statewide support for Donald Trump, he won the candidacy. Finally, the 2020 U.S. presidential election in Maine witnessed a victory for the Democratic candidate, Joe Biden, who won 53.1% of the votes, while his Republican rival, Donald Trump, got 44%. Biden won all 4 electoral votes from Maine. From 1820 (the date first U.S Senate election was held in Maine) to 2021 , 37 elected candidates from the state have served in the U.S Senate , of which 17 were Republicans , 9 were Democrats , 3 were Jacksonians , one was Independent, one was a Whig , one was an Anti- Jacksonian .and 5 senators changed their political affiliations during their careers, of which , one was a Democrat who defected to the Republicans , one began as a Whig and then joined Republicans , one was sometimes a Democrat and sometimes a Jacksonian , one was a Democratic-Republican who later joined Crawford Republicans and finally became a Jacksonian , and a senator switched sides among Democratic-Republican, Adams's Men, Anti-Jacksonian and National Republican parties.

As it could be observed, the number of those senators who served only as Republican Party members from Maine, in addition to those who experienced membership in other parties during their careers, was 19. The same number for Democrats is 11, showing superiority of Republicans in the issue. Republicans also had a strong performance in recent years, and currently (2021), Susan Margaret Collins, a Republican, holds on of the U.S. Senate seats from Maine, while the other seat is held by an independent senator, Angus Stanley King Jr.

William Pierce Frye (with a 30-year record of presence in the U.S Senate, 1881-1911) and Eugene Hale (with a 30-year record of service, 1881-1911), both Republicans, have been the longest-serving U.S senators in the history of Maine. From 1821 (the year first U.S House of representative's election was held in the state) to 2021, 158 elected candidates have entered the U.S. House of representatives as representatives from Maine. 61 were Republicans , 48 were Democrats , 14 were Whigs , 10 were Jacksonians , 2 were Anti-Jacksonians , one was an Adams-Clay Republican , 3 were first Adams-Clay Republicans and then Adams's Men gathering members , one was first a member of Adams's Men gathering and then an Anti-Jacksonian, 2 were

Democratic-Republicans, 2 were Federalists, one was a member of Opposition Party, and 9 representatives changed political affiliation during their careers, of which 2 were sometimes Democratic-Republicans and sometimes Adams-Clay Republicans, 2 were Whigs who joined Republicans, 1 was a Whig who defected to Opposition Party , one began as a Republican and later joined the Opposition Party, one was a Democrat who defected to Jacksonians , one began as a Whig, then joined the Opposition Party and finally became a Republican, one was a Democratic-Republican who defected to the Adams-Clay Republicans and finally joined to the Adams's Men Gathering, and 4 representatives had no clear political affiliation according to available sources.

As the statistics show, the number of those House representatives who served only as Republicans during their careers, in addition to those who experienced membership in other parties, was 65, and the same number for Democrats is 49, showing an edge for Republicans in the history of the U.S. House of representatives' elections in Maine, but in recent decades, the Democratic Party has improved its' performance in the issue, and currently both representatives from Maine in the House are Democrats. Janet Trafton Mills, current governor of the state (a Democrat), is the 75th governor of Maine, while during its history, 71 persons served as governors of the state. The 4-number difference here is due to the fact that 4 governors gained the seat in 2 non-continuous terms. For instance, John Fairfield served from 1839 to 1841 as the 13th governor of Maine, and later was able to gain the seat as the 5th governor from 1842 to 1843 as the 16th governor of the state. Since 1820, 71 persons have served as governor of Maine, and among these, 37 were Republicans, 20 were Democrats, 6 were members of Democratic-Republican Party, 3 were Whigs, 2 were members of Independent Party, 2 were National Republicans and a governor was member of Greenback Party.

As it could be seen, Republicans have an upper hand here, but recent decades have witnessed tense competition among these 2 parties, and none have been able to hold the governor's seat for a long time. Currently (2021), a Democrat is the governor of Maine.

Conclusion: Noting that Republicans have won 31 U.S. presidential elections in Maine (Democrats won 16 including 8 recent contests) and had 19 U.S senators and 65 House representatives and 37 governors in the history of the state , while the numbers for the Democratic Party are 11, 49, and 20 , but currently (2021), Republicans have a U.S. Senate seat from the state and the other seat is held by an independent , and both representatives representing Maine in the U.S House of representatives are Democrats , and the current governor of the state is from the same party; it could be concluded that Maine has been a Republican Party bastion during most of its' history, but now (2021), sympathy toward the Democratic party among the voters in Maine is much stronger.

Missouri

Missouri is a Midwestern state of the U.S. and its'Capital is Jefferson City. Missouri lands were bought from France along with Louisiana in the famous "Louisiana Purchase", by Thomas Jefferson the then U. S President of the time in 1803. Finally, Missouri joined the U.S. as its 24th state on 10 August 1821. The state remained neutral during the Civil War, but some people from Missouri joined the Confederate Army. According to the latest census, Missouri has a population of 6,137,428 inhabitants.79.1% of the population is white, 11.8% black, 0.6% Native Indians and Alaskans, 4.4% Latino, 2.2% Asian, 0.2% Hawaiians and other Islanders, 2.4% others. Washington University in St. Louis (one of the most credible universities in the U.S), Saint Louis University (dating back to 1818), the University of Missouri, Missouri University of Science and Technology (which contains a 200-kW nuclear reactor), Barnes-Jewish (one of the best hospitals in the U.S) are among education and scientific centers in Missouri. Rice, cotton, soybean, corn, beef, turkey and pork are among main agricultural and livestock are products of Missouri. Along with defense and aviation industries, which are the main sectors of industry in the state, motor vehicles and machinery, electrical devices, plastic and chemical products, drinks, lead, zinc, and iron (in recent decades, because of environment-related concerns, extraction and processing of these metals has reduced) are among other industrial products in the state. Missouri has suitable infrastructure for transporting different goods to different parts of the country, and hosts distribution depots of many large corporations like Walmart and Dollar General.

1-O'REILLY AUTO PARTS (auto parts retailer that provides automotive aftermarket parts, tools, supplies, equipment, and accessories) 2-ENTERPRISE HOLDING (car rental agencies) 3-BJC HEALTHCARE (non-profit health care organization) are among large corporations which have headquarters in Missouri. Among tourist Destinations in the state, these could be named: 1-St. Louis Gateway Arch, a symbolic structure, symbol of St. Louis city and and "a gate to enter the West" 2-Branosn, known as the world capital of the live country music. 3- Silver Dollar City, a park with different handicrafts exhibited, in which craftsmen build glass tools, baskets, iron tools, do pottery, and make candies and candles. Marvel cave is also here. It carries on the tradition of the 1880s mining town, which once stood at the entrance to the cave. The cave was first discovered by the Osage Indians in the 1500s and since that time has attracted explorers looking for the Fountain of Youth, miners of marble and bat guano, and archaeologists. 4-Wilson's Creek National Battlefield, site of a battle during the Civil War 5-Mark Twain Boyhood Home and Museum.

This prominent poet and author lived from his 7 to 18 in this house. 6-Harry S. Truman Presidential Library and Museum, including historical assets and works of art showing professional service of Harry Truman and his family from 1945 to 1953, Truman statue in the White House, his family residence, and tombs of Truman and his wife 7-Route 66 Car Museum, a collection containing more than 70 cars, trucks and vehicles related to Batman movie personality. 8-Arabia Steamboat Museum, consisted of material and objects saved from a sunk ship, weighted nearly 400 thousand pounds. 9-Springfield, a small and beautiful city with many parks and other attractions. Among symbols of the city, Nathanael Greene/Close Memorial Park, with its passages, gardens and playgrounds, its beautiful Japanese garden, Mizumoto, is notable. Another attraction of the city is the Fantastic Caverns, only way to tour the fascinating underground landscape is on a 55-minute jeep-drawn tram ride.

This engaging jeep-drawn tram ride makes the Fantastic Caverns America's only ride-through cave system. 10-American Jazz Museum, along with Wonders of Wildlife National Museum & Aquarium, and many other lakes, parks and historical sites, shape the tourism sector in Missouri. 1- Harry. S. Truman, 33rd President of the U.S 2- Samuel Langhorne Clemens, known by his pen name Mark Twain, American writer, humorist. "Adventures of Huckleberry Finn" is his masterpiece 3- Marianne Moore, American poet 4- Thomas Stearns Eliot, poet, essayist, publisher, playwright, literary critic and editor. 5- Marshall Bruce Mathers III, professional name Eminem, Famous Singer, composer and Rap music producer, are among famous people from Missouri.

Since 1821 to now, 51 presidential elections have been held in Missouri, and the Democratic Party has won 30 of them, while Republicans emerged the winner in 19 contests, and Democrat-Republicans gained victory in 2 rounds. From 1820 to 1948, there were 33 rounds of U.S. presidential elections held in Missouri, of which Democrats won 24 of them, while Republicans gained 7 victories, and the Democratic-Republican Party scored 2 wins, but after 1952, the political sphere of the state changed gradually in favor of Republicans, and in recent 12 elections, they have been winners in all 6 recent contests, while the Democratic Party won 6 elections.

In the 2020 Republican Party presidential primaries in Missouri, Donald Trump was elected by gaining 96.8% of the votes, while his rival, Bill Weld, got 0.7%. In the 2020 Democratic presidential primaries in Missouri, Joe Biden won the candidacy through winning 60.1% of the votes, while his closest rival, Bernie Sanders, took 34.6%.Finally, the 2020 U.S presidential election in Missouri witnessed a victory for the Republican Party candidate, Donald Trump, who got 56.8% of the votes, while Democratic candidate, Joe Biden got 41.4%. All 10 electoral votes from Missouri were added to the Trump's vote basket. It's worth noting that in 100-year period (from 1904 to 2004) except an election (1956), victorious candidates in Missouri have been elected president of the U.S. Since 1821 to 2021, Missouri has sent 46 senators to the U.S. Senate.

Among these 46 senators, 23 were Democrats, 15 were Republicans, one was a Whig , one was a member of the Unconditional Union Party, one was a Jacksonian, and 5 were senators who changed their political affiliations during their careers, of which one served as a Democrat and a Jacksonian, 2 switched sides among Republicans and the Unconditional Union Party; one experienced membership in the Democratic-Republican, Jacksonian and Democratic parties, and a senator switched sides among Democratic-Republicans, Adams-Clay Republicans, Adams's Men gathering and Anti-Jacksonians. As it could be observed, the number of those senators who served only as Democratic Party members from Missouri, in addition to those who experienced membership in other parties during their careers, was 25. The same number for Republicans is 17, showing the slight superiority of Democrats in the issue, but recent years have witnessed better performance by Republicans, and one of the U.S Senate seats belonging to the state has been held by Republicans since 1987, and the other seat has the same situation since 2019.

Both current (2021) serving U.S senators from the state, Joshua David Hawley and Roy Dean Blunt, are members of the Republican Party.

Thomas Hart Benton represented the state for 30 years (1821-1851) in the Senate while he changed his party membership several times (Democratic, Democratic-Republican and Jacksonian), and Christopher Samuel Bond from the Republican Party held his seat for 24 years (1987-2011). These were the longest-serving Senators in the history of Missouri.

But, in the U.S. House of Representatives elections in Missouri since 1821 until now (2021) , 306 candidates have been elected. 165 of these were Democrats , 105 were Republicans ,4 were members of Greenback Party , 2 were Whigs , 2 were from Native American Party (also known as Know-Nothing Party), 2 were Jacksonians, 2 were members of Unconditional Union Party, one was a Unionist (both names of the same party in 2 different periods), 2 were Independent Republicans, one was a member of Adams's Men gathering , one was an Anti-Jacksonian (as mentioned in previous parts , both names for a single party in different periods), one was a Liberal Republican , one was a member of Opposition Party, one was an Independent Democrat, and 16 representatives changed political affiliations during their careers , of which 5 were sometimes Republicans and sometimes members of the Unconditional Union Party, 3 served as Whigs and members of the Opposition Party, 2 acted as Democrats and Republicans , one switched sides among Democrats and the Unconditional Union Party , one was sometimes a Democrat and sometimes a Unionist, one was sometimes an Independent Democrat and sometimes a member of the Native

American Party, one switched sides among Democrats and Jacksonians, one served as a Democratic-Republican and an Adams-Clay Republican and a representative switched sides among the Democrats, Whig and the Opposition Parties.

As the statistics show, the number of those House representatives who served only as Democrats during their careers, in addition to those who experienced membership in other parties, was 171, and the same number for Republicans is 112, showing an edge for Democrats in the history of the U.S. House of representatives elections in Missouri, but since the last years of the 20th century (1996), Republicans have gained more popularity among U.S. House of representative elections voters in the state, and currently (2021), 6 out of 8 House representatives who have seats from Missouri, are Republicans, while 2 seats are held by the Democratic Party members.

Clarence Andrew Cannon, a Democrat with 41 years of presence in the U.S. House of representatives was the longest-serving House representative in the history of Missouri and the U.S.

Michael Lynn Parson, current governor of Missouri (a Republican), is the 57th governor in the history of the state, but the number of those persons who acted as the governor of Missouri was 55. The 2-number difference here is due to that 2 governors gained the seat in 2 non-continuous terms. For instance, Christopher Samuel Bond served from 1973 to 1977 as the 47th governor and later, was able to gain the seat as the 49th governor from 1981 to 1985.

History of gubernatorial elections in Missouri shows 55 elected governors. 37 were members of Democratic Party, 12 were Republicans, 3 were Democratic-Republicans, 2 were members of Unconditional Union Party and one was from the Liberal Republican Party.

As it could be observed by having 37 elected governors (vs 17 for Republican Party), Democrats have been superior in the issue. But, Republicans have improved their situation in recent years, and 3 out of 4 recent governors in Missouri have been members of their party. Michael Lynn Parson, current governor of Missouri, is also a Republican.

Conclusion: Noting that Democrats have won 30 U.S. presidential elections in Missouri (Republicans won 19 including 6 recent contests), had 25 U.S. senators and 171 House representatives and 37 governors in the history of the state (the numbers for Republican Party are 17,112, and 12) , they have been superior in political history of Missouri , but the Republican Party has worked better in recent decades, and both senators currently (2021) representing the state in the U.S Senate are Republicans; 6 out of 8 House seats belonging to the state are being held by them (2 are Democrats) , and the current governor of the state is also a Republican, so it could be concluded that while Missouri has been a Democratic Party bastion during most of its history, today it is a Republican Party stronghold.

Arkansas

Arkansas state, located in southern America and its capital, Little Rock were parts of Arkansas territory, which were bought from the French through the famous "Louisiana Purchase" by president Thomas Jefferson and joined the U.S as its 25th state of the U.S. on 15 June 1836. Hot Springs city, Arkansas, is famous for its mineral-water springs, old architecture and beautiful nature. Arkansas is well-known for its vast forests and beautiful lakes, and the nickname "The natural State" reflects it. Before the civil War, agriculture was the main sector of economy in all of the southern states, and through working in the farms, slaves played an important role in this sector. This was the main reason for Arkansas to join the Confederation in the War and seceding from the Union. Although nearly 10 thousand men from the state joined the Union Army during the Civil War, the Union won the War, but racial segregation laws in schools of the southern states, and black students were not able to enter schools with white children. On 17 May 1954, referring to 14th amendment of the Constitution the Supreme Court of the U.S ruled that racial segregation of public schools was unconstitutional in the United States and had to be annulled in every part of the U.S. After ratification of this law, the National Association for the Advancement of Colored People tried to register black students in all of the schools in the southern states. In Little Rock, the board of directors of Little Rock Central High School declared its acceptance to the decision made by the Supreme Court. Virgil Blossom, former principal of schools, provided a plan for the integration of schools in the state, and the plan was ratificated on 24 May 1955 through a decisive vote. The plan came into effect in Autumn semester of 1957. Followed up by NAACP, 9 black students, who became famous as Little Rock Nine, were registered in Little Rock Central High School.

On 4 September 1957 and upon entrance of these 9 black students to the school, Orval Eugene Faubus, governor of Arkansas, opposed the decision and ordered the Arkansas National guard to hinder the presence of black students in the schools. But, president Eisenhower released the order number 10730 which made the national guard of the state a federal force under command of president of the U. S as the chief commander of the U. S military forces. Under orders from the president, these 9 students entered the school, fully protected by military forces, making that day a historical date for every freedom-lover in the world.

According to the last census, Arkansas had a population of 3,017,804 inhabitants, of which 72% were whites, 15.7% were blacks, 7.8% were Latinos, 1.7% were Asians, 1 % were Native Americans and Alaskans, 0.4% were Hawaiians and other Pacific islanders, and the rest 2.2% were from other races and ethnicities.

The University of Arkansas (where students can work in 2 radio stations and a student newspaper with a history of more than 100 years, helped by several student organizations), Harding University, Hendrix College (a small liberal arts college in Conway, Arkansas, associated with United Methodist Church, Lyon College, University of Arkansas at Little Rock, UNIVERSITY OF ARKANSAS FOR MEDICAL SCIENCES, and Pulaski Technical College are among scientific and education centers in Arkansas. Nearly half of the rice produced in the U.S. comes from Arkansas, and Arkansas in among top states in producing wheat, soybean, cotton, corn, chicken, timber, cow and beef. Peanuts, fruits, ornamental trees, grass, alfalfa, milk, cheese, butter, eggs, turkey, pork, fishes (specially catfish, which the state ranks 3rd in breeding in the U.S), are among agricultural and livestock products of the state. Defense and aviation, arms and ammunition, steel and transportation are among other industries in the state. Headquarters of some large corporations like 1-WALMART (largest retail corporation in the world) 2-TYSON FOODS (The company is one of the world's largest processors and marketers of chicken, beef, and pork) 3-Dillard's (upscale American department store chain, selling different goods, from clothes and shoes to cosmetics) 4-J.B. HUNT TRANSPORT SERVICES (American transportation and logistics company) 5-WINDSTREAM (provider of voice and data network communications, and managed services, to businesses) 6-ARVEST BANK and BANK OZK are located in Arkansas.

Among tourist destinations in the state, these could be named: 1-Hot Springs National Park, with many mineral springs, registered in 1921 2-Little Rock Central High School National Historic Site. In 1957, under pressure by president Eisenhower and escorted by military forces, for the first time, 9 black students entered a school with white students 3-William J. Clinton Presidential Library and Museum, in Little Rock city. 4-Buffalo National River , with its stunning nature , a good place for walking , camping and horseback riding 5-Crater of Diamonds State Park , the world's only diamond-bearing site accessible to the public 6-Thorncrown Chapel , made by glass , wood , in middle of a forest 7-Garvan Woodland Gardens , with floriculture and beautiful nature, containing peafowl 8-Arkansas Air Museum, containing old race, military and civil aircraft 9-Old State House Museum, which witnessed many events including voting to secede from the Union on the eve of the Civil War 10-MacArthur Museum of Arkansas Military History, birthplace of General Douglas MacArthur , commander of the U.S military forces in Pacific theater during WWII 11-Downtown Eureka Springs, a historical district with old buildings and architecture 12-Blue Spring Heritage Center , a collection of beautiful gardens, natural spring, and remains of an old watermill 13-River Market District, a roofed market near Arkansas river in Little Rock city , with many food-selling kiosks and different foods 14-The 1886 Crescent Hotel and Spa, dating back to 130 years ago 15-Beckham Creek Cave House or Lodge, built in the heart of a rocky mountain.

These, along many other national parks, lakes and historical sites, shape the tourism sector in Arkansas. 1-Bill Clinton , 42nd president of the U.S 2-Sarah Huckabee Sanders , White House press secretary, serving under President Donald Trump 3-John R. "Johnny" Cash , one of the most famous country style music singers in the U.S 4-Douglas MacArthur, commander of the U.S military forces in Pacific theater during WWII 5- Ernest Gideon Green, Elizabeth Ann Eckford, Jefferson Allison Thomas, Terrence James Roberts, Carlotta Walls

LaNier , Minnijean Brown-Trickey , Gloria Cecelia Ray Karlmark and Melba Joy Pattillo Beals , 8 of 9 members of Little Rock Nine group , are among famous people from Arkansas.

From 1836 (the date Arkansas joined the U.S as its 25th state) to 2020, 47 presidential elections have been held in the U.S, and Arkansas has taken part in 46 contests (1864 election wasn't held in the stated because of secession from the Union and the Civil War), resulting in 33 Democratic victories, 11 Republican wins (including a rejected voting in 1872 because of problems and chaos in the state) and an American Independent Party win. 1872 election results were rejected because of irregularities in the voting process. From 1836 to 1968, 33 elections were held in which Democrats won 30, Republicans won one, and the American Independent won one round of the state electoral vote and a period, as mentioned above, is related to the elections of 1872, which were rejected due to confusion and problems in voting. But since 1968, the Arkansas people have shifted from Democrats to Republicans and of the 13 remaining rounds in the election, Republicans won 10 rounds, six of which were related to the last six elections, and three were won by Democrats. As it could be seen, Arkansas was a Democratic bastion for a long time, but in recent decades, Republicans have gained an upper hand in the U.S. presidential elections in the state. In the 2020 Republican presidential primaries in Arkansas, Donald Trump gained the candidacy through winning 97.1% of the votes, defeating Bill Weld, who won 2.1% of the votes.

The 2020 Democratic presidential primaries in Arkansas saw a victory for Joseph Biden, who won 40.5% of the votes, while his closest rival, Bernie Sanders got 22.4% of the votes.

Finally, the 2020 U.S. Presidential elections in Arkansas resulted in a win for Republican Party candidate, Donald Trump, who won 62.4% of the votes, while his Democratic counterpart, Joe Biden, won 34.8% of the votes. All 6 electoral votes from Arkansas were added to Trump's vote basket.

Since joining the U.S in 1836, Arkansas has sent 35 senators to the U.S Senate. Among these senators, 26 were Democrats, 7 were Republicans, and 2 senators changed their political affiliations during their careers, both of them were sometimes Democrats and sometimes Jacksonians. According to the statistics shown above, the number of those senators who only had membership in Democratic Party, or along this had records of membership in other parties, is 28, and the same number for Republican Party is 7, showing a clear edge for Democrats. Many years ago, popularity of the Democratic Party in the state was so strong that in a 118-year period (1879 to 1997), all of 18 senators representing the state in the U.S Senate were Democrats, but recent years have seen a shift in this trend. John Nichols Boozman and Thomas Bryant Cotton are current representatives of Arkansas in the U.S Senate, both Republicans. John Little McClellan, with a 34-year record of service in the Senate (1943-1977) and James William Fulbright with a 29 years' history of presence in the Senate (1945-1974), both Democrats, have been longest-serving senators from Arkansas. Thaddeus Horatius Caraway and Hattie Ophelia Wyatt Caraway, a wife and husband, both members of Democratic Party, once represented Arkansas in the U.S. Senate. From 1836 to now (2021), Arkansas has sent 98 representatives to the House, 72 of them were Democrats, 18 were Republicans ,2 were Liberal Republicans, 1 was from Whig Party, one was a Laborite candidate, and 4 representatives changed their political affiliations during their careers, of which 2 were sometimes Democrats and sometimes members of the Republican Party, one served as Democrat and Jacksonian and one served as Democrat and Independent Democrat.

As the statistics show, those representatives who only served as Democrats, or had history of membership in other parties along this, have been 76 persons. The same number for Republicans is 20, which indicates a clear superiority for Democrats in this issue in Arkansas. But, recent years witnessed a shift in this trend, and right now, all 4 representatives from Arkansas in the U.S. House of representatives are Republicans. William Asa Hutchinson II, current governor of Arkansas (a Republican), is the 46th governor in the history of the state, but the number of those persons who acted as the governor of Arkansas was 45. The 1 number difference here is due to that a governor (Bill Clinton, who later became 42nd president of the U.S) and gained the seat in 2 non-continuous terms. He served as the 40th governor, and later was able to gain the seat as the 42nd governor of Arkansas. From 1836 to now, there have been 45 governors in Arkansas. 38 governors were Democrats and 7 of them belonged to the Republican Party, as we can see, the difference between the two parties is so great that it needs no explanation and

193

shows the powerful superiority of the Arkansas Democrats throughout the history of the gubernatorial election, so that in a 93-year period from 1874 to 1967 all governors were Democratic. But, Republicans have increased their popularity in the issue, and William Asa Hutchinson II, current governor of Arkansas, is a Republican.

Conclusion : Noting that Noting that Democrats have won 33 U.S presidential elections in Arkansas (Republicans won 11 including 6 recent contests) , had 28 U.S senators and 76 House representatives and 38 governors in the history of the state (the numbers for Republican Party are 7 ,20 and 7) , they have been superior in the political history of Arkansas , but the Republican Party has worked better in recent years , and both senators currently (2021) representing the state in the U.S. Senate are members of their party , while all 4 House seats belonging to the state are being held by them, and the current governor of the state is also a Republican. So, it could be concluded that while Arkansas has been a Democratic Party stronghold throughout most of its history, but for 20 years ago, a tilt towards Republicans has emerged in the state, and now the state has turned into a bastion for the Republican Party.

Michigan

The forested state of Michigan and its capital, Lansing, are located in the American Midwest, formerly known as the Michigan territory. On 26 January 1837, Michigan territory joined the U.S. as its 26th state, after ratification of the Constitution. The state consist of two separate land areas, each of them surrounded from 3 directions by four of the Great Lakes. The areas are connected through Mackinac Bridge, one of the longest suspended bridges in the world. Nearly half of the Michigan state area is covered by mountains, lakes and the state has thousands of miles of coastline. During the Civil War, Michigan remained loyal to the Union, and nearly 90 thousand soldiers from Michigan served in the Union Army. During the Civil War, Colonel Benjamin Pritchard and the 4th Michigan cavalry regiment, led by him, arrested Jefferson Davies and defeated the president of the Confederation. Detroit, the largest city of Michigan, is home to 2 automotive industry giants, General Motors and Chrysler, and is known as the "Automobile Capital of the World". Dearborn city, which the Ford company headquarters are located, has the biggest Muslim population percent in the U.S and is home to the largest Arab diaspora in the country. According to the last census, Michigan had a population of 9,986,857 inhabitants, of which 74.7% were whites, 14.1% were blacks ,5.3 % were Latinos, 3.4% were Asians, 0.7% were Native Americans and Alaskans, and 2.5% were from other races and ethnicities. The University of Michigan-Ann Arbor, Michigan state university (which has one of the largest campuses in the United States), Michigan Technological University and the University of Detroit Mercy are among scientific and education centers in the state. Wheat, potatoes, soybean, corns, sugar beat, grape, apple, peach, pier, strawberries, flowers, milk, cows, sheep and chicken are among agricultural and livestock products in Michigan. Automotive, aviation, pharma, medical equipment, house appliances, machinery, plastic and chemical production are among other active industries in Michigan. Huron Portland Cement (largest cement factory in the world), largest limestone mine in the U.S, one of the largest Holstein cow herds globally, MICHIGAN SUGAR factory (3rd largest sugar producer in the U.S) all are located in the state. Some large corporations like : 1-Ford , General Motors , Chrysler , automotive industry giants 2- Whirlpool (multinational manufacturer and marketer of home appliances) 3-LEAR (manufactures automotive seating and automotive electrical systems) 4-MEIJER (supercenter chain) 5-FEDERAL-MOGUL (manufacturer and supplier of products for automotive, commercial, aerospace, marine, rail and off-road vehicles) 6-DOW CHEMICAL COMPANY (producing chemical products) 7-DOMINO'S PIZZA have headquarters in Michigan. Among tourist destinations in Michigan, these could be named: 1- Mackinac Island, with old architecture and stunning nature. Instead of cars, old horse carriages are used here 2- Sleeping Bear Dunes National Lakeshore and Lake Michigan, with beautiful islands inside 3-Fort Mackinac village.

From 1715 to 1781 fur trade was common here 4-Windmill Island , actually , a park full of flower gardens with Dutch style and a windmill (built in Netherlands in 1760 and transported to this island in 1964) 5-Gerald R. Ford Presidential Museum , containing assets and information related to Gerald Ford , 38th president of the U.S 6-Heritage Hill Historic District , first district established in Grand Rapids city 7-The Ford Piquette Avenue Plant , second automotive production site of Ford company 8-The Henry Ford Museum & Greenfield Village. The museum was founded by Henry Ford, and defines American lifestyle and technological innovations from past to present, and assets like: the vehicle which president John.F. Kenndy assassinated inside it and the Fokker plane in which Admiral John Byrd made the first flight over the North Pole using in 1926 it, are exhibited here 9-The Masonic Temple of Detroit. It is a classical Gothic architecture structure built with

Indiana limestone. The temple was dedicated in 1926 and is the largest temple of its kind in the world. 10-Henry Ford Estate, Henry Ford's residence 11-Zingerman's Del food shop, with its famous sandwiches. These, along many other lakes, islands and beautiful parks and other attractions, shape the tourism sector in the state.

Michigan has been the birthplace of some famous people , among them :1-Henry Ford , founder of Ford company 2-Michael Moore, documentary director and critic 3-Francis Ford Coppola, one of the best-known directors and producers in the history of Hollywood, Godfather movie trilogy is his masterpiece 4-Madonna, singer, lyricist , actress and international entrepreneur, the song " La Isla Bonita" is her masterpiece 5-Steven Seagal , movie producer and among top martial artists in the world 6-Lawrence "Larry" Page , who along Sergey Brin founded Google company. 7-Charles Lindbergh, American aviator who took off with his single-engine plane from New York on 20 May 1927, and after 33 hours and 21 minutes of non-stop flight and crossing 3600 miles above Atlantic Ocean, was able to land in Le Bourget, Paris, France 8-Arthur Millspaugh. From 1922 to 1927 and again from 1942 to 1945 served as senior employee by Iranian government for financial reforms. Albert Kahn, German-American architect, who was born in Germany but later immigrated to the U.S. and resided in Michigan, because of numerous designs, he is known as " architect of Detroit ". Many industrial and financial buildings including automotive industry plants have been designed by him.

Since 1836 (the year Michigan joined the U. S), 47 U. S. presidential elections have been held in the U. S., and Michigan has taken part in all of them. Republicans won 27 rounds. The Democratic Party scored 17 victories, Whigs won a contest, Progressive Party was able to gain a victory and 1892 elections saw a spilt of electoral votes according to Congressional District method. As mentioned before in the article about Maine state, number of U.S Senate senators and House representatives from each state shows number of electoral votes belonging to the state. Every federal district has an electoral vote, and every state has 2 other electoral votes because of its U.S senators. According to the "winner-take-all electoral vote allocation" rule which is the common method in all U.S states except Maine and Nebraska, any candidate which wins a federal district takes an electoral vote from that area, and if he/she wins sum of the votes in all federal districts in a state, 2 votes allocated to the U.S. senators representing the state will also be taken by him/her. In the 1892 U.S. presidential election, Michigan had 14 electoral votes (the state had 12 federal districts). Republicans won 7 federal districts, and Democrats gained 5 of them. Generally, Republicans had more popular votes in the state, and took 2 votes allocated to the U.S Senators and gained 9 out of 14 electoral votes from Michigan. Appliance of this method in elections depended on state legislation, and has changed several times in different periods.

Taking a look at statistics presented above , It's clear that Republicans have an upper hand in the history of U.S presidential elections in Michigan (27 wins vs 17 victories for Democratic Party) , but for a better analysis , history of the U.S presidential elections in Michigan, could be divided to 2 periods : The first period, from 1836 to 1928, a 92 years period, saw 24 rounds of elections, in which Republicans won 17 elections, Democrats gained 4 victories, Whigs scored a win, and Progressive Party was able to gain a single election. Second period, from 1932 to 2020, saw 23 rounds of elections, and Democrats won 13 of them, while Republican Party scored 10 wins. It's worth noting that since 1992 to 2020, except the 2016 election which was won by Republican Party, Democrats won other 7 contests.

In the 2020 Democratic presidential primaries in Michigan, Joe Biden won the candidacy through winning 52.9% of the votes, while his closest rival, Bernie Sanders, took 36.4%.

The 2020 Republican Party primaries in Michigan, witnessed a victory for Donald Trump, who got the candidacy by winning 93.7% of the votes, defeating Bill Weld, who hot 0.9% of the votes.

2020 U.S presidential election in Michigan witnessed a victory for Democratic Party candidate, Joe Biden, who got 50.6% of the votes, while Republican candidate, Donald Trump got 47.8%. All 16 electoral votes from Michigan were added to the Biden's vote basket.

From 1837 (the date first U.S Senate election was held in Michigan) to 2021, 39 elected candidates from the state have served in the U.S Senate, of which 22 were Republicans, 14 were Democrats, 2 were Whigs, and a senator changed his political affiliation during his career: sometimes a Democrat and sometimes a Jacksonian. As it could be observed, the number of those senators who served only as

Republican Party members from Michigan, in addition to those who experienced membership in other parties during their careers, was 22. But Democrats have improved their performance in recent years and decades, and one of the U.S Senate seats belonging to Michigan has been in their hands since 1979, and the other seat has the same situation since 2001. Currently (2021), Richard Mauze Burr and Thomas Roland Tillis, both Republicans, represent the state in the U.S Senate.

Carl Milton Levin (a Democrat with a 36-year record of presence in the U.S Senate, 1979-2015) and Arthur Hendrick Vandenberg (with a 23-year record of service, 1928-1951), a Republican, have been longest-serving U.S senators in history of Michigan. From 1837 to 2021, 285 elected candidates have entered the U.S House of representatives as representatives from Michigan. 167 were Republicans, 107 were Democrats, 4 were Whigs, one was a member of Progressive Party and 6 representatives changed political affiliation during their careers, of which 2 were sometimes Democrats and sometimes Republicans, one served as Republican and member of Progressive Party, one was a member of Opposition Party who also served as a Republican, one was once a Democrat and once a Jacksonian, and a representative switched sides among Republican, Libertarian and Independent. As the statistics show, the number of those House representatives who served only as Republicans during their careers, in addition to those who experienced membership in other parties, was 172 , and the same number for Democrats is 110 , showing an edge for Republicans in the history of the U.S House of representatives elections in Michigan .Currently (2021) , each of Republican and Democratic parties control 7 out of 14 seats belonging to the state in the U.S House of representatives , which indicates a tense competition among them in Michigan.

It's worth noting that John David Dingell Jr (with a 60-year record of service, 1955-2015), and John James Conyers Jr (with a 52-year record of service, 1965-2017), both Democrats who represented Michigan in the U.S House of representatives, have been the longest-serving House representatives in the history of the U.S. Gerald Rudolph Ford Jr, 38th president of the U.S. once represented Michigan in the U.S House of representatives. Gretchen Esther Whitmer, a Democrat and current governor of Michigan, is the 49th governor in the history of the state, while the number of those persons who have held the seat has been 47.

the 2-number difference here is due to that 2 governors gained the seat in 2 non-continuous terms. Since 1837, 47 governors have served in Michigan, and 27 of them have been Republicans, 18 were Democrats and 2 were members of Whig Party. As it could be observed Republicans have been superior in the history of gubernatorial elections in Michigan, but recent years have witnessed a close competition, and the current governor of the state is a Democrat.

Conclusion: Noting that Republicans have won 27 U.S. presidential elections in Michigan (Democrats won 17), It's clear they had an upper hand in the history of the U.S. presidential elections in the state, but Democrats have won all U.S. presidential elections since 1992, except the 2016 elections. Republicans had 22 U.S. senators, 172 House representatives and 27 governors in the history of the state (the numbers for Democratic Party are 15, 110 and 18), but both current senators representing Michigan in the U.S Senate are Democrats (they have been in control of both U.S. Senate seats from Michigan for a long time, one since 1979 and the other since 2001) and now (2021) each of the 2 parties holds 7 out of 14 House seats belonging to the state, and current governor of the state is a Democrat. So, it could be said while Michigan has been a Republican-leaning state through most of its history, sympathy towards Democratic Party among voters in the state has increased in recent decades, and today (2021), Democrats have more popularity in the state.

Florida

Florida state, with its beautiful beaches and numerous golf playgrounds, is located in southeastern America. Tallahassee city is the capital of the state. Miami city is one of the largest harbor cities in the U.S, and also a major tourist destination in Florida. The Nowadays state of Florida was a part of the Florida territory and joined the U.S. as its' 27th state through ratification of the constitution on 3 March 1845. Florida was the first area of the contiguous United States in which European settlers resided. The mainland of the U.S. consisted of 48 states along with the District of Columbia, except states of Alaska and Hawaii and islands like Samoa, Virginia, Northern Mariana, Guam and Puerto Rico which have no land connection with other states. Juan Ponce de León, Spanish explorer, along with his men, were the first Europeans to enter this land in 1513 and called it Pascual, Florida. St. Augustine city, founded in 1565 is the oldest city in the U.S. Pascual, Florida, which in Spanish means festival of flowers or Easter, some believe it was because of the date of their arrival, or maybe the abundance of flowers in this land. During the Civil War, Florida seceded from the Union and joined the Confederation, and through mobilizing 15 thousand soldiers and providing food, played a major role in helping the Confederation Army. There were two large salt factories in Florida, and because of a lack of refrigeration equipment in that era, beef was salted and sent for consumption in the Confederate Army. According to the last census, population of Florida was 21.477.737, showing its demography as follow: 53.2% white, 26.4% Latino, 16.9% black, 3.0% Asian, 0.5 native American and Alaskan, 0.1% Hawaiian and other Pacific islanders and 2.2% others. The University of Florida, University of Miami (Silvester Stallone, Hollywood actor has been graduated here), Florida State University, University of South Florida, John F. Kennedy Space Center (site of launching NASA space rockets and shuttles) and National High Magnetic Field Laboratory are among scientific and education centers in the state.

Florida is a strong state in agriculture and forestry, which its revenue for the state is more than 100 billion dollars a year. After oranges, which 80% of its production in the U.S. is done in Florida, the state produces watermelons, tomatoes, soybean, corns, peanuts, alfalfa, tobacco, cotton, Sugar cane, citrus, beef and sea foods, along many other agricultural and livestock products.In producing pharma drugs and medical researches, Florida is a very advanced state and ranks among 5 top states in the U.S. The state is also host to many research centers on geology and marine sciences, and also hosts many environment protection centers.

Oil, natural gas, gold, airplanes and other aviation products, motor vehicles, computers and communication equipment are among industrial products in Florida. Generally, Florida has a strong economy and 4th largest GDP among the U.S states. Some large corporations like: 1- DARDEN RESTAURANTS, a chain restaurant with multiple brands, main HQ in Orlando, Florida. 2- JABIL, providing industrial services 3- Carnival Cruise Line (international cruise line, providing tourist and travel services) 4- GENESIS (focused on improving performance of financial agencies, and provides a unique package of advisory and training abilities on risk management and institutional target fields. 5- ROYAL CARIBBEAN GROUP (cruise line, providing tourist and travel services) 6- Arquitectonica (one of the best-known architecture Firms in the world) 7- BURGER KING, fast food restaurant chain 8- PUBLIX (supermarket chain) have headquarters in Florida.

Among tourist destinations in Florida , these could be named :1- Walt Disney World , famous entertainment complex, which attracts millions of tourists annually 2- Kennedy Space Center , site of launching NASA space rockets and shuttles 3- Miami Beach , a very expensive and stunning tourist area 4- Art Deco Historic District , with unique buildings in many shapes and colors , built after devastating storm of 1926 5- Everglades National Park , a 1.5 million acres area , home to alligators, American crocodiles, Florida panthers, deer, turtles, egrets, manatees, river otters, and many other species 6- Daytona 500 International Speedway, site of Daytona 500 car races 7- SeaWorld Orlando, one of the largest complexes containing marine wild life 8-Dry Tortugas National Park. Actually, it's a castle built in Middle of sea in 1800 9-St. Augustine's Historic District and the Castillo de San Marcos National Monument, one of the oldest towns in Florida, with attractive and old architecture, along with Castillo de San Marcos National Monument, oldest military fortress in North American, dating back to 17th century. 10-Edison and Ford Winter Estates, winter houses of Thomas Edison and Henry Ford are located here 11-St. Augustine Lighthouse & Maritime Museum, built between 1871 and 1874 12-Universal Studios. These, along many other beautiful beaches, forest parks, historical buildings and largest number of golf playgrounds in the U.S (1250 playgrounds), good facilities, hot weather, hosting major car and golf races and containing alligators, different birds and other fresh-water animals, and having a good environment for diving, swimming and boating, helps Florida to have one of the strongest tourism sectors in the U.S.1-Vincent Lamar Carter, American basketball player 2-James Douglas Morrison, musician, poet, writer, director, and singer in The Doors, one of the most controversial and effective Rock music bands in 1960s. 3-Julian Edwin "Cannonball" Adderley, Alto saxophone instrumentalist, many times called as most melodic instrumentalist of his own age, are among famous people from Florida.

Since 1845 (the date Florida joined the U.S) to 2020, 44 presidential elections were held in the U.S, and Florida took part in all of them except the 1864 election (because of the Civil War). Of these 43 contests, the Democratic Party won 25 times in the state, Republicans had 17 victories, and Whigs gained a single contest.

To have a better inspection, the history of U.S. presidential elections in Florida could be divided into 2 different parts. The first period, from 1848 to 1948, witnessed 25 contests, in which Democrats gained 20 victories, Republicans scored 4 victories, and Whigs were able to win a single election. Second period, from 1952 to 2020, saw 18 rounds of elections, and Republicans won 13 of them, while Democratic Party was able to gain 5 victories. As it could be seen, historically, Democrats have been superior in the issue, while Republicans have worked better in recent decades, and both recent elections in 2016 and 2020 in Florida were gained by them. In the 2020 Republican Party presidential primaries in Florida, Donald Trump was elected by gaining 93.8% of the votes, defeating Bill Weld who got 3.2%. In the 2020 Democratic presidential primaries in Florida, Joe Biden won the candidacy through winning 62% of the votes, while his closest rival, Bernie Sanders, took 22.8%. Finally, the 2020 U.S presidential election in Florida witnessed a victory for Republican Party candidate, Donald Trump, who got 51.2% of the votes, while Democratic candidate, Joe Biden got 47.9%. All 29 electoral votes from Florida were added to the Trump's vote basket.

An important point about Florida is the political orientation of its Latino voters. Typically, states with large Latino populations are Democratic bastions, because of Latino concerns about migration rules and public services, but Florida is not the same. Most of the Latino population in Florida comes from Cuba, fleeing from Castro and his government and carrying strong Right-wing political views. Cuban Latinos in Florida are a powerful and advanced community. Marco Rubio and Ted Cruz, both Republican Senators come from Cuban families living in Florida. Latino votes of Florida had a major impact on result of the recent elections, and sometimes scandalous impacts. In 2000 elections, Florida Electoral College votes was a key to victory for each of candidates, G.W. Bush from Republican party and his Democratic counterpart, Al Gore. In all state judiciary levels and even state supreme court (highest level in the state), Al Gore won the race, but Bush took the issue to the US supreme court. The US supreme court voted in favor of G.W. Bush and made him the 43rd president of the US. From 1845 (the year first U.S Senate election was held in Florida) to 2021, the state has sent 35 senators to the U.S Senate. 23 were Democrats, 11 were Republicans, and 1 was a Whig.

To put the history of U.S Senate elections in Florida under scrutiny, it would be better to divide its' history into two periods, the first one lasting from 1845 to 1969 saw 24 elected Senators, of which there were 19 Democrats, 4 Republicans and one was a Whig candidate. It's worth noting that in a 94-year period-1875 to 1969-all 16 elected Senators from Florida were Democrats and Florida Republicans had no seat in the Senate, all those 4 Republicans elected before1875.

But in the second period, from 1969 to 2021, 7 of 11 elected Senators were Republicans, and Democrats only held 4 seats, which shows a tilt towards Republican party in the Sunshine State. But taking a look into length of their terms, it could be seen 4 Democrat Senators were present in the Senate for 54 years, while 7 Republicans had a 36-year presence. This shows superiority of Democrats in the issue.

During most of its history, Democrats had an upper hand in the U.S. Senate elections in Florida, but Republicans have worked better in recent decades, and currently (2021), both senators representing the state in the U.S Senate, Richard Lynn Scott and Marco Antonio Rubio, are Republicans. Duncen.U. Fletcher (27 years of service, 1909-1936) and Spessard. L.Holland (with 25 years of presence in the U.S Senate, 1946-1971) have been longest-serving Senators of Florida, both Democrats. Since 1845 to 2021, 156 elected candidates have entered the U.S. House of representatives as representatives from Florida. 86 were Democrats, 67 were Republicans, 1 was a Whig, and 2 representatives changed their political affiliations during their careers, both sometimes Democrats and sometimes Republicans. It could be said that the House of Representatives elections in Florida have seen three different periods, in the first period in 19th century, from 1845 to 1900, Florida sent 18 representatives to the House, including 13 Democrats, 4 Republicans and a Whig representative. In 20th century, Florida had 79 representatives in the US House of representatives, 55 of them Democrats and 24 Republicans. Would be interesting to point that from 1900 to 1953, every Floridian representative was from

Democratic party, but second half of the century saw a surge for Republicans, who sent 24 candidates to the House, equal to their Democratic counterparts. In 21th century, until now, Florida has sent 59 representatives to the House, including 40 Republicans and 19 Democrats.

As the statistics show, the number of those House representatives who served only as Democrats during their careers, in addition to those who experienced membership in other parties, was 88, and the same number for Republicans is 69, showing an edge for Democrats in the history of the U.S. House of representatives' elections in Florida. But Republicans have worked better in recent decades, and currently (2021), 16 out of 27 House representatives who have seats from Florida, are Republicans, while 10 seats are held by Democratic Party members and a seat is empty.

Charles Edward Bennett, a Democrat (years of service in the U.S.

House of representatives 1949-1993) was one of the longest-serving representatives in the history of the U.S.

Ronald Dion DeSantis, current governor of Florida (a Republican), is the 46th governor in the history of the state, but number of those persons who acted as governor of Florida was 45. The 1 number difference here is due to that a governor, William Dunnington Bloxham, gained the seat in 2 non-continuous terms. He served as 13th and 17th governor of Florida. Since 1845, 45 governors have served in Florida. Among these 45 governors, 33 were Democrats, 9 were Republicans, one was a Whig, one was a member of Prohibition Party and a governor, William Marvin, served temporarily as 7th governor under orders from president Andrew Johnson, and had no political affiliation. Democrats had a bright history in Florida governorship, having 33 governors before 1999, while Republicans only had 9. but from 1999, Republicans gains surged, and for past 20 years Florida governorship has remained in their hands, and all 4 recent governors from Florida have been Republicans. It's worth noting that John Milton, was 5th governor of Florida, and after the defeat of Confederation Army, his corpse was found on 1 April 1865. Some reports spoke of an accident and some related his death to suicide. After him, Abraham Kurkindolle Allison, speaker of the state senate took the post according to the law. On 19 May 1865, a day before capture of Tallahassee by the Union Army, he resigned and hided, but wasn't that lucky and was captured. Then William Marvin, appointed by president Andrew Johnson, temporarily took the post of Florida governor as the 7th governor of the state.

Conclusion: Noting that Democrats have won 25 U.S presidential elections in Florida (Republicans won 17 contests including 2 recent contests) , and had 23 U.S senators, 88 House representatives and 33 governors in the history of the state (the numbers for Republican Party are 11 , 69 and 9) , but both current U.S senators from the state are Republicans , 16 out of 27 House representatives are Republicans while 10 are Democrats and a seat is empty , and 4 recent governors of Florida have been members of Republican Party , it could be concluded while The Democratic Party has had an upper hand in the political history of the state , Republicans have gained more popularity in recent years , and currently (2021), Florida is a Republican-leaning state.

Texas

Texas state, which its name reminds many of Western movies and cowboys, along its capital, and Austin, are located in the southern part of the U.S. Until 1836, Texas was a part of Mexico, and in that year, Texans declared their independence and formation of the Republic of Texas. After several years, on 29 December 1845, Texas joined the U.S. as its' 28th state. After Alaska, Texas is 2nd largest state in the U.S, and Dallas, Fort Worth and Huston are the main cities in the state. During the Civil War, Texas was among 11 rebel states who declared their secession from the Union, and through mobilizing 90 thousand soldiers, gunpowder production in Marshal city and providing food, played a major role in helping the Confederate Army. According to the last census, Texas had a population of 28,995,881 inhabitants. Demographic composition of the state can be seen in these numbers: 41.2% of the population is white, 39.7% are Latinos, 12.9% are blacks, 5.2% are Asians, 1% Native Indians and Alaskans, 0.1% are Hawaiians and people from other Pacific islands, and the rest 2.1% are from other races and ethnicities. Rice University, University of Texas at Austin (one of the largest universities in the U.S) , Southern Methodist University (Laura Bush, wife to George.W.Bush ,former president of the U.S graduated here) , Texas A&M University , University of Texas at Dallas, University of Houston , Texas Medical Center (largest medical center in the world) , The University of Texas MD Anderson Cancer Center (on of 3 largest cancer centers in the U.S), Texas Children's Hospital (one of the largest and best equipped children's hospitals in the world), Johnson space center and many important pilot training and aviation centers are all among scientific and education centers in

Texas. Texas is also host to 15 active military bases. Cotton, grains, grapefruit, watermelons, honeydew melons, olive, honey, cows, beef, sheep, chicken, eggs and dairy products, are among agricultural and livestock products in the state. Texas has the largest number of cows in the U.S. and ranks among 5 large states in agricultural and livestock production. Texas has the largest oil and natural gas reserves in the U.S. and ranks number 1 in the production of these materials. Construction, petrochemical industry, leather, food products, electronic industry, electrical power, IT and computer are among other active industries in Texas. In the film industry, entertainment and video games, Texas is one of the top states, and Austin city is a major center of film industry. Extraction and production of copper, Uranium, silver, lead, iron, zinc, gold and Manganese shape another part of the industry sector in the state.

Some large corporations like: 1- FOXCONN ASSEMBLY LLC (Computer and Peripheral Equipment Manufacturing Industry) 2- AT&T (one of the largest communication companies in the world) 3- KELLER WILLIAMS REALTY (active in real estate and technology fields) 4- DELL (American multinational computer technology company that develops, sells, repairs, and supports computers and related products and services) 5- AMERICAN AIRLINES 6- PIZZA HUT pizza restaurant chain, have headquarters in Texas. Among tourist destinations in Texas, these could be named: 1- San Antonio's River Walk, a good place for boating. There are numerous cafes along the river , and a calm and suitable passage for walking could be found here 2- Alamo castle , dating back to 1718 , well-known for its role in Texas War of Independence 3- Big Bend National Park , with its unique views , rocky mountains near a river 4- Guadalupe Mountains National Park , living place of many wild species , including golden eagles 5- The Fort Worth Stockyards, a historical site for catling cows which was established in 1866 , it was here that millions of cattle were rested, sorted, or shipped out to other points across the state.6- Galveston's Beaches & Strand Historic District , with shallow and calm waters and old Victorian style mansions 7- The USS Lexington , an aircraft carrier which took part in WWII , now turned into a museum 8- Gruene Historic District , Gruen historical hall (oldest dance salon in Texas , dating back to 1878) is located here 9- Fort Worth Botanic Garden

, established in 1934 in a 109-acre field 10- Hit the El Paso Mission Trail , beginning point of the trail which contains a large part of diverse and historical heritage of Texas 11- Sundance Square , a historical district of Fort Worth , containing historical, commercial , retail and entertainment buildings.

These, along many other museums, parks, and historical sites shape a part of tourism sector in Texas, which helps the state gain billions of dollars of revenue annually. Dwight David "Ike" Eisenhower, Lyndon B. Johnson, 34th and 36th presidents of the U.S, Selena Marie Gomez, singer, lyricist, actress and producer, Denton Arthur Cooley. one of the most prominent heart surgeons in the world, Lance Armstrong, controversial bicycle runner and Hilary Erhard Duff, actress, Pop music singer and lyricist, and David Koresh, religious leader of Davidian sect are among famous people from Texas. Because of its large population, Texas has 38 electoral votes and plays an important role in U.S. presidential elections. Since 1848 (the year Texas took part in a U.S presidential election for the first time) to 2020, 44 U.S presidential elections have been held in the country, and Texas took part in all of them except two contests, both because of the Civil War (1864 and 1868 elections). Of these contests, Democratic party won 27 times in the state and Republicans had 15 victories.

For a better inspection, history of the U.S presidential elections in Texas could be divided into 2 periods. First part, from 1848 to 1948, saw 24 elections held in Texas. Democrats won 23 times, and Republicans were able to gain a single victory. Second period, from 1952 to 2020, witnessed 18 presidential elections, of which Republicans won 14 contests, and the Democratic Party scored 4 victories. Republicans have been the sole winners of 11 recent U.S. presidential elections in the state. In the 2020 Republican presidential primaries in Texas, Donald Trump gained the candidacy through winning 94.1% of the votes, defeating Bill Weld, who won 0.8% of the votes. The 2020 Democratic presidential primaries in Texas saw a victory for Joseph Biden, who won 34.5% of the votes, while his closest rival, Bernie Sanders, got 30% of the votes.

Finally, the 2020 U.S Presidential elections in Texas resulted in a win for Republican Party candidate, Donald Trump, who won 52.1% of the votes, while his Democratic counterpart, Joe Biden, won 46.5% of the votes. All 38 electoral votes from Texas were added to Trump's vote basket.

Since 1846 (the year first U.S Senate election was held in Texas) to 2020, the state has sent 32 senators to the U.S Senate. 24 were Democrats, 6 were Republicans, and 2 senators changed their political affiliations during their careers, of which one was once a Democrat and once a member of Native American Party (also known as Know Nothing Party) and one served as Republican and Liberal Republican. According to the statistics shown above, the number of those senators who only had membership in Democratic Party, or along this had records of membership in other parties, is 25, and the same number for Republican Party is 7, showing a clear edge for Democrats. Before 1961 Only 2 Republicans were able to represent Texas in the U.S Senate. But Republicans have improved their performance in this issue in recent years, and they have held one of the U.S Senate seats from Texas since 1961, and the other seat has the same situation since 1993. Rafael Edward Cruz (also known as Ted Cruz) and John Cornyn III, both Republicans, are current (2021) U.S Senators from Texas. Thomas Terry Connally, with a 24-year record of service in the Senate (1929-1953) and Charles Allen Culberson with a 24 years' history of presence in the Senate (1899-1923), both Democrats, along with John Goodwin Tower (a Republican with 24 years of presence in the U.S Senate, 1961-1985) have been longest-serving senators from Texas. Lyndon.B. Johnson, 36th president of the U.S, once represented Texas in the U.S Senate during his political career.

From 1846 to 2020 , 279 persons have represented Texas in the U.S House of representatives (among them people like G.W.Bush and Lyndon.B.Johnson , presidents of the U.S) , of which 206 were Democrats , 66 were Republicans , one was an Independent Democrat , one was a member of Greenback Party , one was a member of Native American Party , one was a member of Independent Party And 3 representatives changed their political affiliation during their careers , all of them Democrats who also served as members of Republican Party.

As the statistics show, those representatives who only served as Democrats, or had history of membership in other parties along this, have been 209 persons. The same number for Republicans is 70, which indicates a clear superiority for Democrats in this issue in Texas. Between 1845 and 1949 only 6 Republican candidates from Texas were able to enter the U.S House of representatives. But recent years witnessed a shift in this trend, and right now 22 out of 36 Texas seats in the House belongs to Republican Party, while Democrats hold 13 seats and the other seat is empty. Samuel Taliaferro Rayburn (with a 48-year record of presence in the U.S House of representatives), John William Wright Patman (with a 47-year record of service), George Herman Mahon (with a 44-year record of service), Jack Bascom Brooks (42 years of service) and William Robert Poage (41 years of service), all Democrats, have been longest-serving U.S House representatives in the history of Texas and also some of the longest-serving representatives in the history of the U.S.

Gregory Wayne Abbott, current governor of the state, who is a Republican, is actually 48th governor of Texas, but those persons who gained the seat numbered 45. It should be noted that the 3-number difference here is due to that 3 governors gained the seat in 2 non-continuous terms.

From 1845 to 2021, 45 persons served as governors of Texas. Among these, 39 were Democrats and 6 were Republicans. As it could be observed, Democrats have a clear upper hand in the history of gubernatorial elections in Texas, and from 1874 to 1979, more than a century, no Republican candidate has been able to gain the governor's seat in the state, but recent decades saw a major shift in this trend, and since 1995, all 3 recent governors have been members of Republican Party. George.W. Bush, 43rd president of the U.S, had record of serving as governor of Texas during his political career.

Conclusion: Noting that Democrats have won 27 U.S presidential elections in Texas (Republicans won 15 including 11 recent contests), It's clear they had an upper hand in the history of the U.S presidential elections in the state. Democrats had 25 U.S senators, 209 House representatives and 39 governors in the history of the state (the numbers for Republican Party are 7 , 70 and 6) , but both current senators representing Texas in the U.S Senate Republicans and 22 out of 36 House seats belonging to Texas is filled by Republicans (13 for Democrats and a seat is empty) , and all 3 recent governors have been members of Republican Party , so it could be said while Democrats have been superior in general political history of Texas , Republicans are more popular in the state since decades , and today (2021) , Texas is a Republican Party stronghold.

Iowa

Iowa state and its capital, Des Moines, are located in American Midwest. The Nowadays state of Iowa was a part of Iowa territory, which was bought from the French government in the famous deal called "Louisiana purchase" in 1803, under president Thomas Jefferson. After a while and on 27 December 1846, Iowa joined the U.S as its 29th state. During the Civil War, about 70 thousand men from Iowa served in the Union Army, and fertile agricultural lands of the state played a major role in providing food and supplies to the Union. There is a small city in the state, which would be interesting for Iranians, because of its name. Persia city, where according to evidence, when Chicago-Milwaukee-St. Paul railway project was going on, some Persian (Iranian) migrants took part in the project, and when the city was established on 1882, settlers of the city chose to name it "Persia", in memory of Iranian railway workers. According to the last census, Iowa had a population of 3,155,070 inhabitants. 85% of the population was white, 4.1% were blacks, 6.3% were Latinos, 2.7% were Asians, 0.5% Native Indians and Alaskans, 0.2% were Hawaiians and people from other Pacific islands, and the rest 2% were from other races and ethnicities. University of Iowa, Iowa State University, Drake University and Clarke University, are among scientific and education centers in the state. Iowa has fertile soil for agriculture and animal husbandry. Corns, soybean, grapes, pork, eggs and dairy products are among agricultural and livestock products in Iowa. Chemical fertilizers and pesticides, heavy machinery, primary metals, turbines, electrical equipment, Ethanol (Iowa is the largest producer of Ethanol in the U.S), are among industrial products of the state. Iowa is among top states in renewable energy field and some large corporations like :1- CASEY'S GENERAL STORES (convenience stores in the Midwestern and Southern United States along with fuel stations) 2- PRINCIPAL FINANCIAL GROUP (global financial investment management and insurance company) 3- HNI (manufactures office furniture) 4- HY-VEE (supermarket chain) have headquarters there. Among tourist destinations in Iowa, these could be named: 1- The Iowa State Capitol, with its stunning architecture 2- Maquoketa Caves State Park. 10 caves are accessible 3- Amana Colonies, including 7 villages, dating back to 19th century 4- RAGBRAI, Annual Great Bicycle Ride Across Iowa, a week-long race with a passage full of music festivals, drinks and watermelons for catering 5- Herbert Hoover National Historic Site, birthplace of Herbert Hoover, 31st president of the U.S. Also, tombs of Hoover and his wife are located here 6-The Grotto of the Redemption in West Bend, which is truly a unique attraction in Iowa. Also called the West Bend Grotto, it is comprised of nine separate grottos all built from precious stones and gems and handcrafted by a local pastor and a few other helping hands 7-Brucemore , an old and beautiful mansion 8-Paramount Theatre, it's building dates back to 1920 9-African American Museum of Iowa , showing different aspects of African-American history and culture in the U.S and the world 10-Salisbury House & Gardens , a 42-room mansion , built in 1920 by Carl Weeks and his wife Edith 11-Iowa State Fair, a 2-week fair which aims to help agricultural spirit of the state remains alive. During the fair, festivals, live music, different foods and amusements make a happy sphere. These, along other tourist attractions shape the tourism sector in Iowa.

1-Herbert Clark Hoover, 31st president of the U.S 2-James Alfred Van Allen, famous space science expert 3-Alton Glenn Miller, prominent Jazz musician, orchestra leader 4-Marion Mitchell Morrison, actress, director, producer and Academy Awards winner 5-Peggy Annette Whitson, researcher and astronaut, are among famous people from Iowa.

As it was said in the introduction of this book, initial inter-party competitions for choosing the U.S presidential candidate is done in primary method. In this method, registered party members put their votes in vote boxes in favor of the party candidates. The other method is called "Caucuses", which is only in use in Iowa, Nevada, North

Dakota, Wyoming and in Republican Party in Kentucky, while since 1970 other states use primary method. In caucuses method a mixture of party members and leaders choose the party candidate in each state through a workgroup. It should be noted that the caucuses method has a weak point compared to the primary method and its process of vote counting. In the caucuses party members and leaders gather in places like stadiums, and after calling name of a candidate, those who favor him/her gather in a specified point, and each body is counted as a vote. This can cause some problems and irregularities. In Alaska state, initial inter-party elections were held in Caucuses method until 2016, and then Republican and Democratic parties in the state adopted primary method.

Since 1848 to 2020, 44 U.S presidential elections have been held in the country and Iowa has taken part in all of them. Republicans won 31 rounds and Democratic Party scored 13 victories.

To have a better inspection, the history of U.S presidential elections in Iowa could be divided into 2 different parts. The first period, from 1848 to 1984, witnessed 35 contests, in which Republicans won 28 elections and Democratic Party was able to gain 7 wins. 19 elections were held between 1856 and 1928, of which Republicans 18 of them and Democrats only emerged victorious in a single contest.

Second period, from 1988 to 2020, saw 9 rounds of elections, and Democrats won 6 of them, while Republican Party scored 3 wins, 2 of them recent elections in 2016 and 2020.

In 2020 Republican presidential caucuses in Iowa, Donald Trump won the candidacy through winning 97.1% of the votes, while his closest rival, Bill Weld, took 1.3%.

In 2020 Democratic presidential caucuses in Iowa, Pete Buttigieg won the candidacy through getting 26.2% of the votes, while his closest rival, Bernie Sanders, took 26.1%.

2020 U.S presidential election in Iowa witnessed a victory for Republican Party candidate, Donald Trump, who got 53.1% of the votes, while Democratic candidate, Joe Biden got 44.9%. All 6 electoral votes from Iowa were taken by Trump. From 1848 (the year first U.S Senate elections was held in Iowa) to 2021, 34 persons have represented the state in the U.S Senate. 23 were Republicans, 10 were Democrats, And a senator experience membership in Republican Free-Soil parties.

According to the statistics presented above, the number of those senators who served only as Republican Party members from Iowa, in addition to those who experienced membership in other parties during their careers, was 24. The same number for Democrats is 10, showing clear superiority of Republicans in the issue. From 1848 to 1996 (78 years) out of 17 elected U.S Senators in Iowa, 14 were Republicans, 2 were Democrats (first round of U.S Senate elections in Iowa) and a Republican senator defected to Free Soil Party.

Charles Ernest Grassley and Joni Kay Ernst, currently (2021) represent Iowa in the U.S Senate. Charles Ernest Grassley (with 40 years of presence in the U.S Senate, 1981-present (2021)) and William Boyd Allison (with a 35-year record of service, 1873-1908), both Republicans, have been longest-serving U.S Senators in history of Iowa. From 1846 to 2021, 188 elected candidates have entered the U.S House of representatives as representatives from Iowa. 127 were Republicans, 54 were Democrats, 3 were Whigs, 3 were members of Greenback Party, and one was an Independent Republican. As the statistics show, Republicans have an upper hand in the issue. Currently (2021), 3 out of 4 seats belonging to Iowa in the U.S House of representatives is held by Republicans, and Democrats control a single seat.

Kimberly Kay Reynolds, a Republican and current governor of Iowa, is the 43rd governor in the history of the state, while number of those persons who have held the seat has been 41. the 2-number difference here is due to that 2 governors gained the seat in 2 non-continuous terms. Since 1846, 41 governors have served in Iowa, and 30 of them have been Republicans, 10 were Democrats and 1 was a member of Whig Party.

As it could be seen, Republicans have been superior in history of gubernatorial elections in Iowa, and since 2011, both recent governors of the state have been members of Republican Party.

Conclusion : Noting that Republicans have won 31 U.S. presidential elections in Iowa (Democrats won 13) including 2 recent contests , had 24 U.S. senators and 127 House representatives and 30 governors in the history of the state (the numbers for Democratic Party are 10 , 54 and 10) , both senators representing Iowa in the U.S Senate are Republicans and 3 out of 4 House seats belonging to the states are being held by them (1 is held by Democrats) , and current governor of Iowa is also a Republican , it could be concluded that Iowa has been a Republican Party stronghold during most of its history, just like today (2021).

Wisconsin

Wisconsin state and its capital, Madison are located in American Midwest. Initially, the state of Wisconsin was a part of the Wisconsin territory, which joined the U.S. in 28 May 1848 as its 30th state. During the Civil War, Wisconsin remained loyal to the Union, and through mobilizing 91 thousand soldiers and providing food and agricultural products, played an important role in helping the Union Army. The largest city in the state is Milwaukee. Formerly, the share of Milwaukee lead mines production in the country was about 50%. According to the last census, population of the state was 5822434. 80.9% of population is white, while 7.1% are Latinos, 6.7% are Blacks, 3% Asian, 1.2% Native American and Alaskan, 0.1 Hawaiians and other Pacific islanders, and 2% others. The University of Wisconsin-Madison (established in the same year the state joined the U. S, 1848, and people like Richard Bruce Cheney, vice president in G.W. Bush administration were graduated here), Marquette University, Edgewood College, Concordia University Wisconsin and University of Wisconsin-Milwaukee are among scientific and education centers in the state. Wisconsin is well-known for its agricultural and dairy products. Agriculture and animal husbandry shape a large portion of the economy in the state. Wisconsin is the largest cheese producer among the U.S states, and has the title "America's Dairyland". Milk, cheese, apples, corns, soybean, potatoes, Tobacco, beef and processed vegetables, are among main goods produced in Wisconsin. The state also produces a large amount of alcoholic drinks, especially beer. Paper, home furniture, computer components, chemical products, aerospace industry products, transportation industry products, and non-metal mineral materials. 1-CELLULAR LOGISTICS (biotechnology company) 2- KOHL'S (chain store) 3- REGAL BELOIT (manufacturer of electric motors) are among large corporations which have headquarters in Wisconsin.

Among tourist destinations in Wisconsin , these could be named : 1-Annual EAA airshow in Oshkosh city ,one of the largest gatherings of aviators and aviation companies in the world 2- Taliesin rural preservation, which belonged to Frank Lloyd Wright , prominent American architect 3- Door County , a peninsula with facilities for fishing , boating , diving , swimming walking , cycling and Kayaking 4-The Harley-Davidson Museum, Milwaukee , an exhibition for different models of the company motorcycles 5- The Dells of the Wisconsin River , a beautiful valley with stunning nature 6- All Steamed Up at the National Railroad Museum , A highlight is the Eisenhower collection, which includes the Dwight D. Eisenhower, a streamlined vintage British engine used to pull the leader's military train across Europe during WWII. 7- Take a Hike on Wisconsin's Wonderful Trails, an amazing trail in mountainous rocks, a good place for walking 8- Olbrich Botanical Gardens, with a 16-acre area 9- Wisconsin Veterans Museum, an exhibition for the history of American soldiers from the Civil War to 1991 Gulf War 10- Pendarvis State Historic Site, with buildings dating back to mid 19th century 11- Pabst Mansion, once owned by Captain Frederick Pabst, built in 1893. These, among other museums, parks and historical sites, shape the tourism sector in Wisconsin. 1- Laura Elizabeth Ingalls Wilder, American writer, author of " Little House on the Prairie" book series 2- August William Derleth, author and anthologist 3- Reginald Lebowski, American professional wrestler 4- Lester William Polsfuss, guitarist, lyricist and a pioneer in using electric guitars are among famous people from Wisconsin.

Since 1848 to 2020, 44 presidential elections have been held in the state, and Republican Party has won 25 of them, while Democratic Party was able to secure 17 wins and Progressive party emerged winner in a single contest.

By putting the history of presidential elections in Wisconsin under scrutiny, it could be seen that before 1988, 35 rounds of presidential elections have been held in the state, and Republicans won 24 of them, while Democrats gained 10 victories, and Progressives secured a win.

But since 1988, Democrats won 8 out of 9 elections, and Republicans won the last contest in 2016. In 2020 Democratic presidential primary in Wisconsin, Joe Biden gained 62.9% of votes and defeated Bernie Sanders, who got 31.8% of votes. At the same time, Donald Trump won the Republican primary by gaining 97.9% of votes, while 1.8 of voters preferred to write "Uninstructed" on their ballot casts.

Finally, 2020 presidential election in Wisconsin witnessed a victory for Democratic candidate, Joe Biden who was able to win 49.45% of votes, while Donald Trump from Republican Party gained 48.82%. Wisconsin presented 10 electoral votes to Biden, the candidate that became the president. As it could be seen, Republican Party has enjoyed having an upper hand in the history of presidential elections in Wisconsin, but it should be noted that except a single term, Democratic Party has been able to won most of recent elections in the state, showing a strong potential for an important shift among the voters towards their party.

Since 1848, Wisconsin voters have chosen 28 senators to serve in the U.S Senate, and 16 of them were Republicans, 11 were Democrats, and a senator served as member of Republican and Progressive parties during his career. As it could be observed, Number of those senators who served only as Republican Party members from Wisconsin, in addition to those who experienced membership in other parties during their careers, was 17. The same number for Democrats is 11, showing superiority of Republicans in the issue.

But while Democrats have kept one of the U.S, Senate seats belonging to Wisconsin since 1957, Republicans have improved their performance in recent years, and currently (2021) Tammy Suzanne Green Baldwin, a Democrat, along with Ronald Harold Johnson, a Republican, represent Wisconsin in the U.S Senate. Throughout the history of Wisconsin, William Proxmire had the longest record of serving in the U.S. Senate and held his seat for 32 years (1957-1989). Alexander Wiley, another long-serving U.S. senator from the Republican Party who represented Wisconsin, served 24 years (1939-1963). From 1848 until now, Wisconsin has sent 186 elected candidates to the U.S House of representatives.107 of them were Republicans , 66 were Democrats , 3 were Progressives , 1 was from Socialist Party , another one was a Whig Party member , a Laborite Party member was able to gain a seat , Free Soil

Party secured a victory , And six representatives switched their political affiliation during their career , of which 4 swinged among Republican and Progressive parties , one switched side among Democrats and Independent Democrats , and a Republican party member also served as member of Opposition Party. As the statistics show, the number of those House representatives who served only as Republicans during their careers, in addition to those who experienced membership in other parties, was 112 , and the same number for Democrats is 67 , showing an edge for Republicans in the history of the U.S House of representatives elections in Wisconsin .Currently (2021) , 5 out of 8 House representatives who have seats from Wisconsin , are Republicans , while the rest 3 seats are held by Democratic Party members.

Frank James Sensenbrenner Jr, a Republican, and David Ross Obey, a Democrat, who each represented Wisconsin in the House for 42 years, were the longest-serving House representative from the state, and also 2 of the longest-serving House representatives in the History of the U.S.

Anthony Steven Evers, current governor of the state, is actually 46th governor of Wisconsin. But number of those persons who served as governors of the state during its history has been 45. the 1 number difference here is due to that a governor, Philip Fox La Follette, gained the seat in 2 non-continuous terms, and served as 27th and 29th governor of Wisconsin. Since 1848 (the year Wisconsin joined the U.S as its 30th state), 45 governors have served in the state. Among these 45 governors, 30 were Republicans, 13 were Democrats, one was a Whig, And a governor, Philip Fox La Follette, experienced membership in Republican and Progressive Parties during his career. As the numbers show, Republicans had an upper hand in the history of gubernatorial elections in Wisconsin, but recent years have seen a tense competition among the 2 main parties, and Anthony Steven Evers, current governor is a Democrat.

It should be noted that Orland Steen Loomis, 31st governor of Wisconsin died before official beginning of his term.

Conclusion: Noting that Republicans have won 25 U.S presidential elections in Wisconsin (Democrats won 18 including 8 out of 9 recent contests), It's clear they had an upper hand in the history of the U.S presidential elections in the state. Republicans had 17 U.S senators ,112

House representatives and 31 governors in the history of the state (the numbers for Democratic Party are 11, 67 and 13) , but between current senators representing Wisconsin in the U.S Senate one is a Republicans and one is a Democrat , 5 out of 8 House seats belonging to the state are being held by Republican Party members (3 for Democrats) , current governor of the state is a Democrat ,so it could be concluded that Wisconsin has been a Republican Party bastion during most of its history , but currently , sympathy toward Democrats among the voters in the state is stronger.

California

California state, and its capital, Sacramento, located in western part of the U.S, are famous for moderate weather, numerous beaches, beautiful national parks, famous Los Angeles palm trees, movie stars and the Hollywood Walk of Fame, along with Dolby Theatre, where Academy Awards ceremony is held annually. California is the most populated state in the U.S, and hosts largest film studios in the world in Hollywood neighborhood. Silicon Valley area is center of the largest IT corporations globally. California was annexed to the U.S. as a result of Treaty of Guadalupe Hidalgo in 1848, after the American-Mexican War, and finally joined the U.S as its 31st state on 9 September 1850. Political atmosphere of the northern part of the state is much more liberal than the southern part, and every year, in the last days of June, one of the largest LGBT gathering and marches is held in San Francisco city. First sparks of anti-war movement in the Vietnam War era also emitted here during 1960s, in Berkeley University. Along with Koreans, Mexicans, and generally Latinos, Iranian-American society of California is among large communities in the state, actually largest Iranian diaspora in the world. According to the last census, California had a population of 39512223 inhabitants, of which 39.4% were Latinos, 36.5% were whites, 15.5% were Asians, 6.5% were blacks, 1.6% were Native Americans and Alaskans, 0.5% were Hawaiians and other Pacific islanders, and 4% were from other races and ethnicities. Stanford University, California Institute of Technology, University of California-Los Angeles (known as UCLA) and University of California,

Berkeley are among scientific and education centers in the state, and also among top universities in the world. Pistachio, walnut, almond, fig, peanut, lettuce, apricot, nectarine, orange, dates, grapes, lemon, plum, watermelons, strawberries, avocado, peaches, cotton, tomatoes, flowers, alfalfa, are among numerous agricultural products of California, which ranks 1st among the U.S states in the issue, and produces 13% of all agricultural products in the U.S. Beef, chicken, fishes, oyster, and generally, sea foods are among main products of California. Napa Valley, in northern California is a major center of winemaking in the U.S. Google , Facebook , Intel , Yahoo, Netflix , Apple , Visa Card , HP and many other large corporations like : Tesla motors , Chevron (oil company) , Walt Disney (one of the largest entertainment and media corporations in the world) , Wells Fargo (bank) , CIT Bank , Silicon Valley Bank ,GAP (shoe and clothes producer) , UBER taxi service , TACO BELL (chain restaurant) , IHOP , BJ's Restaurants , LA Fitness chain (gym chain) , along with Hollywood film studios , are among big corporations which have headquarters in California.

Among tourist destinations in the state , these could be named: 1-Beautiful beach city of San Francisco , with its famous Golden Gate Bridge 2-Yosemite National Park , containing many mountains , valleys rivers and waterfalls , one of the most-visited national parks in the U.S 3-Disneyland , with numerous kinds of amusement 4-Death Valley National Park , a desert area containing hills , rocks and salt flats 5-Sequoia and Kings Canyon National Parks , containing largest trees in the world 6- Redwood National and State Parks have the largest trees of this type in the world.7-Universal Studios Hollywood , with different and unique amusements 8-Hearst Castle , actually a 165-room mansion built by William Randolph Hearst , famous journalist , newspaper publisher and rich merchant 9-Big Bear Lake near Big Bear city , containing tall trees , surrounding a beautiful and fantastic city 10-Santa Catalina Island , a stunning place with glass-roof boat tours , good for diving and boating 11-Hollywood area , with its old architecture salons 12-Santa Monica and its famous pier , playground and other entertainment sites 13-Richard Nixon Presidential Library and Museum 14-Lake Tahoe . These, along many other attractions have made tourism sector a main source of revenue for California.

Richard Milhous Nixon, 37th president of the U.S, and Leonardo

Wilhelm DiCaprio, actor, producer and Academy Awards winner, are among famous people from California.

Since 1852 to 2020, 43 presidential elections were held in the U.S, and California took part in all of them. Of these 43 contests, Republican Party won 23 times in the state (including 1896 election which witnessed a split of electoral votes , resulting in a single vote for Democrats and other votes for Republicans) , Democrats had 19 (1880 and 1892 elections witnessed split of electoral votes , in both contests Republicans gained a single votes and other votes were won by Democratic Party) , and 1912 elections saw a split of electoral votes between Democratic and Progressive parties , in which Progressive Party won through gaining 11 votes , while Democrats won 2 . To have a better inspection, the history of U.S presidential elections in California could be divided into 2 different parts. The first period, from 1852 to 1948, witnessed 25 contests, in which Republicans gained 14 victories, Democrats scored 10 victories, and Progressive Party had a single win.

Second period, from 1952 to 2020, saw 18 rounds of elections, and Republicans won 9 of them, while Democratic Party was able to gain 9 victories, too, but 8 of these victories have been among 9 recent contests. As it could be seen, historically, Republicans have been superior in the issue, while Democrats have worked better in recent decades, and all 8 recent elections in California were gained by them.

In 2020 Democratic presidential primaries in California, Bernie Sanders won the candidacy through winning 35.5% of the votes, while his closest rival, Joe Biden, took 28%.

In 2020 Republican Party presidential primaries in California, Donald Trump was elected by gaining 92.2% of the votes, defeating Bill Weld who got 2.7%.

Finally, the 2020 U.S presidential election in California witnessed a victory for the Democratic Party candidate, Joe Biden, who got 63.5% of the votes, while Republican candidate, Donald Trump got 34.3%. All 55 electoral votes from California were taken by Biden.

From 1850 (the year first U.S Senate election was held in California) to 2021, the state has sent 45 senators to the U.S Senate.24 were Democrats, 20 were Republicans, and 1 was a member of Anti-Monopoly Party.

As it could be observed, Democrats have an upper hand in the history of the U.S Senate elections in California (24 senators vs 20 for

Republican Party), and have worked better in recent years, too. One of the U.S Senate seats belonging to the state has been in control of Democrats since 1969, and the other seat has the same situation since 1992.

Dianne Goldman Berman Feinstein and Alex Padilla, both Democrats, currently (2021) represent California in the U.S Senate.

Dianne Goldman Berman Feinstein, a Democrat with a 29-year's record of service in the U.S Senate (1992-present) and Hiram Warren Johnson with 28 years of presence in the U.S Senate (1917-1945), a Republican, have been longest-serving U.S senators in the history of the state.

Richard Nixon, 37th president of the U.S, once served as U.S senator representing California.

Since 1850 to 2021, 386 elected candidates have entered the U.S House of representatives as representatives from California. 196 were Democrats , 177 were Republicans , 3 were members of People's Party , one was Independent , one was a Progressive , one was a member of Prohibition Party (a Party which aimed to prohibit the sale and consumption of alcohol) And 7 representatives changed their political affiliations during their careers , of which 2 served as Republicans and members of Progressive Party , one switched sides among Republican and Unionist parties , one was sometimes a Democrat and sometimes a member of Labor Party , one experienced membership in Democratic and Progressive parties , one was once a Democrat and once a Republican , and a representative switched sides among Republican , Progressive and Independent.

As the statistics show, the number of those House representatives who served only as Democrats during their careers, in addition to those who experienced membership in other parties, was 199, and the same number for Republicans is 182, showing an edge for Democrats in the history of the U.S. House of representatives' elections in California. Also, Democrats have worked better in recent decades, and currently (2021), 42 out of 53 House representatives who have seats from California, are Democrats, while 11 seats are held by Republican Party members.

George Edward Brown Jr (with a 43-year record of presence in the U.S House of representatives), Henry Arnold Waxman, George Miller III and Fortney Hillman Stark Jr (all 3 served 40 years), all Democrats, have been longest-serving House representatives in the history of California, and also are counted among the longest-serving House representatives in the history of the U.S.

Gavin Christopher Newsom, current governor of California (a Democrat), is the 40th governor in the history of the state, but number of those persons who acted as governor of California was 39. The 1 number difference here is due to that a governor, gained the seat in 2 non-continuous terms, and statistics here are according to the number of the persons who served in the post, not number of terms. Since 1850, 39 governors have served in California. Among these 39 governors, 21 were Republicans, 11 were Democrats, 3 were Independent Democrats, 2 were members of Anti-Lecompton Democratic Party, one was a member of Native American Party (also known as Know Nothing Party), and a governor was member of Unionist Party. As it could be observed, Republicans have been superior in the issue historically, but Democratic Party has worked better in recent years, and both recent governors of California have been Democrats.

Former United States President Ronald Reagan and former bodybuilding champion and Hollywood celebrity Arnold Schwarzenegger have both served as governors.

Conclusion: Noting that Republicans have won 23 U.S. presidential elections in California (Democrats won 19 contests including 8 recent contests) , and Democrats had 24 U.S senators and 199 House representatives (the numbers for Republican Party are 20 and 182), while both current U.S senators from California are members of Democratic Party , and 42 out of 53 House representatives are Democrats while 11 are Republicans, Republicans had 21 governors in the history of the state (Democrats had 11) , and both recent governors of California have been members of Democratic Party , it could be concluded while the 2 main parties had a tense and close competition in the most of political history of California, nowadays California is a state with strong affiliation to Democratic Party , and large Latino and migrant population play an important role in this issue , mostly because of Democratic Party policies on migration and social services.

Minnesota

T he state of Minnesota is located in the northern United States and the Midwestern region of the United States. Its capital is Saint Paul. The nowadays state of Minnesota is consisted of a part of initial U.S land along with a part of the lands acquired through famous Louisiana Purchase (a purchase in which the U.S government under president Thomas Jefferson bought large areas from the French government in 1803) and some lands bought from the British in 1818 and joined the U.S. as its 32nd state on 11 May 1858. Minneapolis–Saint Paul urban area is consisted of two cities which have joined together after a while, now known as Twin Cities. Minneapolis city once was famous for its numerous watermills, known as flour milling capital of the world. Minnesota state contains many lakes, and sometimes is called "10 thousand lakes land". Most of the initial European settlers of Minnesota were Scotts and Germans, and the state has remained as the cultural center of German-American and Scottish-Americans in the U.S. By the beginning of the Civil War, Minnesota remained in the Union, and although was a small and less-populated state, began mobilizing its men to help the Union Army. 25 thousand soldiers from Minnesota served in the Union Army during the Civil War. According to the last census, Minnesota had a population of 5639632 inhabitants, of which 79.1% were whites, 7% were blacks, 5.6% were Latinos, 5.2% were Asians, 1.4% were Native Americans and Alaskans, 0.1% Hawaiians and other Pacific Islanders, and 2.6% were from other races and ethnicities. University of Minnesota (one of the most credible universities in the world and the U.S, Yiannis Chryssomallis, nicknamed Yanni, musician, pianist and keyboard player has been graduated here), University of St. Thomas, Bethel University, St. Catherine University and Mayo Clinic (one of the most credible medical universities in the world) are among scientific and education centers in the state. Wheat, corn, soya, bulgur, pea, wild rice, milk, pork, turkey, deer, ostrich and bison are among agricultural and livestock products of Minnesota.

Aviation industry products, different sensors, metal industry, agriculture equipment, glass and window, medical equipment, transportation equipment and package industry, are main industries in the state.

During the 20th century, iron ore extraction was very common in Minnesota, but recent decades have witnessed a decrease in the issue. Extraction of crude oil and production of oil derivatives including methanol is another part of industry in Minnesota. For Instance, Flint Hills Resources Pine Bend has capacity of refining 375 thousand crude oil barrels per day.

Some large corporations like :1-UnitedHealth Group Incorporated (active in health and insurance services) 2-Cargill (global food corporation, one of the largest corporations in term of revenue in the world) 3-BEST BUY (multinational consumer electronics retailer) 4-U.S. BANK and Target (retail corporation) have headquarters in Minnesota. One of 12 U.S Federal Reserve branches in located in the state, too.

Among tourist attractions in the state, these could be named: 1-Superior National Forest & Boundary Waters Canoe Area Wilderness, with lakes , rivers and untamed nature 2-International Wolf Center , a research and education center focused on Wolves 3-Mall of America , one of the largest shopping centers in the U.S 4-Split Rock Lighthouse State Park and its old lighthouse 5-Munsinger Clemens Gardens, a good place for walking and watching the nature 6-Victorian Buildings on Summit Avenue , largest and longest set of Victorian style buildings in the U.S , along the most prominent buildings in the city , Cathedral of St. Paul and James J. Hill House , who was a senior executive manager of railway construction , known as "The Empire Builder" 7-Fort Snelling , training site of the Union Army forces in Minnesota during the Civil War 8-Lake Itasca , oldest state park in Minnesota . These.

along with many other attractions shape the tourism sector in the state. 1-Bob Dylan, singer, musician, poet, writer and Nobel prize winner in literature 2-Winona Laura Horowitz, American actress (known as Winona Ryder). She was candidate of Academy Awards 2 times 3-Seann William Scott (actor) and James George Janos (also known as Jesse Ventura), former governor of Minnesota and presenter of "Conspiracy Theory" TV program are among famous people from Minnesota.

Since 1860, Minnesota has taken part in 41 U.S presidential elections. Democrats won 20 rounds, Republican Party scored 20 victories, and Progressive Party was able to gain a single contest. To have a better inspection, the history of U.S presidential elections in Minnesota could be divided into 2 different parts. The first period, from 1860 to 1928, witnessed 18 contests, in which Republican won 17 elections, and Progressive Party scored a single victory.

Second period, from 1932 to 2020, saw 23 rounds of elections, and Democrats won 20 of them (including 12 continuous victories from 1976 to 2020), while Republican Party scored 3 wins.

As the statistics show, both parties each have won 20 U.S presidential elections in the history of Minnesota. Republicans were decisive winners in late past, but since 1932, a major shift in the political sphere of the state has taken place, and Democrats emerged much stronger, winning all 12 U.S presidential elections in the state since 1976.

In the 2020 Democratic presidential primaries in Minnesota, Joe Biden won the candidacy through winning 38.6% of the votes, while his closest rival, Bernie Sanders, took 28%.

In the 2020 Republican presidential primaries in Minnesota, Donald Trump won the candidacy through winning 97.7% of the votes, while his closest rival, Bill Weld, took 0.3%.

2020 U.S presidential election in Minnesota witnessed a victory for Democratic Party candidate, Joe Biden, who got 52.4% of the votes, while Republican candidate, Donald Trump got 45.3%. All 10 electoral votes from Minnesota were added to the Biden's vote basket.

From 1858 (the date first U.S Senate election was held in Minnesota) to 2021, 40 elected candidates from the state have served in the U.S Senate, of which 22 were Republicans, 13 were Democrats, 3 were members of Farmer–Labor Party, one was a member of Independent Party, and a senator experienced membership in Republican and

Farmer–Labor parties.

To have a better inspection, the history of the U.S. Senate elections in Minnesota could be divided into 2 different part. First part, from 1858 to 1949 saw 24 elected U.S Senators, of which 18 were Republicans, 3 were Democrats and 3 were members of Farmer-Labor Party and a senator who changed parties during his tenure and was a member of the Republican Party and the Farmers and Workers Party.

But in the second period, from 1949 to 2020, 16 persons served as U.S senators representing Minnesota, of which 10 were Democrats, 5 were Republicans and one was an Independent. As it could be observed, the number of those senators who served only as Republican Party members from Minnesota, in addition to those who experienced membership in other parties during their careers, was 23. The same number for Democrats is 13, showing superiority of Republicans in the issue, but in the recent decade (2010-2020), the popularity of the Democratic Party in the issue has increased, and both current U.S Senators from Minnesota, Amy Jean Klobuchar and Christine Elizabeth Smith, are Democrats.

Knute Nelson (with a 28-year record of presence in the U.S Senate, 1895-1923) from Republican Party and Henrik Shipstead (with a 24-year record of service, 1923-1947), with membership in Republican and Farmer-Labor parties, have been longest-serving U.S senators in history of Minnesota.

From 1858 (the year first U.S House of representatives' election was held in the state) to 2021, 144 elected candidates have entered the U.S House of representatives as representatives from Minnesota. 86 were Republicans, 42 were Democrats, 12 were members of Farmer-Labor Party, 2 were members of People's Party, and 2 representatives changed political affiliation during their careers, of which one was once a Democrat and sometimes a Republican, and one served as Republican and Independent Republican.

As the statistics show, the number of those House representatives who served only as Republicans during their careers, in addition to those who experienced membership in other parties, was 88, and the same number for Democrats is 43, showing an edge for Republicans in the history of the U.S House of representatives' elections in Minnesota. Currently (2021), 4 out of 8 House representatives who have seats from

Minnesota, are Republicans, while same number goes for Democrats. Timothy James Walz, current governor of the state and a member of Democratic–Farmer–Labor Party, is actually 41st governor of Minnesota. But number of those persons who served in the post is 40. the 1 number difference here is due to that a governor, Rudolph George Petrich Sir, gained the seat in 2 non-continuous terms, and served as 34th and 36th governor of Minnesota in 2 separate terms. Since 1858 to 2021, 40 persons have served as governor of Minnesota. Among these 40 governors, 24 were Republicans, 4 were Democrats, 6 were members of Democratic-Farmer-Labor Party (since 1944, the party has changed its name to Democratic Party in Minnesota), 3 were members of Farmer-Labor Party, 2 were Independent Republicans, and a governor switched sides among Reform Party and Minnesota Independent Party.

As it could be seen, this shows a clear upper hand for Republicans in the issue. From 1858 to 1899, except 2 first years which saw a Democrat governor, all of other governors of the state were Republicans, but It's worth noting that just similar to U.S. Senate and House elections in the state, since 2011 Democrats have worked better, and both recent governors have been members of Democratic-Farmer-Labor Party (Democratic Party branch in Minnesota). Tim Walz, a Democrat, is the current (2021) governor of Minnesota.

Conclusion : Noting that Republicans and Democrats each have won 20 U.S. presidential elections in Minnesota , while Democrats have won all 12 recent elections in the state, and Republicans had 23 U.S senators, 88 House representatives and 24 governors in the history of the state (the numbers for Democratic Party are 13 , 43 and 10) , but both current senators representing Minnesota in the U.S Senate are Democrats and each of the 2 parties hold 4 out of 8 seats belonging to Minnesota in the U.S House of representatives , while both recent governors of the state have been Democrats, so it could be concluded that while Minnesota has been a Republican Party bastion during most of its history, but currently, sympathy toward Democrats among the voters in the state is stronger.

Oregon

The coastal state of Oregon and its capital, Salem, are located in the northwestern part of the U.S. The state is well-known for its stunning nature, and initially was a part of Oregon territory. Oregon joined the U.S. as its 33rd state on 14 February 1859. Portland and Eugene are its' important cities. As a newly-established state, Oregon remained loyal to the Union during the Civil War. According to the last census, Oregon had a population of 4,217,737 inhabitants. 75.1% of the population is white, 13.4% are Latinos, 4.9% are Asians, 2.2% are blacks, 1.8% Native Indians and Alaskans, 0.5% are Hawaiians and people from other Pacific islands, and the rest 4% are from other races and ethnicities. University of Oregon, Oregon State University, Pacific University, George Fox University, Portland State University of which the College of Engineering and Computer Science was named Fariborz Maseeh College because of the financial support of Fariborz Maseeh, an Iranian philanthropist, and Oregon Health & Science University are among the scientific and educational centers of this state. Oregon has a diverse and rich agriculture sector. Berry, pear, potatoes, onions, wine grape, cherries, alfalfa and sweet corn are among main agricultural products of Oregon. Oregon is among top producers of hazelnut, Salmon fish and processed fruits in the U.S, and also is known as one of the largest centers for Mustang race horse breeding in the world. Cow, sheep, eggs and different kinds of ships and Christmas trees are other agricultural and livestock products of Oregon.

Digital technology products, timber, paper, paper paste, three-layer boards and canned fish are among industrial products of Oregon.

Along with Mist-Gas natural gas filed, which plays an important role in the economy of Oregon, sand and gravel are main mineral products of the state.

Some large corporations like :1- NIKE (producing sport shoes and sport clothing) 2- DAIMLER TRUCKS NORTH AMERICA (manufacturing heavy trucks) 3-PRECISION CASTPARTS (American industrial goods and metal fabrication company that manufactures investment castings, forged components, and airfoil castings for use in the aerospace, industrial gas turbine, and defense industries) 4- LITHIA MOTORS (automotive retailer) 5- FRED MEYER (American chain of hypermarket superstores) have headquarters in Oregon.

Among tourist destinations in Oregon , these could be named : 1- Crater Lake National Park , not actually a crater, but rather an ancient caldera of an extinct volcano,Mount Mazama 2- Columbia River Gorge National Scenic Area , an amazing and natural area with numerous waterfalls , specially Multnomah Falls , which has unique beauty 3- Cannon Beach , with large rocks nearby 4- Washington Park, Portland , a collection of amazing parks and gardens 5- Pittock Mansion , formerly house of Henry Pittock , founder of Oregonian newspaper 6- Oregon Coast Aquarium and Yaquina Lighthouse in Newport city 7- Shelton-McMurphey-Johnson House , an incredible Victorian mansion , dating back to 1888 8- Willamette Heritage Center , along with historical theater salons , old carousels and calm nature . These, along other destinations, shape the tourism sector in the state. 1- Linus Carl Pauling, scientist, peace activist, writer, one of the founders of the fields of quantum chemistry and molecular biology, Nobel prize winner in chemistry and peace. 2- Raymond Clevie Carver Jr , poet and author of short stories 3- Philip Hampson Knight , one of the founders of Nike company 4- Beverly Cleary, prominent children's and junior's literature writer 5- Steve Roland Prefontaine , American runner 6- Hin-mah-too-yah-lat-kekt , also known as Chief Joseph, Young Joseph, or Joseph the Younger , a leader of a band of the of Nez Perce, a Native American tribe 7- Marion Eugene Car , first ace of the Marines Corps air fleet during WWII , are among famous people from Oregon.

Since 1860 to 2020, 41 U.S presidential elections have been held in the country, and Oregon took part in all of them. Of these contests, Republican party won 24 times in the state, Democrats had 16 victories, and 1892 election in the state saw a split of electoral votes between Republican Party and People's Party, Republicans won 3 votes and People's Party gained a single vote. For a better inspection, history of the U.S presidential elections in Oregon could be divided into 2 periods. First part, from 1860 to 1984, saw 32 elections. Republicans scored 24 wins while Democrats gained 7 contests, and 1892 saw a split of electoral votes in favor of Republican Party, as mentioned above. But in second period, from 1988 to 2020, which witnessed 9 contests, Democrats were sole winners. As it could be observed, Republicans have been superior in the history of U.S. presidential elections in Oregon, but recent years were better for Democrats, and after 9 continuous victories in recent decades, Oregon could be counted as a Democratic Party stronghold. The 2020 Democratic presidential primaries in Oregon saw a victory for Joseph Biden, who won 67.6% of the votes, while his closest rival, Bernie Sanders got 20.8% of the votes.

The 2020 Republican presidential primaries in Oregon resulted in a win for Donald Trump, without any rivals.Finally, the 2020 U.S Presidential elections in Oregon resulted in a win for Democratic Party candidate, Joseph Biden, who won 56.5% of the votes, while his Republican counterpart, Donald Trump, won 40.4% of the votes. All 7 electoral votes from Oregon were added to Biden's vote basket.

Since 1859 (the year first U.S Senate election was held in Oregon) to 2020, the state has sent 37 senators to the U.S Senate.19 were Republicans, 17 were Democrats, and a senator experienced membership in Democratic and Republican parties during his career. According to the statistics shown above, the number of those senators who only had membership in Republican Party, or along this had records of membership in other parties, is 20, and the same number for Democratic Party is 18, showing a clear edge for Republicans. It's worth noting that service years of these 20 Republican senators have been much longer than their 18 Democratic counterparts. For instance: Mark Odom Hatfield and Frederick Steiwer served 30 and 11 years in the U.S Senate, and by such a criterion, Republicans have represented Oregon in the U.S Senate for 200 years, while Democrats served 100 years. Democrats have worked better in the U.S. Senate elections in Oregon in the recent years. Jeffrey Alan Merkley and Ronald Lee Wyden, both Democrats, currently (2021) represent the state in the U.S.

Senate.

Mark Odom Hatfield (with a 30-year record of presence in the U.S Senate, 1967-1997), a Republican, and Charles Linza McNary (with a 27-year record of presence, 1917-1944), both Republicans, were longest-serving U.S senators in history of Oregon.

During the history of Oregon, 65 elected persons from the state served as representatives in the U.S House of Representatives, and 2 of them served during the period which Oregon was a territory, not a state. 34 were Republicans and 31 were members of Democratic Party.

As it's clear, Republicans have an upper hand in the issue, but Democrats have improved their performance in recent decades, and currently (2021), 4 out of 5 representatives from Oregon in the House are Democrats, and one is a Republican.

Katherine Brown, current governor of Oregon (a Democrat), is the 38th governor in the history of the state, but number of those persons who acted as governor of Oregon was 37. The 1 number difference here is due to that a governor, John Albert Kitzhaber, gained the seat in 2 non-continuous terms. He served as 35th and 37th governor of Oregon.

Since 1859, 37 persons have served as governor of Oregon, of which 20 were Republicans, 16 were Democrats and one was an independent candidate. As it could be observed, it may be suggested that Republicans have an upper hand here, but number of service years by 16 Democratic governors were 3 years longer than their Republican counterparts. Since 1987, all recent governors of Oregon have been members of Democratic Party.

Conclusion: Noting that Republicans have fully won 24 U.S presidential elections in Oregon, and won an election jointly along with People's Party (1892 election) while Democrats gained 16 contests including 9 recent contests , and Republicans had 20 U.S senators and 34 House representatives (the numbers for Democratic Party are 18 and 31), but both current U.S senators from Oregon are members of Democratic Party , and 4 out of 5 House representatives are Democrats while 1 is a Republican , and Republicans had 20 governors in the history of the state (Democrats had 16) , but it should be noted that service years of Democratic governors have been longer , and since 1987 all elected governors of the state have been Democrats , so it could be concluded while Oregon has been a Republican-leaning state through most of its history, it is currently is a Democratic stronghold.

Kansas

ᘇ

K ansas state and its capital Topeka, are located in the American Midwest. Kansas was initially a part of the lands acquired through the famous Louisiana Purchase (a purchase in which the U.S. government under president Thomas Jefferson bought large areas from the French government in 1803). In 1854, following the legal passing of Kansas-Nebraska act, Kansas territory was established. In 1854 and after establishment of the territory, a referendum on slavery issue was held in Kansas, and thousands of Missouri residents illegally took part in the voting, and voted in favor of legalizing slavery in the state. After the referendum and from 1855 to 1859, numerous incidents between pro and anti-slavery groups took place in the state, resulting in death of 55 persons, and later became known as " Bleeding Kansas". Finally, on 29 January 1861, 2 months before the beginning of the Civil War, Kansas joined the U.S as its 34th state and after beginning of the war remained in the Union. Kansas was the first state to ratify the Prohibition act in 1881 and putting it in action. After ratification of the 18th amendment in 1919, the Prohibition became nationwide and lasted until 1933, but terminated in this year. The Prohibition act remained in place in Kansas until 1948, and Kansas acted as the national center for anti-alcohol movement. According to the last census, Kansas had a population of 2913314 inhabitants, of which 75.4% were whites, 12.2% were Latinos, 6.1% were Blacks, 3.2% were Asians, 1.2% were Native Americans and Alaskans, 0.1% Hawaiians and other Pacific Islanders, and 3.1% were from other races and ethnicities. Kansas is a rich state when it comes to agriculture and animal husbandry, and ranks 1st in wheat production in the U.S, and is among the top states in producing corns, soybean, cow, beef and other kinds of meats.

Aircrafts, camping equipment, heating and air conditioning equipment, snow-laying vehicles, prefabricated houses, movable houses, greeting cards, tires, industrial colors, washing machines, cement, rock, clay, sand and gravel, salt, Bituminous coal, plaster, and small amounts of oil and natural gas are among industrial products of Kansas.

The state hosts headquarters of many large corporations like: 1- KOCH INDUSTRIES, led by Charles Koch, active in extraction, refining and distribution of oil products and chemicals, among main backers of Republican Party 2- YRC WORLDWIDE, active in transportation 3- DILLONS (chain store) and AMC THEATRES (movie theater chain).

Among tourist attractions in the state , these could be named : 1- Eisenhower Presidential Library, Museum, and Boyhood Home , actually , the house which Eisenhower (later became 34th president of the U.S) spent his childhood there 2- Boot Hill museum , focused on the history of the western part of the U.S 3- Flint Hills Discovery Center , researching on the history of Flint Hills area 4- Monument Rocks , natural limestone structures 5- Fort Larned National Historic site , containing an old military fort and other buildings 6- The Keeper of the Plains , a square in memory of history and important role of Native Americans in the area 7- Old Cowtown Museum, containing 54 reconstructed historical buildings 8- Kansas Speedway , all shaping the tourism sector in the state. 1- Charles Koch, chairman and CEO of Koch Industries, billionaire and among main backers of Republican Party 2- Charles Luckman, famous as architect of 20th century 3- Charlie Parker, nicknamed "Bird", player of the alto saxophone and Improvisational Jazz musician 4- Robert Michael Gates, former secretary of defense of the U.S are among famous people from Kansas.

Since 1861 (the year Kansas state was established), 40 presidential elections have been held in the U.S, and Kansas has taken part in all of them. Republicans won 33 rounds, Democratic Party scored 6 victories, and People's Party was able to score a single victory.

As it could be observed, Kansas has been a Republican state through most of its history, just like now. Lat victory of Democrats was in 1964. Since 1940, (recent 80 years), this was sole victory of Democrats in the state, and Republicans won all elections since 1968.

Because of decisive statewide support for Donald Trump, Republican Party didn't hold its presidential primaries in Kansas in 2020.

The 2020 Democratic presidential primaries in Kansas saw a victory for Joseph Biden, who won 76.9% of the votes, while his closest rival, Bernie Sanders got 23.1% of the votes.

Finally, the 2020 U.S Presidential elections in Kansas resulted in a win for Republican Party candidate, Donald Trump, who won 56.1% of the votes, while his Democratic counterpart, Joseph Biden, won 41.5% of the votes. All 6 electoral votes from Kansas were taken by Trump.

From 1861 to 2021, 34 elected candidates from the state have served in the U.S Senate, of which 29 were Republicans, 3 were Democrats, and 2 were members of People's Party. These results also indicate that most of Kansas voters have been staunch Republicans during the history of the state. All 3 Democratic senators served before 1940, and after that year, all U.S Senators from Kansas have been members of Republican Party.

Roger Wayne Marshall and Gerald Wesley Moran, both Republicans, currently (2021) represent the state in the U.S Senate. Arthur Capper (with a 30-year record of presence in the U.S Senate, 1919-1949) and Robert Joseph Dole (with a 27-year record of service, 1969-1996), both Republicans, have been longest-serving U.S senators in history of Kansas.

From 1861 to 2021, 123 elected candidates have entered the U.S. House of representatives as representatives from Kansas. 84 were Republicans, 26 were Democrats, 12 were members of the People's Party and a representative served as Republican and member of Liberal Republican Party. As the statistics show, the number of those House representatives who served only as Republicans during their careers, in addition to those who experienced membership in other parties, was 85, and the same number for Democrats is 26, showing a clear edge for Republicans in the history of the U.S House of representatives' elections in Kansas. In recent decades, Republican Party has worked much stronger, and since 1995, except 3 representatives who were members of Democratic Party, all other House representatives from Kansas have been Republicans. 3 out of 4 current representatives representing the state in the U.S House of representatives are Republicans and one is a Democrat. Since 1861 to now (2021), 48 persons have served as governors of Kansas, of which

34 were Republicans, 13 were Democrats and one was a member of People's Party. These numbers show superiority of Republican Party in the history of gubernatorial elections in Kansas, but recent 50 years have witnessed a closer competition among the 2 main parties, and Laura.J. Kelly, current governor of Kansas, is a Democrat.

Conclusion : Noting that Republicans have won 33 U.S presidential elections in Kansas (including 3 all 14 recent contests) while Democrats had 6 victories and Republicans had 29 U.S senators , 85 House representatives and 34 governors in the history of the state (the numbers for Democratic Party are 3 , 26 and 13) , both current senators representing Kansas in the U.S Senate are Republicans and 3 out of 4 House seats belonging to the state are being held by them (1 for Democrats) , and Democrats have 37 governors in the history of the state (vs 7 Republicans) , while current governor of Kansas is a member of Democratic Party , so it could be concluded that Kansas has been a bastion of Republican Party during most of its history , just like today (2021) .

West Virginia

Wiest Virginia state and its' capital, Charleston, are located in
the southeastern part of the U.S. The state was initially a part
of Virginia, and in 1861, on the beginning of the Civil War,
the Northern parts of Virginia state, which constitute the nowadays
state of West Virginia, declared their opposition to seceding from the
Union, seceded from Virginia and remained under supervision of the
federal government. Finally, on 20 June 1863 and in the middle of the
Civil War, on the condition of gradual emancipation of the remaining
slaves in the state, West Virginia joined the U.S as its 35th state. Along
with Nevada, West Virginia was the second state to join the U.S. during
the Civil War. 32 thousand men from the state served in the Union
Army during the Civil War, while 9 thousand joined the Confederate
Army. According to the last census, West Virginia had a population
of 1,792,147 inhabitants, of which 92% were whites, 3.6% were blacks,
1.7% were Latinos, 0.8% were Asians, 0.3% were Native Americans
and Alaskans, and 1.8% were from other races and ethnicities. West
Virginia University, Marshall University, Davis and Elkins College,
Bluefield State College, and Robert C. Byrd Telescope, located in Green
Bank, largest single dish radio telescope in the world, functioning on
millimeter to meter wavelengths, are among scientific and education
centers in the state. West Virginia is known as "The Mountain State"
because of its topography, consisting of mountains, hills and valleys.
Because of this, animal husbandry is more common than agriculture
in the state. Cow, calf, beef, sheep, lamb, pork, turkey, chicken, fishes,

dairy products, eggs and wool are among main livestock products of the state. Wheat, potatoes, soybean, peaches, tobacco and alfalfa are main agricultural products of West Virginia. Chemical industries and oil products like: tires, glue, industrial chemicals, and pharma industry shape a large part of industry sector in the state. Metal products, wood products, aviation products, transportation equipment are among other industrial products in the state. Along with coal and natural gas (main mineral products of the state, West Virginia ranks 2nd in coal production among the U.S states, after Wyoming), oil, gravel, crushed stone and salt are produced in the state. Biotechnology has also made great strides in this state and is one of the pioneers of this industry.1- BRAND ENERGY AND INFRASTRUCTURE SERVICES, active in large industrial structure building, insulation, mechanical industry and other industrial fields 2- ESMARK (active in mining and metal industry) 3- GABE'S (discount department store chain), are among large corporations which have headquarters in West Virginia.

Among tourist destinations in the state, these could be noted: 1- Harpers Ferry, the city which John Brown's attack on federal arsenal happened there. John Brown believed in use of violence to abolish the slavery. He attacked federal arsenal located in Harpers Ferry (part of Virginia in that era, later part of West Virginia) in October 1859, with an intention to arm the slaves and expanding the movement to the south and end the slavery. The move was suppressed, but paved the way towards the Civil War and abolition of slavery 2- New River Gorge National River, opposite to its name, a very old trail, along with its famous bridge. The nearby area is a good place for walking, fishing, watching birds, camping, cycling and rock climbing. 3- Blackwater Falls State Park, named because of its dark water, one of the best tourist areas in the state with many waterfalls and unmated nature 4- Whitewater Rafting, one of the best entertainments in the state 5- Snowshoe resort with its ski resort 6- The Greenbrier, a historical hotel and mineral water springs nearby. The hotel was used as a detention center for keeping German and Japanese diplomats who were captured after declaration of war against the U.S in WWII 7- West Virginia Penitentiary , established in 1876 and closed in 1995 , a popular place for paranormal researchers looking for evidence of spectral phenomena 8- Trans-Allegheny Lunatic Asylum or the Mental Illness Hospital, which, apart from the Kremlin in Moscow, is the largest man-made stone building in the Western Hemisphere, built between 1881 and 1885. 9- Cass Scenic Railroad State Park, with a steam locomotive trip 10- Seneca Caverns. These along with other attractions, shape the tourism sector in West Virginia. 1- Harold Franklin Hawkins, country style singer 2- Stoney Cooper, prominent guitar and violin 3- Kevin Pittsnogle, former basketball player 4- Isabella Maria Boyd, a Confederate spy who gave valuable information to Confederate General Stonewall Jackson, are among famous people from West Virginia.

Since 1864 to 2020, 40 presidential elections were held in the U.S, and West Virginia took part in all of them. Of these 0 contests, Democratic Party won 20 times in the and Republicans had 20 victories, too, and among these victories, 1916 election saw a split of electoral votes in favor of Republicans (7 vs 1). To have a better inspection, the history of U.S presidential elections in West Virginia could be divided into 2 different parts. The first period, from 1864 to 1928, witnessed 17 contests, in which Republicans gained 11 victories (including 1916 elections which witnessed split of the electoral votes in favor of them), and Democrats scored 6 victories.

Second period, from 1932 to 2020, saw 23 rounds of elections, and Democrats won 14 of them, while Republican Party was able to gain 9 victories and 6 of these victories have been 6 recent contests. As it could be seen, in this period both parties gained the same number of victories, but the Republicans have worked better in recent decades, and all 6 recent elections in West Virginia were gained by them, showing their increasing popularity in the state.

In the 2020 Republican Party presidential primaries in West Virginia, Donald Trump was elected by gaining 94.5% of the votes, defeating Joe Walsh who got 1.8%.

In the 2020 Democratic presidential primaries in West Virginia, Joe Biden won the candidacy through winning 65.3% of the votes, while his closest rival, Bernie Sanders, took 11.9%.

Finally, the 2020 U.S presidential election in West Virginia witnessed a victory for Republican Party candidate, Donald Trump, who got 68.6% of the votes, while Democratic candidate, Joe Biden got 29.7%. All 5 electoral votes from West Virginia were taken by Trump.

From 1863 (the year first U.S Senate election was held in the state) to 2021, West Virginia has sent 33 senators to the U.S Senate.19 were Democrats, 12 were Republicans, and 2 were senators who changed their political affiliations during their careers, both sometimes Republicans and sometimes members of Unconditional Union Party.

As it could be observed, Democrats have an upper hand in the history of the U.S Senate elections in West Virginia (19 senators' vs 14 for Republican Party). One of the U.S Senate seats belonging to the state has been held by Democrats since 1959, and the other seat is in control of Republican Party sine 2015. Shelley Wellons Moore Capito, a Republican and Feinstein and Joseph Manchin III, a Democrat, currently (2021) represent West Virginia in the U.S Senate.

Robert Carlyle Byrd, with a 51-year's record of service in the U. S Senate (1959-2010) and John Davison Rockefeller IV with 30 years of presence in the U. S Senate (1985-2015), both Democrats, have been longest-serving U. S senators in the history of the state. Robert Byrd also was among longest-serving U.S senators in the history of the U.S, too. Since 1863 to 2021, 103 elected candidates have entered the U.S House of representatives as representatives from West Virginia. 50 were Republicans, 48 were Democrats, 4 were members of Unconditional Union Party, And a representative experienced membership in Republican and Unconditional Union parties during his career.

As the statistics show, the number of those House representatives who served only as Republicans during their careers, in addition to those who experienced membership in other parties, was 51, and the same number for Democrats is 48, which may be showing an edge for Republicans in the history of the U.S. House of representatives' elections in West Virginia, but the number of service years of these 48 Democratic representatives are much higher than their Republican counterparts. For example, Nick Rahall served 38 years (1977-2015) in the House. 51 Republican representatives together served 245 years, while 48 Democratic representatives had a sum of 430-year record service. These shows historical superiority of Democrats in the issue, but all 3 current representatives of the state in the House are Republicans. James Conley Justice II, current governor of West Virginia (a Republican), is the 36th governor in the history of the state, but the number of those persons who acted as governor of West Virginia was 34. The 2-number difference here is due to that 2 governors, gained the seat in

2 non-continuous terms, and statistics here are according to number of persons who served in the post, not number of terms. For example, Arch Alfred Moore Jr served as 28th governor of the state from 1969 to 1977 and later was able to gain the seat again as 30th governor, serving from 1985 to 1989. Since 1863 (the Year West Virginia joined the U.S as a new state) to 2021, 34 governors have served in West Virginia. Among these 34 governors, 19 were Democrats, 13 were Republicans, and 2 were governors who switched their political affiliations during their careers, of which one served as Democrat and Independent, and the other one was sometimes a Democrat and sometimes a Republican.

As it could be seen, the number of those governors who served only as Democrats during their careers, in addition to those who experienced membership in other parties, was 21, and the same number for Republicans is 14, which may be showing an edge for Democrats in the history of the gubernatorial elections in West Virginia. This shows historical superiority of Democrats in the issue. From 2001 to 2017, all 3 elected governors of the state were members of Democratic Party, but in 2017, James Conley Justice II, current governor of West Virginia, who was a Democrat, was elected as 36th governor of the state, but after a While defected to Republican Party.

Conclusion: Throughout the history of the presidential election, West Virginia Democrats who won 20 voting rounds are equal to Republicans with 20 rounds, of which only one round is related to 1916. The seven-to-one electoral vote is divided between this party and the Democrats. On the other hand, six of the 20 Republican elections are related to the last six elections. Throughout the history of Senate elections, Democrats top Senate with 19 senators versus Republicans with 14 senators. And throughout the House election, Democrats with 48 seats vs. Republicans with 51 seats provided the total number of terms or years of the 48 Democrats is higher than Republicans. Democrats are still leading the way with 21 governors versus Republicans with 14 governors throughout the state election, but of the two current state senators, one is a Democrat and one is a Republican, and all three current representatives, along with the governor, are Republicans. It can be concluded that West Virginia has historically been more pro-Democrat but is now a Republican state.

Nevada

N evada is a U.S. state located in western America, and its' capital is Carson City. Originally, Nevada was a part of Mexico and became part of the U.S. after the Mexican-American War of 1848, according to the Treaty of Guadalupe Hidalego, turning it into a part of the Utah state in 1850. Finally, and eleven years later, in 1861, part of the territory was separated and a new territory called Nevada was formed. Finally, on October 31, 1864, during the Civil War, Nevada joined the United States as the 36th state. Nevadan cities as Reno and Las Vegas are well-known globally for their casinos and entertainment centers. It would be interesting to know that Nevada is the only state of the U.S. known for legalizing prostitution in some of its' districts. According to the last census, Nevada had a population of 3,080,165 inhabitants. Demographic composition of the state can be seen in these numbers: 48.2% of the population was white, 29.2% were Latinos, 10.3% were blacks, 8.7% were Asians, 1.7% Native Indians and Alaskans, 0.8% were Hawaiians and people from other Pacific islands, and the rest 4.6% were from other races and ethnicities. University of Nevada—Reno (which is a center for research on earthquakes, and contains one of the largest earthquake simulation labs in the U.S), University of Nevada—Las Vegas, Sierra Nevada University and College of Southern Nevada are among scientific and education centers in the state. The state also hosts a highly-secret U.S military base called area 51. Because of its arid weather, agriculture is not a common activity in Nevada. Although modern methods of irrigation have facilitated growing crops in the state. Cows, beef, sheep and alfalfa are among main agriculture and livestock products of Nevada. Potatoes, wheat, barley, boulghour, corns, honey, onion, garlic, mint, vegetables and some fruits are among other agricultural products in Nevada. Metal products, computer and electronic devices, chemical and plastic products, printing press and publishment are among industries in Nevada. The state also hosts a large geothermal field, in use for generating electricity.

Opposite to agriculture, extraction and production of minerals is a main economy sector in Nevada. Nevada is the largest producer of gold and silver in the U.S. Goldstrike and Carlin mines are among the largest in the U.S. Nevada also has a large geothermal energy field that can use Earth's heat to generate electricity.

Other minerals like copper, diatom soil, plaster, lithium, molybdenum, iron ore, salt, oil, magnesite, carbonate, limestone and gravel are found in Nevada.

Some large corporations like: 1- JOHNSON ELECTRIC (manufacturing engines, mechanical gears, motion equipment, and other mechanical-electrical parts for applications in transportation, industry and medicine) 2- AMERCO (owner of Amerco Real Estate, Republic Western Insurance, and Oxford Life Insurance and U-Haul companies) 3- CLARK COUNTY SCHOOL DISTRICT 4- MGM RESORTS INTERNATIONAL (entertainment company), Caesars Entertainment and Las Vegas Sands have headquarters in Nevada. Among tourist destinations in Nevada, these could be named: 1-Casinos and entertainment centers 2- Hoover Dam , which has largest water reservoir in the U.S 3- Lake Tahoe, with snowy mountains nearby 4- Lake Mead National Recreation Area , with a beautiful view , a good place for walking and boating 5-Valley of Fire State Park , with colorful rocks and wave rocks 6- Great Basin National Park , containing mountains and forests 7- Burning Man , annual art festival which gathers many visitors every year 8- National Automobile Museum in Reno city , a collection of old and new model cars 9- Animal Ark , a wildlife preservation area with numerous animal species 10- Nevada Historical Society Museum, exhibiting history of Reno city since 10 thousand years ago to the modern history 11- Red Rock Canyon National Conservation Area . These, along many other attractions, shape the tourism sector in Nevada. 1- Andre Agassi, Iranian-American tennis player 2- Kyle

Thomas Busch, professional racing driver 3- Marcus Banks, basketball player 4- Brandon Richard Flowers, singer, musician and lyricist 5- Juanita Brooks, historian and author, are among famous people from Nevada.

Since 1864 to now (2021), 40 presidential elections have been held in the U. S, and Nevada has taken part in all of them. Republicans won 20 of them, comparing to 19 Democratic victories and a victory for People's Party. None of these parties were able to score continuous victories, and a cycle has been going on for a long time. For example, from 1932 to 1948, Democrats won 5 elections one after another, then Republicans gained 2 victories, and again from 1968 to 1988, Republican Party was the sole winner of presidential elections in Nevada.

As it could be observed, Republicans have an upper hand in the history of U.S presidential elections in Nevada and won 20 contests (19 victories for Democrats), but Democratic Party has improved its performance in recent years and has won all 4 recent elections. It's worth noting that from 1912 to 2020, excerpt 1976 and 2016 elections, winner of U.S. presidential elections in Nevada has been the final winner of the elections in the whole country.

Initial inter-party elections in Nevada are not held in primary method, but in caucuses method.

The 2020 Democratic Party caucuses in Nevada saw a victory for Bernie Sanders who won 46.8% of votes vs Joe Biden who got 20.2%. Because of statewide support for Donald Trump, Republican Party didn't hold its 2020 caucuses in Nevada.

Finally, the 2020 U.S presidential election in Nevada witnessed a victory for Democratic candidate, Joseph Biden, who won 50.1% of the votes, while his Republican rival, Donald Trump, got 47.7%. Biden won all 6 electoral votes from Nevada. Since 1864(the year first U.S Senate election was held in Nevada) to now (2021), Nevada has sent 27 Senators to the U.S Senate, of which 14 were Democrats, 11 were Republicans and 2 were senators with multiple political affiliations, and experienced membership in Republican and Silver parties. As it could be observed, the number of those senators who served only as Republican party members from Nevada, in addition to those who experienced membership in other parties during their careers, was 13. The same number for Democrats is 14, showing superiority of Democrats in the issue. It's worth noting that while difference in number of U.S senators from the 2 main parties is just 1, but accumulative number of service years for Democratic senators is 168, while the same number for Republican Party is 84, which shows a clear edge for Democratic Party in the issue.

Right now (2021), Cathrine Marie Cortez Masto and Jacklyn Sheryl Rosen, both Democrats, Represent Nevada in the U.S Senate. Harry Mason Reid, a Democrat with 30 years of service in the U.S Senate (1987-2017) and John Percival Jones, who experienced membership in both Republican and silver parties (with a 30-year record of service in the U.S Senate, 1873-1903) were longest-serving U.S senators in the history of Nevada. From 1864 until now (2021), 40 Representatives from Nevada have been present in the U. S House of Representatives, and both Republicans and Democrats had a same share of the seats (each 20). As of today (2020), Nevada has 3 Democratic representatives and a Republican representative in the U.S House of representatives. In the history of gubernatorial elections in Nevada, since 1864, 30 governors have been elected, among them 14 were Republicans, 14 were Democrats (of these, one was a Silver-Democrat coalition member) and 2 were members of Silver Party. According to these numbers, both 2 main parties (Republicans and Democrats) had equal numbers of governors in the history of Nevada, but number of service years for Democratic governors was 77, and the same number for Republicans is 67. Since 1999 to 2019, all 3 elected governors of Nevada were Republicans, but from 2019, Steve Sisolak, a Democrat who won the election, became 30th governor of Nevada.

Conclusion: Noting that Republicans have won 20 U.S presidential elections in Nevada (Democrats won 19 including 4 recent contests), It's clear they had an upper hand in the history of the U.S presidential elections in the state. Democrats had 14 U.S senators in the history of Nevada , while Republican party had 13 , and both current U.S senators from the state are Democrats .Both parties had each 20 House representatives and 14 governors in the history of the state , while 3 out of 4 House seats belonging to the state are being held by Democrats (1 for Republicans) , and current governor of Nevada is a Democrat ,so it could be concluded that except the U.S Senate elections , the 2 main parties had an equal share in political contests in the history of the state, but today (2021), Nevada is a Democrat-leaning state.

Nebraska

Nebraska state and its capital, Lincoln, are located in the American Midwest. The state is well-known for its cordial people and vast grasslands. Nebraska joined the U.S. as its 37th state on 1 March 1867. Nebraska was the birthplace of Howard Baskerville, American teacher at Memorial school, active in Tabriz, Iran in the early 20th century, who was killed during his efforts to help the Constitutionalist movement in Iran and breaking the siege of Tabriz. He is known as "Constitutionalist Martyr" in Iran. According to the last census, Nebraska had a population of 1934408 inhabitants, of which 78.2% were whites, 11. 4% were Latinos ,5.2% were blacks, 2.7% were Asians, 1.5% were Native Americans and Alaskans, 0.1% were Hawaiians and other Pacific islanders, and 2.3% were from other races and ethnicities. Creighton University, University of Nebraska—Lincoln (Warren Buffet, one of the richest persons in the world graduated here), University of Nebraska-Omaha and Doane University are among scientific and education centers in the state. Potatoes, corn, bean, alfalfa, soybean, sugar beet, sheep, lamb, pork, turkey, chicken, eggs and milk are among agriculture and livestock products of Nebraska. Nebraska is the major center of beef and pork (generally meat) processing, and other products related to beef, including beef packaging. In addition to the processing of beef and pork, which is a successful industry in the state, cow and pig husbandry is a common activity in Nebraska. Manufacturing electrical equipment and home appliances, machinery, processed metal products, railway transportation equipment, off-road vehicles, chemical products including pesticides, fertilizers and pharma drugs are among industries in Nebraska. Railway industry is also very active in the state.

Some large corporations like :1- BERKSHIRE HATHAWAY (belonging to Warren Buffet) 2-UNION PACIFIC (active in railway transportation) 3-CABELA'S (chain stores related to fishing and hunting equipment) 4-MUTUAL OF OMAHA (insurance and financial services company) 5-VALMONT INDUSTRIES (manufacturer of Valley center pivot and linear irrigation equipment, windmill support structures, lighting and traffic poles and steel utility poles) have headquarters in Nebraska. Among tourist destinations in Nebraska , these can be pointed : 1- Omaha's Henry Doorly Zoo and Aquarium , which contains one of the largest roofed deserts and jungles in the world 2- Old Market in Omaha , an old market consisting of retail shops , galleries , coffee shops and restaurants 3- Strategic Air and Space Museum, Ashland , numerous kinds of aircrafts and space vehicles are exhibited here 4- Chimney Rock National Historic Site , dating back to between 24 and 25 million years ago 5- Haymarket District in Lincoln , a district with excellent restaurants and reconstructed historical buildings 6-Indian Cave State Park with beautiful and exciting reliefs , showing scenes from wildlife and nature on the cave walls 7-Carhenge , a site in which vintage cars are arranged in a circle in a style remembering Stonehenge 8-A Scenic Driving Tour of the Sandhills , in beautiful and calm nature 9-Scotts Bluff National Monument . All of these shape the tourism sector in Nebraska. 1-Gerald Rudolph Ford, Jr, 38th president of the U.S 2-Malcolm X, among leaders of the Muslim black community in the U.S. 3-Howard Conklin Baskerville, American teacher at Memorial school in Tabriz, Iran, in the early 20th century who was killed during his efforts to help the Constitutionalist movement in Iran and breaking the siege of Tabriz. He is known as "Constitutionalist Martyr" in Iran. 4- Red Cloud, Native American chieftain 5- Henry Jaynes Fonda, actor in TV, cinema and theater 6- Marlon Brando, Jr, one of the greatest actors of cinema and theater, and Academy Awards winner 7- Warren Edward Buffett, investor, economist and one of richest persons in the world, are among famous people from Nebraska.

Nebraska and Maine are 2 states that don't follow the " winner-take-all electoral vote" allocation in the U.S. presidential elections but according to the "Congressional District Method"; these states are divided into federal districts in accordance to the number of the House representatives. Number of House representatives in each state shows the number of federal districts in the state, and each federal district has an electoral vote. These, adding to 2 votes belonging to the U.S senators from each state, shape whole number of electoral votes from each state. For example, in the "winner-take-all" method, if a state has 9 electoral votes, and a candidate wins 5 out of 7 federal districts, he finally wins all 7 electoral votes from federal districts and 2 votes from U.S. senators, but Maine and Nebraska don't follow this method, and all of the electoral votes from federal districts don't go for the candidate who has gained more votes generally in the state, but the winner of any federal district takes the electoral vote from there. Nebraska has 5 electoral votes (3 federal districts) , and for instance , if a candidate wins 2 federal districts and another candidate wins 1 district , unlike other states , first candidate doesn't get all electoral votes from the state , but he gets 2 electoral votes for 2 federal districts and 2 votes from the U.S senators , while the second candidate gets an electoral vote from the federal district he/she has won (just like the 2008 election in which John McCain won 4 electoral votes from Nebraska and Barack Obama got 1) .

Since 1867 (the year first U.S election was held in Nebraska) to 2020, Nebraska has taken part in 39 U.S presidential elections, of which Republican Party scored 32 victories (2008 and 2020 elections witnessed split of the electoral votes between the 2 main parties, both times 4 vs 1 in favor of Republicans), while Democratic Party gained 7 victories. As it could be seen, Republicans are far superior in the issue, and this shows their strong popularity in Nebraska. From 1940 to 2020, 21 rounds of U.S presidential elections have been held in the state, and Democrats only gained a single victory in 1964, and as mentioned above, in 2008 and 2020 elections they gained a single electoral vote from Nebraska. If we take a closer look at the issue, we see that since 1968, Republicans have won the last 14 rounds of this election. 2020 Republican Party primaries in Nebraska, witnessed a victory for Donald Trump, who got the candidacy by winning 90.7% of the votes, defeating Bill Weld who got 8.6%.

In the 2020 Democratic Party presidential primaries in Nebraska,

Joe Biden won the candidacy by gaining 76.1% of the votes, while his closest rival, Bernie Sanders, got 13.9%.

Finally, the 2020 U.S presidential election in Nebraska witnessed a victory for Republican candidate, Donald Trump, who won 58.2% of the votes, while his Democratic rival, Joe Biden, got 39.2%. Trump won all 5 electoral votes from Nebraska. From 1867 (the date first U.S Senate election was held in Nebraska) to 2021, 38 elected candidates from the state have served in the U.S Senate, of which 28 were Republicans, 8 were Democrats, one was a member of People's Party and a senator experienced membership in Republican and Independent. As it could be observed, Number of those senators who served only as Republican Party members from Nebraska, in addition to those who experienced membership in other parties during their careers, was 29. The same number for Democrats is 8, showing superiority of Republicans in the issue. The trend has been persistent until now (2021), and currently Debra Strobel Fischer and Benjamin Eric Sasse, both Republicans, represent Nebraska in the U.S Senate.

Carl Thomas Curtis (with a 24-year record of presence in the U.S Senate, 1955-1979) and Roman Lee Hruska (with a 22-year record of presence in the U.S Senate, 1954-1976), both Republicans, have been longest-serving U.S senators in the history of Nebraska.

From 1865 (the year first U.S House of representatives' election was held in the state) to 2021, 95 elected candidates have entered the U.S House of representatives as representatives from Nebraska. 62 were Republicans, 25 were Democrats, 7 were members of Populist Party (also known as People's Party), and a representative acted as Republican and independent.

As the statistics show, Number of those House representatives who served only as Republicans during their careers, in addition to those who experienced membership in other parties, was 63, and the same number for Democrats is 25, showing an edge for Republicans in the history of the U.S House of representatives' elections in Nebraska. Currently (2021), all 3 House representatives who have seats from Nebraska are Republicans. John Peter Ricketts, current governor of the state, is 40th governor of Nebraska, while number of persons who served in the post is 39. the 1 number difference here is due to that a governor, Charles Wayland Bryan gained the seat in 2 non-continuous terms, serving as 20th and 23rd governor of Nebraska. Since 1867, 39 persons have served as governor of Nebraska. Among these 39 governors, 26 were Republicans, 11 were members of Democratic Party, and two gained their seat through electoral fusion, meaning they gained the elections thorough coalition among Democratic and People's parties. As it could be seen, Republicans have an edge here, and since 1999, all 3 recent governors (including recent governor, John Peter Ricketts) of the state have been members of their party.

Conclusion: Noting that Republicans have fully won 32 U.S presidential elections in Nebraska (Democrats won 7) including 14 recent contests except 2008 and 2020, and had 29 U.S senators, 63 House representatives and 26 governors (the numbers for Democratic Party are 8, 25 and 13), It's clear that Republican Party has an upper hand in the political history of Nebraska. Currently, both U.S senators and 3 House representatives, who represent Nebraska in the U.S Senate and U.S House of representatives, along with current governor of the state are Republicans. So, it could be concluded that Nebraska has been a Republican state through its history, and situation today is the same.

Colorado

The mountainous Colorado state and its capital city, Denver, are located in western America. The state was initially a part of the lands which were bought from the French government in the famous deal called the "Louisiana purchase" in 1803 (under president Thomas Jefferson's administration). Foundation of Colorado was related to secession crisis before the Civil War and large-scale migration of white settlers who came after the famous gold rush of 1861, resulting in foundation of Colorado territory, and finally, Colorado joined the U.S. as its 38th state in 1 August 1876. According to the last census, Colorado had 5,758,736 inhabitants. 67.9% of Colorado population was white, 21.8% was Latino, 4.6% black, 3.5% Asian, 1.6% Native Indian, 0.2% Hawaiians and 3.1% were from other races and ethnicities. The University of Denver (which its Colorado Women's College is dedicated to women), Colorado School of Mines, University of Colorado Boulder, Colorado State University and United States Air Force Academy are among scientific and education centers in the state. Also, The U.S. Olympic & Paralympic Training Center in Colorado Springs, which is the largest training center of the U.S Olympic and Paralympic committee, is located here. The state is home to Native Americans who have thrived on the American handicraft market by making painted pottery and decorative objects. Most Native Americans generally live in Four Corners. Four Corners is the point where the southwest corner of Colorado, the southeast corner of Utah, the northeast corner of Arizona, and the northwest corner of New Mexico meet. It is the only point in the United States where the four states meet. Apple, corns, wheat, alfalfa, dairy products, cow, beef and dairy products are main agricultural and livestock products of Colorado. The state also produces melons and watermelons, sweet corn, beans, sorghum, peaches, sugar beet, sunflower seed, grape and mushrooms are among other agricultural products from the state.

Manufacturing metal products, electrical and computer devices, furniture, machinery, plastic products, clothing and textile, leather, spacecraft and telescopes for use by NASA, wind blades and turbines, oil and natural gas, coal, gold, silver, zinc, lead, granite, limestone, sand and gravel and meet packaging are main industries in Colorado.

Some large corporations like: 1-JBS USA (active in packaging meat and processing foods) 2-CATHOLIC HEALTH INITIATIVES (public health services company) 3- CHIPOTLE MEXICAN GRILL chain of fast casual restaurants 4-KROENKE SPORTS & ENTERTAINMENT (sports and entertainment holding) have headquarters in Colorado.

Among tourist destinations in the state, these could be named: 1-Rocky Mountain National Park, with its high mountain summons, lakes, grasslands, forests, and interesting wildlife 2-Vail and Nearby Mountain Towns, a good place for skiing, containing numerous restaurants, shopping malls and beautiful hotels 3-Mesa Verde National Park, where Pueblo tribe was living from 7th to 14 centuries. Many archeological sites exist here, but stone houses are more famous 4-Durango and the Silverton Narrow Gauge Railway, with old buildings, which is among main tourist attractions in summers of Colorado. The trail starts from a valley in Durango, and goes on until mountainous Silverton city which once was settled by miners 5-Aspen city and the ski resort nearby. 6-Dinosaur National Monument, a site for exhibiting dinosaur fossils which once lived here 7-Glenwood Springs, with medical uses. These, along other attractions, shape the tourism sector in Colorado. 1-John Rogers Searle, prominent philosopher 2-Talcott Parsons, sociologist 3-Florence Rena Sabin One of the pioneering women in medicine and a medical scientist 4-Kent Rominger, former American astronaut, NASA chief for a while in Johnson Space Center. He holds the Space Shuttle Orbiter flight time record with 1610 hours 5- Lawrence Henry Gipson, historian and winner of Bancroft (1950) and Pulitzer (1962) prizes, are among famous people from Colorado.

Since 1876 (the year Colorado joined the U.S as a state) to 2021, 37 presidential elections have been held in the US, and Colorado has taken part all of them, resulting in 22 Republican Party victories, 14 Democratic wins and a win for Populist Party. As it could be observed, Republican Party has an edge in the issue, and from 1968 to 2004, Democrats only won 1992 election, and other 9 races were gained by Republicans, but since 2008 Democratic Party's star began to bright, and all 4 recent contests were won by Democrats. In the 2020 Democratic Party primaries in Colorado, Bernie Sanders became winner, winning 37% of votes and surpassed his closest rival, Joe Biden who got 24.7% of the votes. In the 2020 Republican Party presidential primaries in Colorado, Donald Trump elected by gaining 92.3% of the votes, defeating Bill Weld who won 3.6%.Finally, the 2020 presidential elections in Colorado saw a victory for Democratic candidate, Joseph Biden. Biden won 55.4 % of votes while her Republican rival Donald Trump took 41.9%. Biden gained 9 electoral votes of the state.

From 1876 (the year first U.S Senate election was held in the state) to 2021, 37 U.S Senators have been elected to represent Colorado in the U.S Senate. 19 of them were Republicans and 16 were from Democratic Party, and 2 senators had multiple political affiliations during their careers, of which one served as Democrat and Republican and one switched sides among Democrats, Republicans and Silver Republican Party. As it could be observed, Number of those senators who served only as Republican Party members from Colorado, in addition to those who experienced membership in other parties during their careers, was 21. The same number for Democrats is 18, showing slight superiority of Republicans in the issue. But recent years have witnessed stronger performance by Democrats, and currently now (2021), Michael Farrand Bennet and John Wright Hickenlooper Jr, both from Democratic Party and Represent the state in U.S Senate.

Henry Moore Teller (service years 1876-1882 and 1888-1902, 20 years) from Republican, Democratic and Silver Republican parties, Edwin Carl Johnson (with an 18-year record of service, 1937-1955), a Democrat, and Gordon Llewellyn Allott (service years 1955-1973), a Republican with an 18-year record of presence in the U.S Senate, have been longest-serving U.S senators in the history of Colorado. Since conduction of First elections to send Colorado representatives to U.S House of representatives in 1877, 73 persons have been elected to serve in the position. 38 were Republicans, 32 were Democrats, 2 were members of Populist Party from Colorado, and a representative who experienced membership in Republican, Democrat and Silver Republican parties was able to enter the House.

As the statistics show, Number of those House representatives who served only as Republicans during their careers, in addition to those who experienced membership in other parties, was 39, and the same number for Democrats is 33, showing an edge for Republicans in the history of the U.S House of representatives' elections in Colorado. currently (2021), 4 out of 7 House representatives who have seats from Colorado are Democrats, while 3 seats are held by Republican Party members, indicating a tense competition.

Jared Schutz Polis, current governor of Colorado (a Democrat), is the 43rd governor in the history of the state, but number of those persons who acted as governor of Colorado was 38. The 5-number difference here is due to that 3 governors gained the seat in 2 non-continuous terms and a governor held the post in 3 non-continuous terms. Since 1876, 28 persons have served as governor of Colorado and among them 20 were Democrats, 17 were Republicans and one was a member of Populist Party. As It's clear, Democrats have been superior in the issue, and also have worked better in recent decades. Since 2007, all 3 recent governors have been members of Democratic Party, and a better inspection shows that since 1975 only a Republican governor has served for 8 years and in the other years Democratic governors have held the post.

Conclusion: Noting that Republicans have won 22 U.S presidential elections in Colorado (Democrats won 14 contests including 4 recent elections), and had 21 U.S senators and 39 House representatives (the numbers for Democratic Party are 18 and 33) , while both U.S Senators representing the state and 4 out of 7 House seats belonging to the state are being held by Democrats (vs 3 Republicans) , and during the history of gubernatorial elections in the state Democrats had 20 governors (Republicans had 17) including 3 recent ones , it could be said the Colorado has been a Republican state through most of its history , but today , Democratic Party is more popular among the voters in the state.

North Dakota

North Dakota state and its capital, Bismarck are located in the American Midwest, neighboring Canada. The state was initially a part of Dakota territory, and joined the U.S as its 39th state on 2 November 1889. Dakota means "friends" in some Native American languages, and also is the name of an Indian tribe, and the state is one of the major settlements of the Native American people in the U.S. According to the last census, North Dakota had a population of 762062 inhabitants, of which 83.7% were whites, 5.6% were Native Americans and Alaskans, 4.1% were Latinos, 3.4% were blacks, 1.7% were Asians, 0.1% were Hawaiians and other Pacific islanders, and the rest 2.3% were from other races and ethnicities. University of North Dakota, North Dakota State University, University of Jamestown and Dickinson State University are among scientific and education centers in the state. Because of its fertile soil, North Dakota has a strong agriculture sector. Wheat, barley, oil seeds, beans, lentils, peas, sunflower seed, flaxseed, sugar beet, potatoes, honey, dairy products, cow, sheep, pork and turkey are among agricultural and livestock products of North Dakota. Generally, North Dakota is among top states of the U.S in agriculture. In addition to shale gas, North Dakota has large oil, coal and lignite coal reservoirs, and after Texas, ranks 2nd in production of oil among the U.S states. These companies have their headquarters in this state: 1. Scheels all sports, 2. Ics construction company, 3. Basin electric power cooperative, 4. Forum communications company. Among tourist destinations in the state, these could be named: 1-Theodore Roosevelt

National Park. Visitors can reach here on foots or by cars 2-National Buffalo Museum, a park which contains one of the largest centers for preservation of American bison's in the world 3- Knife River Indian Villages National Historic Site which consists of a number of traditional Native American villages. 4- Fort Abraham Lincoln State Park, a former military fort 4- Lake Sakakawea, with a 1500-mile coastline 5- Maah Daah Hey Trail, a beautiful area, suitable for walking, hiking and cycling 6- Children's Museum at Yunker Farm, with amusement equipment in an open area, a trail for walking through the nature and educational gardens 8- Plains Art Museum. These destinations shape the tourism sector in North Dakota. 1- Larry Alfred Woiwode, author 2- James Frederick Buchli , NASA astronaut 3- Josh Duhame , Hollywood actor, are among famous people from North Dakota. Since 1892 (the year first U.S presidential election was held in North Dakota) to 2021, the state has taken part in 33 U.S presidential elections, of which Republican Party scored 27 victories, Democratic Party gained 5 wins, and 1892 election witnessed a split of electoral votes among candidates from Republican, Democratic and People's parties.

As we can see, the Republicans of North Dakota are by far the most dominant in the history of this election, and they have done well in recent decades. And from 1940 to 2020, when 21 of these elections were held, except for the 1964 elections, they won the remaining 20 elections. If we want to take a closer look, we see that the 1964 election was the last victory of the Democrats, and since 1968 the Republicans have won all 14 recent elections. In 2020 Republican Party presidential caucuses in North Dakota, Donald Trump emerged victorious without any rivals.

In the 2020 Democratic Party presidential caucuses in North Dakota, Bernie Sanders won the candidacy by gaining 53.3% of the votes, while his closest rival, Joe Biden, got 39.8%.

It's worth noting that initial inter-party elections for choosing the presidential candidate in North Dakota are held in caucuses method. Finally, the 2020 U.S presidential election in North Dakota witnessed a victory for Republican Party candidate, Donald Trump, who got 65.1% of the votes, while Democratic candidate, Joe Biden got 31.8%. All 3 electoral votes from North Dakota were added to the Trump's vote basket. From 1889(the year first U. S Senate election was held in North Dakota) to 2021, the state has sent 24 senators to the U. S Senate.15

were Republicans and 9 were Democrats. It's clear that Republicans have an upper hand in the issue. Currently (2021), both U.S senators representing the state in the U.S Senate, Kevin John Cramer and John Henry Hoeven III, are members of Republican Party.

Milton Ruben Young (with a 36-year record of presence in the U.S Senate, 1945-1981) from Republican Party and Quentin Northrup Burdick (with a 32-year record of service, 1960-1992), a Democrat, have been longest-serving U.S senators in history of North Dakota.

Since 1889 (the year first representative from North Dakota entered the U.S House of representatives), to 2021, 30 elected candidates have entered the U.S House of representatives as representatives from North Dakota. 24 were Republicans, 5 were Democrats, and a representative experienced membership in Nonpartisan League and Republican Party.

As the statistics show, Number of those House representatives who served only as Republicans during their careers, in addition to those who experienced membership in other parties, was 25, and the same number for Democrats is 5, showing a clear edge for Republicans in the history of the U.S House of representatives' elections in North Dakota. Republicans have worked quite good during recent years in the issue, and since 2011, the single seat representing the state in the House has remained in their hands.

Douglas James Burgum, current governor of North Dakota (a Republican), is the 33rd governor in the history of the state, but number of those persons who acted as governor of North Dakota was 32. The 1 number difference here is due to that a governor, William Langer, gained the seat in 2 non-continuous terms, and acted as the 17th and 21st governor of the state.

Since 1889 (the year North Dakota joined the U.S as its 39th state) to 2021, 32 persons have served as governors of the state. Among these 32 governors, 25 were Republicans, 6 were Democrats, and one was a member of People's Party. This shows an upper hand for Republicans in the issue. since 1889 to 1935 only one Democratic governor was able the gain the post. The trend has continued in recent decades, and since 1992 all recent governors of North Dakota have been members of Republican PaConclusion : Noting that Republicans have won 27 U.S presidential elections in North Dakota (Democrats won 5) and had an excellent performance during the recent decades in this issue , winning all 14 recent contests , and had 15 U.S senators , 25 House representatives and 25 governors (the numbers for Democratic Party are 9 , 5 and 6) , while both U.S senators and the single representative representing the state , along with the governor of the state are also Republicans , it could be said that North Dakota has been a Republican bastion through its history , acting as a dam against Democratic Party influence.

South Dakota

S outh Dakota state, which its name reminds one of the famous Mount Rushmore Monument in memory of four prominent U.S. presidents, is an American Midwest state, and Pierre city is its capital. Dakota means "friends" in some Native American languages, and also is the name of an Indian tribe. The state was initially a part of Dakota territory, and joined the U.S. on 2 November 1889 as its 40th state. In 1890, tragic incident of Wounded Knee Massacre, which resulted in the merciless killing of the Native American Lakota tribe members, took place in the state. Federal soldiers attacked Pine Ridge Indian Reservation, which was home to Lakota tribe. The attack ended in chaos and skirmishes and during the fighting, about 150 to 300 residents of the camp were killed, nearly half of them women and children. Some reports spoke about firing by mistake by the soldiers, but at least 20 soldiers who took part in the killing later received medals of honor from the U.S. government. According to the last census, South Dakota had a population of 884,659 inhabitants. Demographic composition of the state can be seen in these numbers: 81.5% of the population was white, 9% were Native Indians and Alaskans ,4.2% were Latinos, 2.3% were blacks, 1.5% were Asians, 0.1% were Hawaiians and people from other Pacific islands, and the rest 2.5% were from other races and ethnicities. The University of South Dakota, South Dakota State University, Augustana University and Dakota Wesleyan University are among education and scientific centers in the state. Wheat, corns, soybean, flaxseed, alfalfa, rye, cows, pork, lamb, chicken, fishes and dairy products are among agricultural and livestock products of South Dakota. Wood products, electrical devices light machinery, extraction and production of gold, cement, sand and gravel are among main industries in the state. 1- SANFORD HEALTH and AVERA HEALTH (providing health services) 2-Black Hills Energy (electric and gas utility) 3-WELLMARK (insurance) are companies which have headquarters in South Dakota. Among tourist destinations in the state , these could be named : 1-Mount Rushmore National Monument , where relic faces of George Washington , Thomas Jefferson , Abraham Lincoln and Theodor Roosevelt have been carved into the rocks 2-Badlands National Park , made of clay and sand 3-Wind Cave National Park , which contains one of the largest karstic cave systems in the world 4-Mammoth Site , where numerous Mammoth fossils are found and now exhibited 5-Deadwood city and beautiful nature nearby , along with Mount Moriah cemetery , where people like Wild Bill Hickok and Calamity Jane are buried , and some other historical buildings 6-Spearfish Canyon , an area with forests , stunning waterfalls and rock walls 7-National Music Museum, where thousands of American , European and non-Western music instruments are kept and exhibited 8-Good Earth State Park at Blood Run , exhibiting history and lifestyle of Native American people for thousands of years 9-The Old Courthouse Museum in Sioux Falls , which shows history of the city and the state , dating back to 1800. These, along other attractions, shape the tourism sector in South Dakota.

1-Crazy Horse and Sitting Bull, native American tribal chiefs 2-Tom Brokaw, author, journalist and news anchor 3-Ernest Orlando Lawrence, physicist and Nobel prize winner 4-Russell Charles Means, writer, Native American rights activist, political activist and actor, are among famous people from South Dakota.

Since 1892 (the year first U. S presidential election was held in the state) to now (2021), 33 presidential elections have been held in the U. S, and south Dakota has taken part in all of them. Republicans won 28 of them, Democratic Party had 4 victories and Progressive Party scored a single win.

To have a better inspection, the history of U.S. presidential elections in South Dakota could be divided into 2 different parts. The first period, from 1892 to 1936, witnessed 12 contests, in which Republicans won 8 elections, Democrats gained 3 victories and Progressive Party scored a single win. Second period, from 1940 to 2020, saw 21 rounds of elections, and Republicans won 20 of them, while Democratic Party gained a single win (1964 election). A better inspection shows that Republicans have been sole winners of all 14 contests since 1968.

The statistics show that the Republican Party has an upper hand in the issue.

In the 2020 Republican Party presidential primaries in South Dakota, Donald Trump emerged victorious without any rivals. In the 2020 Democratic Party presidential primaries in South Dakota, Joe Biden won the candidacy by gaining 77.5% of the votes, while his closest rival, Bernie Sanders, got 22.5%.

Finally, the 2020 U.S. presidential election in South Dakota witnessed a victory for Republican candidate, Donald Trump, who won 61.8% of the votes, while his Democratic rival, Joseph Biden, got 35.6%. Trump won all 3 electoral votes from South Dakota.

From 1889 (the date first U.S Senate election was held in the state) to 2021, 27 elected candidates from South Dakota have served in the U.S Senate, of which 18 were Republicans, 7 were Democrats, and 2 senators changed their political affiliations during their careers, of which one acted as Republican and Silver Republican, and a U.S senator served as independent candidate, Republican, and member of People's Party. As it could be observed, Number of those senators who served only as Republican Party members from Maine, in addition to those who experienced membership in other parties during their careers, was 20. The same number for Democrats is 7, showing superiority of Republicans in the issue. Republicans also had a strong performance in recent years, and currently (2021), John Randolph Thune along with Marion Michael Rounds, both Republicans, represent South Dakota in the U.S Senate. Karl Earl Mundt from the Republican Party with 25 years of experience in the Senate from 1948-1973, he was the most experienced senator in the history of this state. Since 1889, 37 elected candidates have entered the U.S House of representatives as representatives from South Dakota. 26 were Republicans, 9 were Democrats, and 2 were members of Populist Party (also known as People's Party).

As it could be seen, Republicans have an upper hand in the history of U.S House of representatives' elections in South Dakota, and currently (2021) the single seat belonging to the state in the house is held by them. Kristi Lynn Noem the current governor of South Dakota from the Republican Party is the 33rd governor of this state. But the total number of people who served in this position was 32, and the reason for this difference is that one of these governors, William John Janklow, reached this position in two non-consecutive terms. He has twice been registered separately as the 27th and 37th governor and our statistics are not based on the number of courses, but on the number of people who have reached this position. Since 1889 (the year South Dakota joined the U.S as its 40th state), 32 persons have served as governor of South Dakota. It's clear that Republicans have been superior in the issue, and since 1979 all governors in the state have been members of their party.

Conclusion: Given that Republicans winning 28 rounds in South Dakota are ahead of Democrats with 4 rounds. And they have excelled in recent decades, winning all 14 of these elections. And throughout the history of Senate, House and Governor elections, Republicans with 20 senators, 26 representatives and 26 governors, are ahead of Democrats with seven senators, nine representatives and five governors and they have done better in recent years, and both senators and the representative and current governor are Republicans. It can be concluded that South Dakota, like its northern neighbor, has historically been a reliable base for Republicans and is now a highly Republican state.

Montana

Montana state and its capital, Helena, are well known for natural glaciers and resources, and are located in northwestern part of the U.S. Once known as Montana territory, Montana joined the U.S as its 41st state on 8 November 1889. Montana is a main center for breeding of Mustang horse. During its modern history, Montana witnessed several wars between white settlers and Native American tribes who were the original inhabitants of the area, including: Great Sioux War and Battle of the Little Bighorn. Sioux was a large Native American tribe. According to the last census, population of Montana was 1.068.778, showing its demography as follow: 85.9% white, 6.7% native American and Alaskan, 4.1% Latino, 0.9% Asian, 0.6% black, 0.1% Hawaiian and other Pacific islanders and 2.8% others. Montana State University, University of Montana, Carroll College and Montana Technological University are among scientific and education centers in the state. Agriculture and animal husbandry in Montana are among the best in the U.S. Wheat, barley, lentil, flaxseed, sugar beet, alfalfa, potatoes, timber, dairy products, cow, beef and lamb are among main agricultural and livestock products of the state. Montana is also among main producers of beer, especially barrel beer. Extraction and production of gold, silver, copper, lead, coal, vermiculite, talc, palladium, platinum and oil are among mineral industry sectors of Montana. Some large corporations like: 1-GLACIER BANCORP (providing financial services) 2-Town Pump (chain of truck stops, gas stations, casinos, hotels and convenience stores) 3-FRINGE BENEFIT RESOURCES (insurance services) have headquarters in Montana.

Among tourist attractions in Montana , these could be pointed out : 1-Glacier National Park , with natural glaciers and beautiful waterfalls 2-Big Sky Resort , one of the largest ski resorts in the U.S , along many restaurants and amusements 3-Gray wolf at the Grizzly and Wolf Discovery Center , a place for watching life of wolves closely 4-Lewis and Clark Caverns State Park , containing one of the most complex network caves in the U.S 5-The World Museum of Mining , with underground mine tours 6-The C.M. Russell Museum Complex , in memory of this American writer and artist , known as "The Cowboy Artist" 7-Museum of the Rockies , which is actually a dinosaur fossil museum 8- Little Bighorn Battlefield was the site of a bloody war in 1876 between the United States Army and the Native Americans. 9-Yellowstone National Park. Norris Geyser Basin is the hottest, oldest and most dynamic thermal part of Yellowstone. These, along other tourist destinations, form the tourist sector in Montana.

1-Phillip Bradley Bird, producer, director, playwright and animator 2-William Everett Luckey, singer, musician, instrumentalist, caricaturist and animator 3-Charles Marion Russell, painter and artist 4-Dorothy Baker, novelist and Nobel Prize winner 5-Plenty Coups, Native American chieftain, are among famous people from Montana. From 1892 to 2020, 33 US presidential elections were held in Montana, of which Republicans won 22 rounds and Democrats winning 11 rounds of electoral votes. For a better inspection, history of presidential elections in Montana could be divided into 2 parts. First part, from 1892 to 1948, witnessed 15 presidential elections in the state. Democrats gained 9 wins and Republican Party had 6 victories. Second period, from 1952 to 2020, saw 18 elections, and except 1964 and 1992 elections, in which Democrats emerged victorious, Republican Party won other 16 contests. According to the statistics shown above, Republicans have an upper hand in the history of the U.S presidential elections in Montana (they had 22 victories while Democrats had 11 wins), and improved their performance in recent decades, too, winning all 7 recent contests.

The 2020 Republican Party primaries in Montana, witnessed a victory for Donald Trump, who got the candidacy by winning 93.8% of the votes. It's worth noting that 6.2% of the votes (second rank) was occupied by the votes which were written as "No Preference".

In the 2020 Democratic Party presidential primaries in Montana,

Joe Biden won the candidacy by gaining 74.5% of the votes, while his closest rival, Bernie Sanders, got 14.7%.

Finally, the 2020 U.S presidential election in Montana witnessed a victory for Republican candidate, Donald Trump, who won 56.9% of the votes, while his Democratic rival, Joseph Biden, got 40.5%. Trump won all 3 electoral votes from Montana. From 1890 (the year first U.S Senate election was held in Montana) to 2021, 22 elected candidates from the state have served in the U.S Senate, of which 14 were Democrats, 7 were Republicans and a Senator experienced membership in Silver Republican and Republican Party during his career.

As the statistics show, the number of those U.S senators who served as members of Republican Party, in addition to the U.S senators who also served as a Silver Republican was 8, and number of those senators who only served as Democrats was 14, showing an edge for Democratic Party in the issue. Recent years have seen a closer race among the 2 main parties, and currently, Steven David Daines (a Republican) and Raymond Jon Tester (a Democrat) represent the state in the U.S Senate.

Maxwell Sieben Baucus, with a 36-year record of presence in the U.S Senate (1978-2014) and James Edward Murray, with 27-year history of serving in the Senate (1934-1961), both Democrats, were longest-serving U.S Senators from Montana.

From 1889 to 2021, 36 persons have represented Montana in the U.S House of representatives, of which 19 were members of Republican Party, 15 were Democrats, one was a member of People's Party, and a representative served as member of Republican and Silver Republican parties.

As the statistics show, those representatives from Montana who remained Republican during their entire serving record in the House, in addition to those who experienced membership in other parties, were 20 persons, and the same number for Democratic Party is 15. This shows that historically, Republican Party had a better performance in the U.S House of representative elections in the state. But looking at the number of service years, representatives from both parties each have about 105 to 107 years of service, nearly tied in the race for the U.S House. Currently (2021), a Republican represents Montana in the U.S House of representatives.

Gregory Richard Gianforte, current governor of the state (a

Republican), is actually 25th governor of Montana. But number of h the persons who served in the post was 24. the 1 number difference here is due to a governor, Joseph Kemp Toole, gained the seat in 2 non-continuous terms, and served as 1st and 4th governor of Montana.

Since 1889 (the year Montana joined the U.S as its 41st state) to now (2021), 24 persons have served as governor of Montana. Among these 24 governors, 13 were Democrats, 10 were Republicans and one served as member of Democratic and People's parties.

As it could be seen, number of those governors who only served as Democrats, in addition to the governor who also experienced membership in People's Party, was 14. Republicans had 10 governors, showing an upper hand in the issue. But as mentioned above, current governor is a Republican.

Conclusion: Given that Montana Republicans winning 22 rounds are ahead of Democrats with 11 rounds winning the last 7 rounds. Throughout the history of Senate elections, Democrats with 14 senators are ahead of Republicans with 8 senators. And the two current senators in the state are one Democrat and one Republican, and throughout the history of the House of Representatives, Republicans with 20 seats are ahead of the Democrats with 15 seats. And the only current representative in the state is a Republican. Throughout the history of governorship elections, Democrats with 14 governors are ahead of Republicans with 10 governors. However, the current governor of the state is a Republican. It can be concluded that throughout the history of elections, this state had a tendency towards Republicans and now it is a state with a strong tendency towards Republicans.

Washington

Washington state and its capital, Olympia, are located in northwestern part of the U.S. The state was initially a part of Washington territory, and joined the U.S as its 42nd state on 11 November 1889. The state was named in memory of George Washington; 1st president of the U.S. Seattle is the most important city in the state. Name of the state shouldn't be confused with Washington D.C, capital city of the U.S. The state was first place to host the well-known STARBUCKS chain cafe. According to the last census, Washington had a population of 7614893 inhabitants, of which 67.5% were whites, 13. % were Latinos, 9.6% were Asians, 4.4% were blacks, 1.9% were Native Americans and Alaskans, 0.8% were Hawaiians and other Pacific islanders, and 4.9% were from other races and ethnicities.

University of Washington, Gonzaga University, Seattle University, Washington State University and Pacific Northwest National Laboratory (also known as PNNL) are among scientific and education centers in the state. St. Helens volcano is also located in the state. Washington is the largest producer of Apple and red raspberries in the U.S. Grape, pear, cherry, wheat, barley, corn, potato, mint, alfalfa, peas, lentil, eggs, dairy products, flour, cow, beef, fishes, oyster and lobster are among main agricultural and livestock products of the state. Manufacturing aircrafts and other aerospace products, ships, electronic and computer parts, communication and wireless equipment, medical equipment, navigation tools, timber and products related to timber industry like: paper, plywood, coal, cement, broken stones, gold, silver, sand and gravel are among main industries in Washington. Generally, Washington has a strong and diverse economy, and some large corporations like

:1- Amazon 2- MICROSOFT 3- COSTCO WHOLESALE (chain store) 4- T-MOBILE (communications company) 5- NORDSTROM (chain store) 6- STARBUCKS (chain cafe) have headquarters in the state. Among tourist destinations in the state , these could be named : 1- Seattle Center (education-cultural-entertainment center) in Seattle city , containing the famous Space Needle tower 2- San Juan Islands , with numerous seafood restaurants along with Island National Historic Park , site of the Pig War which was fought between the British and the U.S forces because of border disputes 3- Seattle Downtown , with its pier , market , and different amusements 4- Leavenworth city , a Bavarian settlement 5- North Cascades National Park , an untamed area for touring nature and fishing 6- Olympic National Park , with its stunning nature and a good place for walking , cycling , golf , boating and fishing 7- Japanese Gardens, Manito Park , as its clear from the name , a Japanese-style garden 8- Boeing Factory, located north of Seattle in Everett , where some parts of assembling the aircrafts is observable for those interested 9- Whatcom Falls Park , with suitable walking trails 10- Ebey's Landing Historical Park , located in Whidbey Island 11- Olympic Flight Museum . These, along many other tourist attractions, form the tourist sector in Washington.

Bill gates, one of the main founders of Microsoft corporation, Chris Cornell (Rock musician), Michael Andrew McKagan (Bass Guitar instrumentalist) are among famous people from Washington.

Since 1892 (the date first U.S presidential election was held in Washington) to 2020, 33 rounds of U.S presidential elections have been held in the state. Of these contests, Democratic Party won 18 times, Republicans had 14 victories, and Progressive Party was able to gain a single victory.

To have a better inspection, the history of U.S presidential elections in Washington could be divided into 3 different parts. The first period, from 1892 to 1948, witnessed 15 contests, in which Democrats gained 7 victories, Republicans Party scored 7 victories, and Progressives were able to win a single contest.

Second period, from 1952 to 1984, saw 9 rounds of elections, and Republicans won 7 of them, And Democrats were able to gain 2 victories. This part could be named as the Republican period. In the third period, from 1988 to 2020, 9 rounds of U.S. presidential elections were held in the state, and Democratic Party won all of them. This period could be named the Democratic Party era. Voters in Washington began to shift their favor towards Democratic Party in the U.S presidential elections since 1988 and the trend has been going on until now (2021).

In the 2020 Democratic presidential primaries in Washington, Joe Biden won the candidacy through winning 38% of the votes, while his closest rival, Bernie Sanders, took 36.6%.

In the 2020 Republican Party presidential primaries in Washington, Donald Trump elected by gaining 98% of the votes, and second rank belonged to the votes which " WRITE-INS" was written on them, meaning people other than registered candidates.

Finally, the 2020 U.S presidential election in Washington witnessed a victory for Democratic Party candidate, Joe Biden, who got 58% of the votes, while Republican candidate, Donald Trump got 38.8%. All 12 electoral votes from Washington were added to the Bidens's vote basket.

From 1889 (the year first U.S Senate election was held in the state) to 2021, the state has sent 23 senators to the U.S Senate. 12 were Republicans and 11 were Democrats, of which one of them, George Turner, entered the U.S senate through a coalition of Democrats, Silver Republicans and People's Party.

As it could be seen, in the first look, Republicans have an upper hand in the history of the U.S senate elections in Washington (12 U.S senators vs 11 for Democrats), but the number of the service years of the Democratic senators was 130, while the same number for Republicans is 100. Democrats also have worked better in recent decades, and one of the U.S Senate seats belonging to the Washington has been held by them since 1987, and the other one since 2001.

Patricia Lynn Murray and Maria Ellen Cantwell, both Democrats, currently represent Washington in the U.S Senate.

Warren Grant Magnuson with 37 years of experience in the Senate (1944-1981) and Henry Martin Jackson with 30 years of experience in the Senate (1953-1983) both democrats are the most experienced senators of this state. Since 1889 (the year first U.S House of representatives' election was held in the state), to 2021, 85 elected candidates have entered the U.S House of representatives as representatives from Washington. 42 were Republicans, 40 were Democrats, 2 were Progressives, and one was a Silver Republican.

As the statistics show, just like the U.S Senate elections, in the first look, it seems that Republicans have an edge in the issue (42 representatives' vs 40 for Democratic Party). But number of service years for Democratic representatives is 560, while the same number for Republican Party is nearly 460, showing superiority of Democrats in the issue. Currently (2021), 7 out of 10 representatives representing Washington in the House are Democrats, and 3 are members of Republican Party.

Jay Robert Inslee, current governor of Washington (a Democrat), is the 23rd governor in the history of the state, but number of those persons who acted as governor of Washington was 22. The single number difference here is due to that a governor, Arthur Bernard Langlie, gained the seat in 2 non-continuous terms, and served as 12th and 14th governor of the state in separate terms.

Since 1889 (the year Washington joined the U.S as its 42nd state) to 2021, 22 persons have served as governor of Washington. Among these 22 governors, 11 were Republicans, 10 were Democrats and a governor, John Rankin Rogers, experienced membership in Democratic and People's parties during his career.

As the statistics show, the number of those governors who only served as Democrats, in addition to John Rankin Rogers, who along his membership in Democratic Party also served as member of People's Party, was 11, the same number for Republicans. But number of service years for Democratic governors was 68, while the same number for Republicans is 62, showing a slight upper hand for Democrats in the issue. But all 5 recent governors of Washington (since 1985) have been members of Democratic Party, which indicates strong popularity of Democrats in the state during recent decades.

Conclusion: Given that Democrats in Washington winning 18 rounds throughout the history of the presidential election are ahead of Republicans with 14 rounds and it has done better in recent decades and won the electoral votes of the last 9 rounds of election. Democrats throughout the history of Senate, House and Governor elections with 11 senators, 40 representatives and 11 governors vs. Republicans with 12 senators, 42 representatives and 11 governors and considering that in all three sections, the number of rounds and years of Democratic senators, representatives, and governors in power has been greater than that of Republicans. Moreover, both senators of the state are Democrats and of the state's 10 representatives in the US House of Representatives, seven are Democrats and three are Republicans and finally, all five recent governors were Democratic. It can be concluded that Washington State has historically been more in favor of Democratic party and is now mostly a Democratic state.

Idaho

Idaho state and its capital, Boise, are located in northwestern
America. By signing the Oregon treaty, Idaho officially became a
U.S territory in 1846. Since 1863, the area was administrated as
Idaho territory, and finally joined the U.S on 3 July 1890 as its 43rd
state. Name of the state comes from the Shoshone language (a Native
American tribe, original inhabitants of the area), taken from "Ee-da-
how" phrase, meaning "calm down, calm down, the Sun comes over
the mountains". According to the last census, population of Idaho
was 1.787.065, showing its demography as follow: 81.6% white, 12.8%
Latino, 1.7% native American and Alaskan ,1.6% Asian, 0.9% black,
0.2% Hawaiian and other Pacific islanders and 2.6% others. University
of Idaho, College of Idaho, Brigham Young University—Idaho, Lewis-
Clark State College and Idaho National Laboratory (national laboratory
belonging to United States Department of Energy) are among education
and scientific centers in Idaho. In 1951 Idaho saw a breakthrough in
electric power industry, and was the site of generating electricity from
nuclear power for the first time in history. Idaho is an agricultural leader
among U.S states. Potatoes, wheat, barley, sugar beets, sunflower seeds,
onion, peas, lentil, bean, mint, different kinds of fruit, cow, beef, lamb,
pork and fish are among main agricultural and livestock products in
the state. Dairy products and wine are also common products in Idaho.
Largest barrel cheese factory of the world, is located in Gooding, Idaho.
Electronical and computer parts, transportation equipment, medical
equipment, chemical and plastic products, timber and metal products,
machinery, producing and assembling aircraft parts, memory chips and

extracting silver are among main industries in the state.

Some large corporation like: 1- J.R. SIMPLOT (producing agricultural and food products) 2- MICRON TECHNOLOGY (manufacturing computer memory and data-saving hardware like flash memories and USBs) 3- BOISE CASCADE (timber products) 4- ALBERTSONS (food products chain store) 5- WINCO FOODS (food products chain store) have headquarters in Idaho.

Among tourist destinations in the state, these could be named: 1- Sun Valley resort, with tele cabin and a ski resort 2- Sawtooth National Recreation Area, with beautiful nature. A good place for fishing, walking and cycling in mountains 3- Lake Coeur d'Alene suitable area for boating and fishing 4- Hell's Canyon National Recreation Area. Deepest river valley in North America is located here. 5- Shoshone Falls, pouring on large rocks 6- Old Idaho Penitentiary State Historic Site. These, along many other parks and mountains, shape the tourism sector in Idaho.

1- Ezra Weston Loomis Pound, controversial American poet 2- Vardis Alvero Fisher, author of Old Western novels 3- Sarah Palin, Republican Party candidate for vice presidency to John McCain in 2008 U.S presidential election, are among famous people from Idaho.

Since 1892 (the year first U.S presidential election was held in Idaho) to 2020, 33 presidential elections have been held in the state. Of these 33 contests, Republican Party won 22 times in the state, Democrats had 10 victories, and People's Party gained a single contest.

To have a better inspection, the history of U.S presidential elections in Idaho could be divided into 2 different parts. The first period, from 1892 to 1964, witnessed 19 contests, in which Democrats gained 10 victories, Republicans scored 8 victories, and People's Party was able to win a single election.

But in the second period, from 1968 to 2020, which saw 14 rounds of elections, situation changed in full favor of Republicans, who won all of contests.

In the 2020 Republican Party presidential primaries in Idaho, Donald Trump was elected by gaining 94.5% of the votes, defeating Bill Weld who got 2.1%. In the 2020 Democratic presidential primaries in Idaho, Joe Biden won the candidacy through winning 48.9% of the votes, while his closest rival, Bernie Sanders, took 42.5%. Finally, the 2020

U.S presidential election in Idaho witnessed a victory for Republican Party candidate, Donald Trump, who got 63.8% of the votes, while Democratic candidate, Joe Biden got 33.1%. All 4 electoral votes from Idaho were added to the Republican Party's vote basket.

From 1890 to 2021, the state has sent 26 senators to the U.S Senate. 17 were Republicans, 8 were Democrats, and 1 was a member of People's Party.

Republican Party has been superior in the history of U.S Senate elections in Idaho, and also had an excellent performance in recent decades: one of the U.S Senate seats belonging to Idaho has been held by them since 1949, and the other seat has been the same since 1981.

James Elroy Risch and Michael Dean Crapo, both Republicans, currently (2021) represent Idaho in the U.S Senate. William Edgar Borah, a Republican, with a 33-year record of presence in the U.S Senate (1907-1940) and Frank Forrester Church III, with a 24-year history of serving (1957-1981) from Democratic Party, have been longest serving U.S Senators in the history of Idaho.

Since 1889 to 2021, 34 elected candidates have entered the U.S House of representatives as representatives from Idaho. 22 were Republicans, 9 were Democrats, 2 were members of People's Party, and a representative changed his political affiliations during his career, serving as Republican and Silver Republican.

As the statistics show, Number of those House representatives who served only as Republicans during their careers, in addition to the representative who also served as a Silver Republican, was 23 and the same number for Democrats is 9, showing an edge for Republicans in the history of the U.S House of representatives' elections in Idaho. Republicans have also worked better in recent decades, and since 1995 to now (2021), except a single representative who was a Democrat, House seats from the state have been held by them. Both current representatives from Idaho in the U.S House of representatives are members of Republican Party.

Bradley Jay Little, current governor of Idaho (a Republican), is the 33rd governor in the history of the state, but number of those persons who acted as governor of Idaho was 31. The 2-number difference here is due to that 2 governors gained the seat in 2 non-continuous terms.

George Laird Shoup was the last governor of Idaho territory who was appointed by the U.S president Benjamin Harrison, and after joining the U.S as its 43rd state, was elected again as the first governor of the state.

Sine 1890, 31 governors have served in Idaho. Among these, 20 were Republicans and 11 were Democrats. It's clear that Republicans have been superior in the issue, and since 1995, all 5 recent governors of Idaho have been members of Republican Party.

Conclusion : Noting that Republicans have won 22 U.S presidential elections in Idaho (Democrats won 10 contests) including 14 recent races , and had 17 U.S senators, 23 House representatives and 20 governors in the history of the state (the numbers for Democratic Party are 8 , 9 and 11) , and both current U.S senators from the state both House representatives and current governor of Idaho (could be said all 5 recent governors) are Republicans , It could be said that Idaho has been a Republican state during most of its history , just like today (2021).

Wyoming

Mountainous state of Wyoming state and its capital, Cheyenne are located in the western part of the U.S. The state is well known for old legends and old Cowboy cities. Before joining the U.S as a state and when it was a U.S territory, Wyoming was the first territory to recognize the women's suffrage in 1869, and on 6 September 1870, Louisa Ann Swain was the first woman to vote in a General election in the U.S in Wyoming. When Wyoming moved towards joining the U.S, the U.S Congress demanded Wyoming to nullify the women's suffrage, but Wyoming officials answered: "We will stay out of the Union a hundred years rather than come in without our women". Congress surrendered on the issue, and finally, on 10 July 1890, Wyoming joined the U.S as its 44th state. According to the last census, Wyoming had a population of 578759 inhabitants. 83.7% of population is white, 10.1% are Latinos, 2.7% are Native Americans and Alaskans, 1.3% are blacks, 1.1 % are Asians, 0.1% are Hawaiians and other Pacific islanders, and 2.2% are from other races and ethnicities. University of Wyoming, Sheridan College and Laramie County Community College are among scientific and education centers in the state. Wheat, barley, sugar beets, alfalfa, bean, bulghur, sunflower seed, cow, beef, milk and other dairy products, and wool are among main agricultural and livestock products in Wyoming. Processed metal products, food products, machinery, plastics and chemical products, timber, computer and electronical products and home appliance are main industry sectors in the state. Wyoming is a rich state in mineral resources, and is the largest producer of coal in the U.S. Largest trona resources in the world are located in the state, and Wyoming contains 3rd largest Uranium resources in the U.S, along with being among top 10 states in producing oil and natural gas. Wyoming also has large limestone, gemstone, iron ore, gold and plaster resources.

Some large corporations like :1-ADMIRAL BEVERAGE (producer of alcoholic and non-alcoholic drinks) 2-CLOUD PEAK ENERGY (coal extraction company) 3-BOARDWALK REAL ESTATE INVESTMENT TRUST (real estate investor) 4-TACO JOHN'S (fast food restaurant chain) have headquarters in Wyoming.

Among tourist attractions in the state , these could be named : 1-Yellowstone National Park , oldest national park in the world , containing deers , Grizzly bears and gray wolves 2-Grand Teton National Park , a combination of mountains and forest 3-Jackson city with wooden houses and amazing shops 4-Hot Springs State Park , with hot natural springs 5-The Buffalo Bill Center of the West, Cody, consisting of 5 museums 6-The Wind River Range and its stunning nature 7-National Historic Trails Interpretive Center , which exhibits history of Wyoming , its native people and early European settlers 8-Fort Laramie National Historic Site , an old military fort 9-Devils Tower National Monument , a stunning tower made of volcano lava remains 10-Old Trail Town , consisted of 26 old houses , belonging to old Cowboy era 11-Grand Targhee Ski Resort . These, along many other attractions, form the tourist sector in the state.

Floyd Taliaferro Alderson, Cinema actor and Edna Ann Proulx, writer and Nobel prize winner, are among famous people from Wyoming.

Since 1892 (the date first U.S presidential election was held in Wyoming), the state has taken part in 33 U.S. presidential elections. Republicans won 25 contests and Democrats had 8 victories. As the statistics show, Republicans have an upper hand in the history of U.S presidential elections in Wyoming, and also worked better in recent decades, winning all 14 contests since 1968, and the last Democratic victory was in 1964 election.

Inter-party elections in Wyoming are held in caucuses method.

In the 2020 Democratic Party caucuses in Wyoming, Joseph Biden won the contest by winning 72.2% of votes, while his closest rival, Bernie Sanders, got 27.8%.

In the 2020 Republican Party caucuses in Wyoming, Donald Trump emerged victorious through anonymous support of the voters.

Finally, the 2020 U.S presidential election in Wyoming witnessed a decisive victory for Republican candidate, Donald Trump, who won 69.9% of the votes, while his Democratic rival, Joe Biden, got 26.6%. Trump won all 3 electoral votes from Wyoming.

From 1890 (the year first U.S Senate election was held in the state) to 2021, 22 elected candidates from Wyoming have served in the U.S Senate, of which 16 were Republicans and 6 were Democrats. It's clear that Republicans have an edge in the issue, and have held their superiority in recent decades: one of the U.S Senate seats belonging to Wyoming in the U.S Senate has been in their hands since 1962, and the other seat has seen the same situation since 1977.

John Anthony Barrasso III and Cynthia Marie Lummis Wiederspahn, both Republicans, currently represent Wyoming in the U.S Senate.

Francis Emroy Warren, a Republican with 37 years of presence in the U.S Senate (1890-1893, 1895-1929) and Joseph Christopher O'Mahoney, a member of Democratic Party with a 26-year record of service (1934-1954, 1954-1961) have been longest-serving U.S senators in the history of Wyoming.

From 1895 (the year first U.S House of representatives' election was held in the state) to 2021, 19 persons have represented Wyoming in the U.S House of representatives, of which 14 were members of Republican Party and 5 were Democrats. Republicans have an upper hand in the issue, and during recent decades also have worked better than Democrats. Since 1979 all House representatives from Wyoming have been members of Republican Party, and Liz Cheney (daughter of Dick Cheney, Vice president in president G.W. Bush administration), the single representative currently representing the state in the House is a Republican. It's worth noting that Dick Cheney himself also once represented the state in the House for 11 years.

From 1890 until today (2021), Wyoming has seen 33 governors, of which 20 were Republicans and 13 were Democrats. As it could be observed, just like the U.S Senate and U.S House of representatives are superior here, and since 2011, both recent governors of Wyoming, including the current governor, Mark Gordon, have been members of Republican Party.

It's worth noting that Francis Emory Warren, who was appointed by president Benjamin Harrison as governors as governor of Wyoming territory, along with the Wyoming representative in the House persisted on keeping the Women's suffrage in Wyoming in face of nullification demand from the U.S Congress. His efforts were fruitful and Wyoming kept women's suffrage after joining the U.S as a state, and Warren was elected as the first governor of the state.

Nellie Davis Tayloe Ross, 14th governor of Wyoming , was the first woman to serve as governor of a state in the U.S.

Conclusion: Noting that Republicans have won 25 U.S presidential elections in Wyoming (Democrats won 8) including 14 recent contests, it's clear they had an upper hand in the history of the U.S presidential elections in the state. Republicans had 16 U.S senators and 14 House representatives and 20 governors in the history of the state (the numbers for Democratic Party are 6, 5 and 13), and both current senators representing Wyoming in the U.S Senate Are Republicans, just like the single representative from the state in the U.S House of representatives and the current governor. So, it could be said that Wyoming has been a Republican stronghold through most of its history, just like today (2021).

Utah

Utah state and its capital, Salt Lake City, are located in western part of the U.S, along Rocky Mountains. Many initial settlers in Utah were American Mormons, who had escaped marginalization and prosecution. Feuds between federal government and Mormon community of Utah postponed acceptance of Utah as a U.S state. Finally, and after illegalizing the polygamy, Utah joined the U.S on 4 January 1896 AS its 45th state. According to the last census, Utah had a population of 3205958 inhabitants, of which 77.8% were whites, 14.4% were Latinos ,2.7% were Asians, 1.6% were Native Americans and Alaskans, 1.5% were blacks, 1.1% were Hawaiians and other Pacific islanders, and 2.6% were from other races and ethnicities. Nearly 63% of the population in the state is Mormon (a Christian sect), making Utah the most homogenous state in religious affiliation of the inhabitants. Brigham Young University—Provo, University of Utah, Utah State University (Ardeshir Zahedi, former foreign minister of Iran before the 1979 Revolution graduated here) and Westminster College are among scientific and education centers in the state. Wheat, barley, corn, potatoes, onion, dry bean, apple, cherry, peach, apricot, pear, container plants and ornamental trees, alfalfa, mushrooms, cow, lamb, pork, turkey, fishes, dairy products, specially milk, honey and wool are among main agricultural and livestock products in Utah. Computer and electronic parts, communication equipment, microchips and scientific tools, oil extraction, natural gas, copper, magnesium, potassium, sand and gravel, clay, gemstone and salt are main industrial sectors and products in the state. Some large corporations like: 1-ALSCO (linen and uniform-rental business service provider to restaurants, health care organizations, the automotive industry and industrial facilities) 2-VIVINT SMART HOME (public smart home company in the United States and Canada) 3-SKYWEST AIRLINES have headquarters in Utah.

Among tourist destinations in the state , these could be named : 1-Arches National Park with stone arches and sand hills 2-Monument Valley , many films and advertising clips have been filmed here 3-Canyonlands National Park , its most beautiful part is Mesa Arch , a large rock arch 4-Zion National Park , with high rocky mountains and deep verdurous valleys 5-Bryce Canyon National Park , with stone columns which shape a stunning and magical view 6-Salt Lake City Mormon Temple , built 1853-1893 7-Park City and nearby Ski Resorts , the Park City is actually a beautiful city and a good place for ski , host to Sundance Film Festival 8-Grand Staircase-Escalante National Monument , a vast area of rigged land including valleys , arches , hills , waterfalls , forests and marshes 9-Coral Pink Sand Dunes State Park , with its sand hills 10-Park City Historic Main Street. These, along many other destinations, shape the tourism sector in Utah.

Among famous people from Utah, these could be pointed: 1-Virginia Louise Sorensen, winner of Newberry Medal in 1957, for his famous children novel, Miracles on Maple Hill 2-Avard Tennyson Fairbanks, Sculptor who built 10 sculpture and monuments of Abraham Lincoln, including famous ones in Supreme Court building and Ford theater museum 3-Alma Wilford Richards, American athlete and first Olympic Medal winner from Utah 4-Dr. Lloyd Miller, He is known as "Koroush Ali Khan" among Iranians. A musician and Jazz and world music instrumentalist, well-known for his researches on traditional music of Iran and Afghanistan. He was eager to learn about music in both western and eastern cultures. Before him, his mother received a medal of honor from Mohammad Reza Pahlavi, former Shah of Iran, for her book, " Bright Blue Beads". The book aimed to introduce Iranian culture and civilization to the world.

Utah could be divided into 2 different parts. The first period, from 1896 to 1948, witnessed 14 contests, in which Democrats and Republicans each gained 7 contests. Second period, from 1952 to 2020, saw 18 rounds of elections and Republicans won 17 of them, while Democratic Party gained a single win in 1964 and after that all next 14 elections were won by Republican

Since 1896 (the year first U.S presidential election was held in the state) to 2020, Utah has taken part in all 32 U.S presidential elections held in the country. Republicans won 24 rounds and Democratic Party scored 8 victories. To have a better inspection, the history of U.S presidential elections in

Party. These numbers show that Utah voters have a strong sympathy towards Republicans and the Party has an upper hand in the history of U.S presidential elections in the state.

The 2020 Republican Party primaries in Utah, witnessed a victory for Donald Trump, who got the candidacy by winning 87.8% of the votes, while his closest rival, Bill Weld, got 6.9% of the votes.

In the 2020 Democratic Party presidential primaries in Utah, Bernie Sanders won by gaining 36.1% of the votes, while his closest rival, Joe Biden, got 18.4%.

Finally, the 2020 U.S presidential election in Utah witnessed a victory for Republican candidate, Donald Trump, who won 58.1% of the votes, while his Democratic rival, Joe Biden, got 37.6%. Trump won all 6 electoral votes from Utah. From 1896 (the date first U.S Senate election was held in Utah) to 2021, 17 elected candidates from the state have served in the U.S Senate, of which 12 were Republicans and 5 were Democrats. According to the statistics, Republican party has an edge in the issue, and last Democratic U.S senator from Utah, Frank Edward Moss, served 1955-1977, and since then all U.S senators representing Utah have been Republicans. Mitt Romney and Michael Shumway Lee, both Republicans, currently represent Utah in the U.S Senate.

Orrin Grant Hatch (with a 42-year record of presence in the U.S Senate, 1977-2019) and Reed Smoot (with a 30-year record of service, 1903-1933), both Republicans Republican, have been longest-serving U.S senators in history of Utah. From 1789 (the year first U.S House of representatives' election was held in the state) to 2021, 42 elected candidates have entered the U.S House of representatives as representatives from Utah. 26 were Republicans and 16 were Democrats. Republicans have been superior in the history of the U.S House of representatives' elections in Utah, and all 4 current House representatives from the state are Republicans. It's worth noting that Brigham Henry Roberts, an elected candidate from Utah wasn't able to enter the House because of being married to several women (polygamy).

Since 1896 (the Utah joined the U.S as its 45th state) to 2021, 18 persons have served as governors of Utah. Among these 12 were members of Republican Party and 6 were Democrats. Before 1985, both parties had governors in a repeated cycle, but after 1985 gubernatorial election, all 6 recent governors have been Republicans, including

Spencer James Cox, current governor of the state.

Conclusion: Noting that Republicans have won 24 U.S presidential elections in Utah including 14 recent contests (Democrats gained 8 victories), It's clear they had an upper hand in the history of the U.S presidential elections in the state. Republicans had 12 U.S senators , 26 House representatives in the history of the state and 12 governors (the numbers for Democratic Party are 5 , 15 and 6) , and both current senators representing Utah in the U.S Senate are Republicans and all 4 House seats belonging to the state are being held by them , also the current governor of the state is a member of Republican Party , it could be concluded that Utah has been a Democratic Party bastion during most of its history ,and the situation is not different today (2021

Oklahoma

Oklahoma state and its capital, Oklahoma City are located in South Central U.S. Oklahoma state was formed through merging of Oklahoma territory and Indian Territory, and joined the U.S as its 46th state on 16 November 1907. Actually, the nowadays state of Oklahoma was a part of the lands which were bought from the French government in the famous deal called "Louisiana purchase" in 1803 under president Thomas Jefferson administration. But before the forming of the state, the Congress ratified the "Indian Removal Act" in 1830, which forced Eastern Woodlands Indian tribes to migrate to "Indian Territory", which today is a part of Oklahoma state. Until 1840, 100 thousand Native Americans were forced to settle there, and about 15 thousands of them died because of malnutrition, disease and accidents. On 19 April 1995 Oklahoma City was rocked by a large explosion, which ruined a federal building, resulting in death of 168 people. Timothy James McVeigh, responsible for the explosion, after detention declared that his terrorist act was a revenge for death of 80 members of branch Davidians in famous Waco incident. According to the last census, population of Oklahoma was 3956971, showing its demography as follow: 65% white, 11.1% Latino, 9.4% native American and Alaskan, 7.8% black, 2.4% Asian, 0.2% Hawaiian and other Pacific islanders and 6.3% others. University of Oklahoma, University of Tulsa, Oklahoma State University, Oklahoma City University and National Weather Center are among scientific and education centers in the state. Wheat, alfalfa, soybean, rye, watermelon, peanut, cow, beef, pork, chicken and dairy products are among main agricultural and livestock products in the state.

Transportation equipment, industrial machinery, communication and electronic equipment, plastic products, metal products, processed food and paper are among industrial products of the state. Oil, natural gas, coal, crushed stone, lode, sand and gravel are main mineral products of Oklahoma. Some large corporations like :1-HOBBY LOBBY (retail company selling textiles, home décor etc…) 2-HELMERICH & PAYNE (petroleum contract drilling company engaged in oil and gas well drilling and related services for exploration) 3-MIDFIRST BANK 4-SONIC (fast food restaurant chain) have headquarters in Oklahoma.

Among tourist destinations in the state , these could be named : 1-Marland Estate Mansion , with 55 rooms , once belonged to Ernest Whitworth Marland , oil billionaire 2-Oklahoma City National memorial , which actually is a memorial to victims of famous 1995 explosion in the city 3-Oklahoma Aquarium , with numerous kinds of marine species 4-Woolaroc Museum & Wildlife Preserve , home to bisons , muskox , and deer live here 5-Route 66 , with post offices , shops and old restaurants 6-Cherokee Heritage Center , exhibiting life style and history of Cherokee Indian tribe 7-National Cowboy & Western Heritage Museum , introducing western American culture and cowboy lifestyle 8-Bricktown area in Oklahoma city . A water canal for boating is located here, with many shops and restaurants nearby 9-University of Oklahoma, which contains Sam Noble Oklahoma Museum, including a large collection of dinosaur fossils.

1-William Bradley Pitt, also known as Brad Pitt, famous Hollywood actor 2-Chesney Henry "Chet" Baker Jr, also known as Chet Baker, musician and prominent Western Jazz instrumentalist 3-James Garner, cinema and TV actor 4-Troyal Garth Brooks, country music genre singer 5-Wilma Pearl Mankiller, Cherokee activist and social worker 6-Leroy Gordon Cooper, Jr, one of the 7 main astronauts in Mercury space program, are among famous people from Oklahoma.

Since 1908 (the date first U.S presidential election was held in Oklahoma) to 2020, Oklahoma has taken part in 29 U.S presidential elections. Of these contests, Republican Party won 19 times in the state, while Democrats had 10 victories. It's worth noting that 1960 election saw a split of the electoral votes (7 were won by Republicans and a vote was taken by Democrats). As it could be observed, Republicans have an edge in the issue, and all 14 recent U.S presidential elections in Oklahoma have been won by them, from 1968 to 2020. Last Democratic victory was 1964 election.

In the 2020 Republican Party presidential primaries in Oklahoma, Donald Trump elected by gaining 92.6% of the votes, defeating his closest rival, Joe Walsh who got 3.7%.

In the 2020 Democratic presidential primaries in Oklahoma, Joe Biden won the candidacy through winning 38.7% of the votes, while his closest rival, Bernie Sanders, took 25.4%.

Finally, the 2020 U.S presidential election in Oklahoma witnessed a victory for Republican Party candidate, Donald Trump, who got 65.4% of the votes, while Democratic candidate, Joe Biden got 32.3%. All 7 electoral votes from Oklahoma were added to the Trump's vote basket.

From 1907 (the year first U.S Senate election was held in Oklahoma) to 2021, the state has sent 18 senators to the U.S Senate.9 were Republicans and 9 were Democrats. The 2 main parties have an equal share in number of U.S senators in the history of the state, but number of service years of Democratic senators has been 125, while Republicans served 105 years. This shows superiority of Democrats in the issue. But Republicans have worked better in recent decades, and one of the U.S Senate seats belonging to Oklahoma has been held by Republicans since 1969, and the other seat has seen the same situation since 1994, while no Democratic candidate from Oklahoma has been able to enter the U.S Senate during this period.

James Mountain Inhofe and James Paul Lankford, both Republicans, currently (2021) represent Oklahoma in the U.S Senate.

James Mountain Inhofe (with a 27-year record of presence in the U.S Senate, 1994-present), Donald Lee Nickles (with a 24-year record of service, 1981-2005), both Republicans, and John William Elmer Thomas, a Democrat with a 24-year record of serving in the U.S Senate (1927-1951), have been longest-serving U.S senators in history of Oklahoma.

During the political history of Oklahoma, 89 elected candidates have represented the state in the U.S House of representatives, of which 50 were Democrats, 37 were Republicans, one was a member of Silver Party, and a representative switched sides among Republican and Democratic parties.

As the statistics show, the number of those House representatives who served only as Democrats during their careers, in addition to the single representative who experienced membership in Republican Party, was 51, and the same number for Republicans is 38, showing an edge for Democrats in the history of the U.S House of representatives' elections in Oklahoma. If we put the issue under scrutiny in recent decades, it could be seen that every several years, voters in the state have shifted towards one of the 2 main parties. For instance, after 1927 Democratic and Republican parties were in a close race, but from 1927 to 1967, for 40 years, Democrats were superior. After 1967, the trend saw a tilt towards Republicans, and currently (2021), all 5 House representatives from Oklahoma are members of Republican Party.

John Kevin Stitt, current governor of Oklahoma (a Republican), is the 28th governor in the history of the state, but number of those persons who acted as governor of Oklahoma was 26. The 2-number difference here is due to that 2 governors, George Patterson Nigh and Henry Louis Bellmon gained the seat in 2 non-continuous terms. Nigh served 17th and 22nd governor of Oklahoma, and Bellmon served as 18th and 23rd.

Since 1907 (the year Oklahoma joined the U.S as its 46th state), 26 persons have served as governors of Oklahoma. Among these 26 governors, 21 were Democrats, 5 were Republicans. As it could be observed, Democrats have worked very good in the issue. Until 1963, all governors were members of Democratic Party, and in this year, first Republican governor was elected. But recent years have seen strong popularity of Republicans among gubernatorial elections voters in the state, and since 2011 both recent governors of the state have been Republicans.

Conclusion: Noting that Republicans have won 19 U.S presidential elections in Oklahoma (Democrats won 10 contests) including all 14 recent contests since 1968. Each of the 2 main parties had 9 U.S senators in the history of the state, but number of service years for Democratic senators was much more. Democrats have edge in the history of the U.S House of representatives' elections and gubernatorial election in Oklahoma: they had 51 representatives and 21 governors, while Republicans had 38 representatives and 5 governors. But both current U.S senators, all 5 House representatives and current governor of the state are Republicans. So, it could be said while in a general view Democrats have been a bit superior in the political history of Oklahoma, but today (2021) the state is a Republican stronghold.

New Mexico

N ew Mexico is famous for its spicy food and for being the world's largest hot air balloon festival in the southwestern United States, bordering Texas and Mexico. Its capital is Santa Fe. New Mexico is the neighbor to Texas state and Mexico. Nearly half of the nowadays state of New Mexico was initially a part of Mexico and was annexed to the U.S after Mexican-American War, according to Treaty of Guadalupe-Hidalgo in 1848. Initially governed as New Mexico territory, the entity finally joined the U.S. as its 47th state on 6 January 1911. According to the last census, New Mexico had a population of 2,096,829 inhabitants. Demographic composition of the state can be seen in these numbers: 49.3% of the population is Latino, 36.8% are whites, 11% Native Indians and Alaskans,2.6% black, 1.8% are Asians, 0.2% are Hawaiians and people from other Pacific islands, and the rest 2.6% are from other races and ethnicities. University of New Mexico, New Mexico State University, Los Alamos National Laboratory (a large federal-owned scientific center. First nuclear bomb in the world was tested and exploded here), Sandia National Laboratories, Apache Point Observatory (containing SDSS telescope, one of the largest wide-angle optical telescopes in the world) are among scientific and education centers in the state. New Mexico also hosts several U.S Air Force bases, including: Holloman Air Force Base, Cannon Air Force Base, Kirtland Air Force Base, White Sands Missile Range, and half of the Fort Bliss military base. New Mexico has a diverse economy, and from agriculture, animal husbandry and producing dairy products to oil, natural gas, minerals and natural resources are among economic sectors in the state. Onion, potato, pumpkin, watermelon, lettuce, cabbage, corn, Beans, milk and cheese are main agricultural products of New Mexico. The state ranks among top states in producing milk and cheese. New Mexico is 3rd state in producing oil, and has large mineral resources including Uranium, potassium and coal. Albuquerque Studios in the state may help to expand its juvenile film industry.

Several large corporations like :1- HONEYWELL (active in aerospace industry, emerging technologies, Performance Materials and Technologies (PMT) and Safety and Productivity Solutions (SPS)) 2- GCC DACOTHA (producing construction material) 3- AKAL SECURITY (Security company) have headquarters in New Mexico.

Among tourist attractions in the state, these could be named: 1- Carlsbad Caverns National Park, consisted of 120 known caves 2- White Sands National Monument, containing sand hills with unique attractivity 3- Albuquerque International Balloon Fiesta, largest hot air balloon festival globally 4- Bandelier National Monument. The area contains native ecosystems with natural structures, made of volcano stones 5- Taos Pueblo city, ancient city dating back to 1000 years ago, with houses made of clay 6- Cumbers-Toltec Scenic Railway. Visitors can experience an entertainment tour with steam locomotive here 7- Gila Cliff Dwellings National Monument. Rock houses made by Native American tribes 1300 years ago 8- Chaco Culture National Historical Park, a center containing 15 huge ruined buildings and hundreds of small buildings, dating back to 800-1200 AD 9- The Very Large Array radio telescope, located in western Socorro hills and St.Augustin plain in the Karl G Jansky radio observatory. The observatory is in use for research on blackholes and other astrologic phenomena. These, along many other destinations, shape the tourism sector in New Mexico.1- Demi Gayness Kutcher, actress 2- Neil Patrick Harris, actor, singer, TV host and director 3- Robert Mirabal, musician and Native American float instrumentalist 4- Angelico Chavez, priest, historian, writer, poet and painter 5- Sidney McNeill Gutierrez, NASA astronaut, are among famous people from New Mexico.

Since 1912 (the year first U.S presidential election was held in the state) to 2020, 28 U.S presidential elections have been held in the country, and New Mexico took part in all of them. Of these contests, Democratic party won 16 times in the state and Republicans had 12 victories.

For a better inspection, history of the U.S presidential elections in New Mexico could be divided into 2 periods. First part, from 1912 to 1964, saw 14 elections, and Democrats won 9 times, while Republicans gained 5victories.Second period, from 1968 to 2020, witnessed 14 presidential elections, of which Republicans and Democrats each won 7 contests, and Democratic Party has emerged winner in all 4 recent elections, showing an increase in its popularity among the voters in New Mexico.

2020 Democratic presidential primaries in New Mexico saw a victory for Joseph Biden, who won 73.3% of the votes, while his closest rival, Bernie Sanders got 15.1% of the votes.

In 2020 Republican presidential primaries in New Mexico, Donald Trump gained the candidacy through winning 91.4% of the votes, and "uncommitted" votes ranked 2nd with an 8.6% share.

Finally, the 2020 U.S Presidential elections in New Mexico resulted in a win for Democratic Party candidate, Joseph Biden, who won 54.3% of the votes, while his Republican counterpart, Donald Trump, won 43.5% of the votes. All 5 electoral votes from New Mexico were added to Bidens's vote basket.

Since 1912 to 2020, New Mexico has sent 18 senators to the U.S Senate.11 were Democrats and 7 were Republicans. In addition to their superiority in number of the U.S senators, service years of Democratic senators have been much longer (150 vs 66 for Republican senators). Democrats have also worked better in recent years, and one of the U.S Senate seats belonging to New Mexico has been held by them since 1983, and the other seat has seen the same situation since 2009. Currently (2021), Martin Trevor Heinrich and Ben Ray Luján, both Democrats, present the state in the U.S Senate.

Pietro Vichi Domenici, with a 36-year record of service in the Senate (1973-2009) from Republican Party and Jeff Bingaman, with a 30 years' history of presence in the Senate (1983-2013), a Democrat, have been longest-serving U.S senators in the history of New Mexico.

From 1911 (the year first U.S House of representatives' election was held in New Mexico) to 2021, 34 persons have represented New Mexico in the U.S House of representatives, of which 22 were Democrats and 12 were Republicans. While Democrats have an upper hand in the issue, including in recent years, but currently (2021), out of 3 seats belonging to the state in the House, one is held by a Republican, one by a Democrat and a seat is empty.

Michelle Lynn Lujan Grisham, current governor of New Mexico (a Democrat) is 32nd governor of the state. But number of those persons who acted as governor of New Mexico was 28. The 4-number difference here is due to that 2 governors, gained the seat in 3 non-continuous terms.

Since 1911 (the year New Mexico joined the U.S as its 47th state), 28 persons have served as governors of the state. Among these 28 governors, 18 were Democrats and 10 were Republicans. While Democrats have been superior in the history of gubernatorial elections in the state and current governor is a Democrat, recent years have witnessed a close race among the 2 main parties in the issue. out of 5 recent governors since 1991, 3 were Democrats and 2 were Republicans.

Conclusion: Noting that Democrats have won 16 U.S presidential elections in New Mexico (Republicans won 12 contests) including all 4 recent contests, and had 11 U.S Senators, 22 House representatives and 18 governors (the same numbers for Republicans are 7, 12, 10). It's clear they have an edge in the political history of the state. Currently (2021), both U.S Senators representing New Mexico are Democrats, out of 3 seats belonging to the state in the House, one is held by a Republican, one by a Democrat and a seat is empty, and current governor of the state is a member of Democratic Party. It could be said that New Mexico has been a Democratic Party bastion during most of its history, just like today (2021).

Arizona

The state of Arizona was part of Mexico with its famous cacti in the western United States, centered in Phoenix. Part of the state was annexed to the United States and New Mexico after the US-Mexico War in 1848. The southern parts were ceded to the United States under a treaty called the Gadsden Purchase, drafted in 1853 and finalized on June 8, 1854, between the United States and Mexico. January 18, 1863 Arizona secedes from New Mexico and finally joins the United States on February 14, 1912 as the 48th state. According to the last census, Arizona had a population of 7,278,717 inhabitants. Taking a look into demographics of the state, recent data shows that 54.1% of Arizona population is white, 31.7% are Latinos, 5.3% are Native Indians and Alaskans, 5.2 are % blacks, 3.7% are Asians, 0.3% are Hawaiians and other U.S islanders, and others form 2.9% of its demography. University of Arizona, Arizona State University-Tempe, Northern Arizona University, Arizona Christian University, Fred Lawrence Whipple Observatory (which contains Multiple Mirror Telescope, one of the largest telescopes in the world), Mount Graham International Observatory (hosting Heinrich Hertz Submillimeter Telescope), Kitt Peak National Observatory and National Solar Observatory are among scientific and education centers in the state. Lettuce, cotton, melon, wheat, barley, citrus, potato, cow, beef, pork, chicken, eggs, dairy products and cattle food are among main agricultural and livestock products of Arizona. Electronical and computer parts, turbine engines, guided missiles, helicopters, aerospace industry products, machinery, metal products and soft drinks are among main industrial products in the state. Apart from copper, which Arizona is its largest producer in the U.S, gold, silver, molybdenum, sand, uranium, zinc, mercury, tungsten, limestone, coal, potassium and cement are other main mineral products of Arizona.

Some large corporations like: 1- KYOCERA SOLAR (manufacturing solar energy equipment) 2- PET SMART.INC (privately held American chain of pet superstores, which sell pet products, services, and small pets) 3- REPUBLIC SERVICES (waste disposal company) 4- SPROUTS FARMERS MARKET (supermarket chain) 5- CIRCLE K (international chain of convenience stores) have headquarters in Arizona. Among tourist destinations in the state, these could be named: 1- tombstone city, which the architecture and environment here resemble old American 2- Antelope Canyon at Page, a rocky valley near Page city. Colorful stone columns with ridges light coming through make a beautiful view for visitors 3- Organ Pipe Cactus National Monument, an international biosphere reserve. Its main property is namesake organ pipe cactus 4-Tumacacori National Historical Park, which is located in south of Tuscon, containing ruins of 3 old churches dating back to colonial Spanish rule era, in a 47-acre area in southern Arizona. San José de Tumacácori and Los Santos Ángeles de Guevavi were built in 1691, and are oldest monasteries in Arizona. Third monastery, San Cayetano de Calabazas, was built in 1756. 5-Canyon De Chelly National Monument, rocky settlements of Native American tribes, dating back to 1000 years ago 6-Jerome city, which once was a crowded city because of mines nearby, but slowly turned into a ruin, and now, after reconstruction of some buildings, has an amazing composition 7-Mission San Xavier del Bac monastery, known as "White Pigeon of Desert", built in 1770 by hermits in southwest of Tuscon. Buildings of the monastery, specially their decorations, are good examples of Baroque style architecture of Spanish colonial era.

The site is still used by Tohono O'odham Native American tribe as a ritual site 8-Watson Lake, surrounded by rocky hills nearby, and Monument Valley. These, along with other museums, parks and historical sites, shape the tourism sector in Arizona.1- Judith Ann Jance, novelist 2-Richard Shelton, poet and writer 3-Pearl Zane Grey, adventure novel author 4-Linda Maria Ronstadt, singer, are among famous people from Arizona. Since 1912 until now (2021), Arizona has taken part in 28 U.S presidential elections. Republican Party has won 19 contests, and Democrats were victorious in 9 races.To have a better inspection, we can divide the history of the presidential elections in Arizona to 2 periods. In the first period, from 1912 to 1948, 10 presidential elections have been held in this state. Democratic Party won 7 times and Republicans won 3 times. Democrats won 5 consecutive elections from 1923 to 1948. However, in the second period, from 1952 to 2020, Arizona people took part in 18 US presidential elections. In these 18 contests, Republicans won 16 times and Democrats won the state electoral vote 2 times. Notable point in this election is the fact that from 1952 to 2016, Republicans won all rounds except for 1996 election in which Democrats won and in 2020 they could win electoral votes after many years.

Because of statewide support for Donald Trump, Republican party didn't hold its presidential primaries in Arizona in 2020.

The 2020 Democratic presidential primaries in Arizona saw a victory for Joseph Biden, who won 44.4% of the votes, while his closest rival, Bernie Sanders got 32.9% of the votes.

Finally, the 2020 U.S Presidential elections in Arizona resulted in a win for Democratic Party candidate, Joe Biden, who won 49.36% of the votes, while his Republican counterpart, Donald Trump, won 49.06% of the votes. All 11 electoral votes from Arizona were added to Biden's vote basket.

From 1912 (the year first Senate election was held in the state) to 2021, 14 Senators have represented Arizona in the U.S Senate: 7 Democrats and 7 Republicans. It's clear that the 2 main parties are tied in number of U.S senators in the state, but Democrats have worked better in recent years, winning both U.S Senate seats belonging to Arizona.

Currently (2021), Mark Edward Kelly and Kyrsten Lea Sinema, both Democrats, represent Arizona in the U.S Senate.

Carl Trumbull Hayden, with a 42-year record of service in the Senate (1927-1969), a Democrat and John Sidney McCain III, also known as John McCain with a 31 years' history of presence in the Senate (1987-2018), a Republican, have been longest-serving senators in history of Arizona.

Since 1912 to now (2021), Arizona has sent 44 elected candidates to the U.S House of Representatives, 23 of them were Democrats, 20 were Republicans, and a representative switched sides between Republicans and Democrats.

As the statistics show, those representatives who only served as Democrats, or had history of membership in other parties along this, have been 24 persons. The same number for Republicans is 21, which in the first look indicates superiority of Democrats in this issue. But number of service years of Republican senators has been 218 (vs 180 years for Democrats), much longer than their Democratic counterparts, which gives them an upper hand in the history of U. S House of representatives' elections in Arizona.Currnetly (2021) a close race is going on, and out of 9 House representatives from Arizona, 5 are Democrats and 4 are members of Republican Party.

Gubernatorial elections in Arizona from 1912 to 2020 resulted in election of 23 governors. Share of Democratic Party in these contests was 13 wins, and Republicans gained 10 victories. While Democrats have an edge in history of gubernatorial elections in the state, recent years show Republican superiority. Both elected governors in recent 10 years were Republican candidates. Current governor of Arizona is Doug Ducey, a Republican.

Conclusion: Republicans have won 19 rounds of U.S presidential elections in Arizona (while Democrats had 9 victories, including the last contest in 2020), both parties has 7 U.S senators in the history of the state, but both current U.S senators representing the state are Democrats. Democrats sent 24 of their party members to the House, while the number for Republicans is 21, and Republican representatives had longer service years. Currently (2021), out of 9 House representatives from Arizona, 5 are Democrats and 4 are members of Republican Party. Democrats had 13 governors in history of Arizona, while 10 Republican Party members were able gain the governor's seat in the state, including the recent governor. So, it could be said that while the 2 main parties had a close contest during political history of Arizona, today (2021), Democrats are in a stronger position.

Alaska

Alaska state and its capital, Juneau are located in northwestern edge of North America. The state is the largest U.S state by size, and large oil, gold and other mineral reservoirs along with unique nature including natural glaciers, have made Alaska one of the richest and most attractive states in the U.S. Northern areas of Alaska, which are inhabited by Eskimos, have long winters, with weeks without sunrise. Hearing the name of Alaska recalls of immigrants and adventurers who came to this area in search for gold in severe cold and snow, some of them lost their wealth and even lives. Alaska once was a Russian colony, until William H. Seward, Secretary of State in president Andrew Johnson (17th president of the U.S) administration succeeded in persuading the U.S Senate to purchase the area from Russian government. On 30 March 1867 the Alaska treaty was ratified by representatives from the U.S and Russia, evaluating price of the area 7.2 million dollars, and finally, Alaska was handed over to the U.S government on 18 October 1867. On the official transfer day, while Russian and American soldiers stood near each other to perform the ceremony (taking down the Russian flag and raising the American flag), the Russian flag got stuck by the rod and a Russian soldier climbed from the rod to free the flag, but a strong wind began to blow, throwing the flag on bayonets of standing soldiers, horrifying everyone, because such accident was taken as ominous. According to historians, after seeing this scene, Princess Maria Maksutova, wife of the last Russian governor of Alaska, fainted. But raising the American flag went forward smoothly. From 1867 to 1884, the area was called "Department of Alaska", and later, from 1884 to 1912, Alaska was administrated as a district. In 1912,

Territory of Alaska was established, and finally, on 3 January 1959, Alaska joined the U.S as its 49th state.

According to the last census, Alaska had a population of 731545 inhabitants, of which 60.2% were whites, 15.6% were Native Americans and Alaskans, 7.3% were Latinos, 6.5% were Asians, 3.7% were blacks, 1.4% were Hawaiians and other Pacific islanders, and the rest 7.5% were from other races and ethnicities. University of Alaska—Anchorage, Alaska Pacific University, University of Alaska-Southeast, University of Alaska-Fairbanks and Ilisagvik College are among scientific and education centers in the state. With its large natural resources like: oil, gold, copper, silver, lead, coal, Alaska is a rich state. Because of the cold and harsh weather, agriculture is not a common activity in Alaska. Alfalfa, barley, oat, potatoes, cow, beef and milk are main agricultural and livestock products of Alaska. But fishing and hunting of marine livings are widespread in Alaska. Hunting reindeers is also common.

Some large corporations like: 1-CHUGACH ALASKA (active in petroleum industry and mining) 2-AFOGNAK NATIVE (active in oil and timber industries) 3-CHENEGA (a successful company belonging to Alaskan Native people) have headquarters in Alaska.

With its natural glaciers and unique wildlife, Alaska is a popular tourist destination. Some of major tourist attractions in Alaska are: 1-Denali National Park, home to Grizzley bears, wolves, reindeers and 167 bird species. 2- Tracy Arm Fjord, an area with natural glaciers and untamed wildlife. Visitors can experience tours and trips with boat and ship here 3-Kenai Fjords National Park, an area with natural glaciers, living place of brown bears 4- Alaska Highway, which was built during WWII era. 5-University of Alaska Museum of the North, containing more than a million historical and natural history assets 6-Dalton Highway. In many nights between September and April, auroras can are observable here 7-Alaska Native Heritage Center, a place for storytelling and dancing gatherings of Native people of Alaska, also an exhibition for art works and handicrafts 8-Inside Passage, an area for trips with tourist ships in nature, containing incredible wildlife 9-Wrangell-St. Elias National Park & Preserve, with natural glaciers, lakes, mountain springs, abandoned mines, and beautiful wildlife 10-Klondike Gold Rush National Historical Park, site of beautiful reconstructed buildings, recalling famous Gold Rush to Alaska 11-Alaska Railroad. Visitors can experience a tour through stunning nature here by train 12-Iditarod National Historic Trail, a historical trail for sleighing in old times. These, along many other destinations, have made Alaska a rich tourist state. 1-Dana Stabenow, science-fiction and adventure novel author 2-Elizabeth Peratrovich, civil rights activist 3-John Ben Benson Jr, designer of Alaska state flag 4-Scott Carlos Gomez, former ice hockey professional player 5-Ray Mala, Native Hollywood actor, are among famous people from Alaska.

Since 1960 to now (2021), Alaska has taken part in 16 U.S presidential elections, of which Republicans won 15 and Democratic Party emerged victorious in a single contest in 1964. In a simpler definition, Republicans won the first election and Democrats gained the second contest, and the rest 14 races all were won by Republican Party. Alaska could be counted as non-penetrable bastion of Republican Party. Because of statewide support for Donald Trump, the 2020 Republican Party primaries were not held in the state. In the 2020 Democratic Party presidential primaries in Alaska, Joe Biden won the candidacy by gaining 55.3% of the votes, while his closest rival, Bernie Sanders, got 44.7%. Finally, the 2020 U.S presidential election in Alaska witnessed a victory for Republican candidate, Donald Trump, who won 52.8% of the votes, while his Democratic rival, Joe Biden, got 42.8%. Trump won all 3 electoral votes from Alaska. It's worth noting that until 2016, initial inter-party elections for choosing U.S presidential election candidates in Alaska were held in caucuses method, and this trend changed to primary method in 2020.

From 1959 (the date first U.S Senate election was held in Alaska) to 2021, 8 elected candidates from the state have served in the U.S Senate, of which 4 were Democrats and 4 were Republicans. While number of U.S senators from each party is equal, but number of service years of these 4 Republican senators has been 85 years, comparing to 37 years for Democratic senators.

Currently (2021), Lisa Ann Murkowski and Daniel Scott Sullivan, both Republicans, represent the state in the U.S Senate. Theodore Fulton Stevens Sr (with a 41-year record of presence in the U.S Senate, 1968-2009) from and Frank Hughes Murkowski (with a 21-year record of service, 1981-2002, father of Lisa Murkowski, current U.S senator representing Alaska), both Republicans, have been longest-serving

315

U.S senators in history of Alaska. It could be noted that Frank Hughes Murkowski, another member of Murkowski family, served as 8th governor of Alaska 2002-2006.

From 1959 to 2021, 4 elected candidates have entered the U.S House of representatives as representatives from Alaska. 2 were Democrats and 2 were Republicans. Just like the U.S Senate elections, number of service years of Republican representatives is much larger than their Democratic counterparts (52 years' vs 8 years). Don Young is the state's only current Republican MP since 1973, with 48 years in the US House of Representatives and one of the longest-serving in US history.

Among 12 persons who have served as governors of Alaska during its history, 6 were Republicans, 4 were Democrats, one was an independent candidate, and a governor switched sides among Alaskan Independence Party and Republican Party. As the statistics show, Number of those House representatives who served only as Republicans during their careers, in addition to the governor who also served as a member of Alaskan Independence Party, was 7, while 4 Democrat governors served in the history of Alaska. This shows an upper hand for Republican Party in the issue. But number of service years for governors from both parties is the same: 27 years. It's worth noting that last Democratic governor of Alaska served 1994-2002, and after that none of Democratic Party members have been able to gain a gubernatorial election in the state.

Mike Dunloway, current (2021) governor of Alaska, is a Republican. Sarah Palin, Republican candidate for vice president post in 2008 U.S presidential election in John Mc Cain's campaign once served as governor of Alaska.

Conclusion : Noting that Republicans have won all U.S presidential elections in Alaska except 1964 election , and had 4 U.S senators with much longer service years than Democratic senators (each party had 4 U.S senators) , and situation is the same in U.S House of representatives elections in the history of the state (each party had 2 representatives but Republican House representatives had much longer service years) , and Republicans had more governors (7 vs 4 for Democrats) , adding to that both U.S Senators and the single House representative from Alaska along with current governor of the state are members of Republican Party , It could be said Alaska has been a Republican stronghold through its history , and today (2021) situation is similar.

Hawaii

Hawaii state (also known as Hawaii archipelago) and its capital, Honolulu are located in the Pacific Ocean. The state is famous for its incredible nature, including beaches, beautiful jungles and attracting volcanoes, along with moderate weather, and hosts millions of tourists annually. Hawaii joined the U.S. as its 50th state on 21 August 1959. According to the last census, the population of Hawaii was 1415872, showing its demography as follow: 37.6% Asian, 21.7% white, 10.7% Latino, 10.1% Hawaiian and other Pacific islanders, 2.2% black, 0.4% native American and Alaskan, and 24.2% others.Hawaii is not an industrial state, and its natural resources are scarce, which causes it to have to import industrial materials from other states, an issue making housing and other life costs high in the state, but cultivating sugar cane, pine apple and catling cows is widespread in the state. Bananas, papaya, mango, avocado and aster flower are other agricultural and garden products of the state. HAWAIIAN AIRLINES and HAWAII PACIFIC HEALTH are among large corporations which have headquarters in Hawaii. Hawaii is one of the best-known tourism centers in the world with attractions like: 1-Waikiki Beach and Hanauma Bay, both have very beautiful and unique nature 2-Volcanoes National Park, Haleakala National Park and Nā Pali Coast State Wilderness Park, which have their special attractivity 3-Kona Coffee Living History Farm. Visitors can learn about history of coffee and its production from guides here 4-Hana Road, a dreamy passage between the jungle and the ocean, with numerous waterfalls 5-Waipio Valley, with stunning nature, on the beach 6-Pearl Harbor and USS Arizona Memorial in U.S naval base in Hawaii, which was attacked by the Japanese warplanes on the eve of

Sunday, 7 December 1941 and resulted in the U.S entrance to WWII. Hawaii has many other tourist attractions, and these make the state a global tourism hub.

Barack Hussein Obama II, 44th president of the U.S and Nicole Scherzinger, singer, poet, dancer and model, are among famous people from Hawaii.

Since 1960 (the date the first U.S. presidential election was held in Hawaii) to 2020, the state has taken part in all 16 U.S. presidential elections held in the country. Of these contests, the Democratic Party won 14 times in the state, while Republicans had 2 victories. 9 out of 14 Democratic victories gained in 9 recent elections, and actually, Republicans had no victories in Hawaii after 1984. This shows strong popularity for the Democratic Party among the voters in the state.

The 2020 Democratic presidential primaries in Hawaii saw a victory for Joseph Biden who won 63.2% of the votes, while his closest rival, Bernie Sanders got 36.8% of the votes.

Because of statewide support for Donald Trump, the 2020 Republican Party primaries were not held in the state.

Finally, the 2020 U.S. Presidential elections in Hawaii resulted in a win for the Democratic Party candidate, Joe Biden, who won 63.7% of the votes, while his Republican counterpart, Donald Trump, won 34.3% of the votes. All 4 electoral votes from Hawaii were added to Biden's vote basket. From 1959 to 2021, 7 elected candidates have entered the U.S. Senate from Hawaii, of which 6 were Democrats and one (Hiram Leong Fong, years of service 1959-1977) was a Republican, and after Fong, none of Republican candidates have been able to enter the U.S. Senate from Hawaii, which shows an edge for Democrats on the issue.

Currently (2021), Mazie Keiko Hirono and Brian Emanuel Schatz, both Democrats, represent Hawaii in the U.S. Senate.

Daniel Ken Inouye (with a 49-year record of presence in the U.S Senate, 1963-2012) from Democratic Party and Hiram Leong Fong (with an 18-year record of service, 1959-1977), a Republican, have been the longest-serving U.S senators in the history of Hawaii.

Since 1959 (the year first U.S House of representatives' election was held in the state) to 2021, 15 elected candidates have entered the U.S House of representatives as representatives from Hawaii. 13 were Democrats and 2 were Republicans. As it could be observed, Democrats have been far superior in the history of U.S House of representatives' elections in Hawaii, and after 2011, no Republican representative from Hawaii has been elected. Both current House representatives from Hawaii are members of Democratic Party.

Since 1959 (the year Hawaii joined the U.S as its 50th state) to 2021, 8 persons have served as governors of the state, and among them, 6 were Democrats and 2 were members of Republican Party. David Yutaka Ige, a Democrat, is current governor of Hawaii. As It's clear, in addition to their better performance in the history of gubernatorial elections in the state, Democrats currently hold governor's seat in Hawaii.

Conclusion: noting that Democrats have won 14 U.S presidential elections in the state including all 9 recent contests (Republicans had 2 victories), and had 6 U.S senators, 13 House representatives and 6 governors (the numbers for Republican Party are 1, 2, 2), it could be seen that they have an upper hand in the political history of Hawaii. Currently, both U.S Senators and both House representatives from Hawaii, and governor of the state are members of Democratic Party, and it could be concluded that Hawaii has been a Democratic Party bastion during its history, just like today (2021).

Washington D.C.

Whearen founders of the U.S. began to form the federal government on 16 July 1790, they separated a part of the northern areas of Virginia state and a part of the southern areas of Maryland state from them, establishing a federal area, and named it in honor of George Washington as the main founder of the U.S. along with Christopher Columbus as the first person to discover America (Washington District of Columbia). The district is also known as Washington D.C, capital of the U.S, and is under supervision of the U.S. Congress and not counted as part of any state. The White House, the capitol, most of the government departments, and the federal buildings like The Library of Congress are located in Washington D. C, and the area is not a state according to law. According to the last census, Washington D.C. had a population of 705,749 inhabitants. 46% of the population is black, 37.5% are Whites, 11.3% are Latinos, 4.5% are Asians, 0.6% are Native Americans and Alaskans, 0.1% are Hawaiians and other Pacific islanders, and 2.9% are from other races and ethnicities. Georgetown University, one of the oldest universities in the U.S, dating back to 1789 and where some famous people like Bill Clinton, 42nd president of the U.S have been graduated and George Washington University where Collin Powel, former Secretary of the State of the U.S graduated are among the most credible education centers in the U.S. and are 2 of the education and scientific centers in Washington D.C. Washington D.C. is not an agricultural or industrial area, and most of inhabitants work in services. Among tourist destinations in the state, these could be named: 1- United States Capitol and Capitol Hill, recognized around the world as a symbol of the United States; the Capitol is the seat of the House of Representatives and the Senate. The huge dome, based on the dome of St. Peter's in Rome, stands out above all other Washington buildings. Like Washington itself, the building has grown over the years since the central portion was built between 1793 and 1812. The last addition, in 1958-62, enlarged the main façade where presidents take the oath. On the other side, a marble terrace offers beautiful views over the mall and the city. An underground passage with historical exhibits leads from the Capitol to one of Washington's little-known places to visit, the Library of Congress.

The Library of Congress is the world's largest library, modeled after the Opera House in Paris. You can visit portions on your own, but free tours disclose even more of its beautiful interior. Displayed here are one of the three surviving complete Gutenberg Bibles, an earlier hand-printed Bible, Thomas Jefferson's draft of the Declaration of Independence, Jefferson's personal library, and galleries filled with exhibits focusing on topics as varied as the musical careers of the Gershwin brothers and the work of editorial cartoonists and graphic artists 2-The Lincoln Memorial , The best-loved of all Washington's memorials, the Lincoln Memorial stands at the far end of the mall, separated from the Washington Monument by the Reflecting Pool. At its center is a 19-foot marble statue of a seated and pensive President Abraham Lincoln surrounded by 36 columns, one for each of the states that existed at the time of Lincoln's death. This is the most famous work designed by noted sculptor Daniel Chester French. Jules Guerin painted the murals on the inside walls, showing important events in Lincoln's life. Since its completion in 1922, the Lincoln Memorial has been the scene of a number of historic events. In 1939, when the all-white Daughters of the American Revolution (DAR) refused to let celebrated African American singer Marian Anderson perform at a concert in nearby Constitution Hall, President Franklin Roosevelt and First Lady Eleanor Roosevelt arranged for her to give an open-air concert on the steps of the Lincoln Memorial, attended by 75,000 people and broadcast to millions of radio listeners.Martin Luther King Jr. delivered his famous "I have a dream..." speech from the memorial steps in 1963, again making history here.Visiting this and other Mall monuments is one of the favorite things to do in Washington, D.C. at night.

The monuments are all lighted, and many, like the Lincoln Memorial, are open 24 hours. The statue of Lincoln is especially powerful lighted at night inside the darkened interior of the temple and framed by the floodlit white columns.3-National Mall and Veterans Memorials. The spacious swath of lawns and pools that forms a wide greenbelt from the Capitol Building to the Lincoln Memorial is also the site of many of Washington's landmark buildings and monuments. Most prominent at its center point is the Washington Monument, and war memorials include those to veterans of World War II, the Korean War, and Vietnam.The Vietnam Veterans Memorial, a poignant wall inscribed with the names of all-American servicemen and women who lost their lives or are missing, is one of Washington's most visited memorials. The nearby Vietnam Women's Memorial has a bronze sculpture of three servicewomen helping a wounded soldier. The Korean War Veterans Memorial contains 19 steel sculptures of soldiers. The newest, American Veterans Disabled for Life Memorial was dedicated in 2014. 4-The White House. The White House is the official residence of the President of the United States.

The home of every president except George Washington, it was originally built by James Hoban in 1792, and after being burned down by British forces in 1814 was rebuilt in 1818.The free White House Visitor Center, a short distance away, has excellent interactive exhibits, which show details about the White House and the presidential families. It includes furniture of past presidents, a model of the residence, historical changes, and videos with insights from presidents about their time living there. he Ellipse, a 54-acre stretch of lawn stretching to Constitution Avenue, hosts summer concerts by the US Army Band. Next door to the White House is the elaborate 1833 Greek Revival Treasury Building and the 1871 Executive Office Building, one of the most striking old government buildings in Washington. From Lafayette Square, one of the city's best-known, statues of Lafayette and others overlook the White House.5-The Washington Monument. The 555-foot white shaft of the Washington Monument is a familiar icon of the National Mall, and a beautiful sight, especially when mirrored in the long Reflecting Pool at its foot. Construction of the obelisk to honor the nation's first president did not proceed smoothly. The plan was approved by Congress in 1783, but ground wasn't broken until 1848.When the tower reached 156 feet in height in 1854, political wrangling and lack of funds stopped the project for several years, and the Civil War caused further interruption so that the tower was not capped until 1885, when it was finally completed by the Army Corps of Engineers. You can still see the separate stages of its building by three changes in the color of its facing stones; inside are engraved stones from states, cities, foreign countries, individuals, and civic groups, many of them donors who helped in its private funding stages. You can take an elevator to the very top for aerial views over the mall and much of Washington. The base of the monument is surrounded by a circle of 50 American Flags.6-National Air and Space Museum. The National Air and Space Museum is one of the world's most popular museums, with a collection of history-making air and spacecraft that includes the original 1903 Wright Brothers Flyer and Charles Lindbergh's Spirit of St. Louis, the first plane to fly solo across the Atlantic Ocean.

More recent flight history is represented here by the Apollo 11 command module, part of the first manned lunar landing mission. Permanent and changing exhibitions illustrate the science, history, and technology of aviation and space flight, covering topics like the use of air power in both world wars, the space race, flight pioneers, and up-to-the-minute flight and space technology. Many of the exhibits are interactive, and all contain actual historical objects, such as a moon rock you can touch. Not only do permanent exhibits illustrate history, they show the how and why of flight and space science, explaining how things fly, how jet engines work, and what keeps the International Space Station in orbit.7-National Museum of African American History and Culture. Focusing on themes of history, culture, and community, the newest of the Smithsonian museums explores changing definitions of American citizenship and equality, at the same time highlighting African American culture and that of the entire African diaspora. Various themes are covered in changing exhibits, which center on themes such as African American food traditions and chefs, the influence of African American sports stars on the breakdown of segregation, and African craftsmanship. Historic artifacts on display include a section of the original Woolworth lunch counter that was the scene of the Greensboro, N.C. sit-in in 1960, and the aircraft known as the "Spirit of Tuskegee." In World War II, it was used to train African American airmen in the

Army Air Forces, men whose work helped trigger the desegregation of the military.

8-Washington National Cathedral. The English-style, Neo-Gothic National Cathedral, one of the world's largest cathedrals, took 83 years to build, from 1907 to 1990. It follows the Gothic building style and techniques, with flying buttresses and solid masonry construction of Indiana limestone. Throughout the cathedral are artistic details to see, from its stained-glass windows to the hand-embroidered kneelers that commemorate war heroes and historic events.

The cathedral is the burial place of President Woodrow Wilson and Helen Keller, and state funerals for Presidents Eisenhower, Reagan, and Ford took place here. The top of the 300-foot central tower is the highest point in Washington.9-Georgetown Historic District. The neighborhood from 27th to 37th Streets, between Rock Creek Park and K Street NW, is the city's oldest, with origins in the early 1700s, before Washington itself. Georgetown University, the nation's oldest Roman Catholic and Jesuit College, is located here.These, along some other parks, lakes, and historical sites, shape the tourism sector in Washington D.C.

Albert Arnold Gore, Jr. (also called Al Gore), environmental activist and American politician, winner of Noble peace prize and former vice president of the U.S (1993-2001) in Bill Clinton administration, David Michael, body builder, actor, hybrid martial artist and former famous wrestler in WWE company and Stephen Tyrone Colbert, comedian, writer, producer, actor, media critic and TV presenter are among famous people from Washington D.C. The district has no U.S senators and House representatives and is being administrated under supervision of the U.S Congress, and once was out of governance of all 50 U.S states, without any right to take part in U.S presidential elections. But after ratification of 23rd amendment of the U.S Constitution in 1961, became able to take part in the U.S presidential elections. From 1964 (the year first U.S presidential election was held in the district) to 2020, Democrats have been winners in all 15 rounds of U.S presidential elections in the district. Washington D.C has 3 electoral college votes.

In the 2020 Democratic presidential primaries in Washington D.C, Joe Biden won the candidacy through winning 77.5% of the votes, while his closest rival, Elizabeth Warren, took 12.1%.

Republican Party presidential primaries in Washington D.C in the same year resulted in a decisive win for Donald Trump, who got 100% of the votes without confronting any rivals.

Finally, the 2020 U.S presidential election in Washington D.C witnessed a victory for Democratic Party candidate, Joseph Biden, who got 92.1% of the votes, while Republican candidate, Donald Trump got 5.4%. All 3 electoral votes from the district were added to the Democratic Party's vote basket.

As the statistics show, Washington D.C has been a staunch Democratic Party stronghold since the beginning of its participation in the U.S presidential elections to now (2021).

Sources

www.house.gov

www.senate.gov

history.house.gov

www.census.gov

www.270towin.com

www.whitehouse.gov

www.dictionary.com

www.businessinsider.com

www.congress.gov

www.nytimes.com

cm.usatoday.com

www.washingtonpost.com

ballotpedia.org

historicmissourians.shsmo.org

www.sos.mo.gov

bioguideretro.congress.gov

history.house.gov

www.nga.org

www.duluthnewstribune.com

www.govtrack.us

gov.idaho.gov

www.zippia.com

www.watchusgrow.org

voteview.com

www.nasda.org

www.worldatlas.com

www.britannica.com

www.netstate.com

www.spiegel.de

www.pbs.org
www.joincalifornia.com
www.usa.gov
www.ct.gov
connecticuthistory.org
www.ct.gov
www.statista.com
www.nj.com
www.history.com
ag.umass.edu
www.farmflavor.com
www.topuniversities.com
sos.maryland.gov
constitutingamerica.org
parks.ny.gov
www.usnews.com
delawaretoday.com
www.arcadiapublishing.com
historyofmassachusetts.org
en.wikipedia.org
slaveryandremembrance.org
neworleanshistorical.org
64parishes.org
www.aoc.gov
www.oxfordreference.com
www.dnr.louisiana.gov
www.blackpast.org
www.blackpast.org
www.mshistorynow.mdah.ms.gov
www.austinrealestate.com
www.lrl.mn.gov
www.trans-alleghenylunaticasylum.com
www.encyclopedia.com
www.newsmax.com

*From Manuscript
to Masterpiece*

Also Available from
J. Kenkade Publishing

ISBN: 978-1-955186-54-9
Visit www.amazon.com
Author: Patrick Baker
Publisher: J. Kenkade Publishing

We live in a world where, although we share the world with different people and ethnicities, we live with hate, malice, envy, and strife toward one another. "A Nation Divided by Racism" addresses these matters within an open dialogue.

Also Available from
J. Kenkade Publishing

ISBN: 978-1-955186-92-1
Visit www.amazon.com
Author: Patrick C. Moore
Publisher: J. Kenkade Publishing

Have you ever wondered what it would feel like to have the keen eye-sight, speed and agility of a Jaguar? Being able to see horrible and unlawful events take place, but in a mere instance have the capability of making sure that these events stopped in the eye of danger? If so, Max Rockafellor has an epic tale of how he became Jag-Man, Inquisitor of the Night!

Also Available from
J. Kenkade Publishing

ISBN: 978-1-955186-93-8
Visit www.amazon.com
Author: Margaret Joanne Rice
Publisher: J. Kenkade Publishing

Set in the Old South after the Civil War– specifically on a tobacco plan-tation in Staunton, Virginia– this story revolves around three key groups of people. Plantation owners, plantation workers, and Native Americans play integral roles in this saga. They often intersect and prove necessary for each other to exist in their sociopolitical climate. The conflict in the story involves an ancient Indian folktale about a baby skull hidden on planta-tion property in a grandfather clock that is shrouded in superstition. This skull is said to have magical powers, and when it disappears, many strange events begin to unfold.

Made in the USA
Coppell, TX
10 June 2022

78672809R00198